श्रीगुरुभ्यो नमः

śrī-gurubhyo namaḥ

श्रीभगवानुवाच ।
इदं तु ते गुह्यतमं प्रवक्ष्याम्यनसूयवे ।
ज्ञानं विज्ञानसहितं यज्ज्ञात्वा मोक्ष्यसेऽशुभात् ॥ १

This
Bhagavad Gītā

---

presented to

---

from

---

on the occasion of

Family Registry

Father

Name

Gotra

Gotra*

Mother

Gotra is a term applied to a group of families or a lineage whose members trace their descent to a common ancestor, usually a sage of ancient times. A wife assumes her husband's *gotra* from the time of marriage. The *gotra* is part of the Hindu identity and is often recited at the commencement of sacred ceremonies.

Great Grandfather

Gotra

Grandfather

Great Grandmother

Gotra

Great Grandfather

Gotra

Grandmother

Great Grandmother

Great Grandfather

Gotra

Grandfather

Great Grandmother

Gotra

Great Grandfather

Gotra

Grandmother

Great Grandmother

Family Registry

Father

Name

Gotra

Gotra

Mother

Great Grandfather

Gotra

Grandfather

Great Grandmother

Gotra

Great Grandfather

Gotra

Grandmother

Great Grandmother

Great Grandfather

Gotra

Grandfather

Great Grandmother

Gotra

Great Grandfather

Gotra

Grandmother

Great Grandmother

Marriage Record

and

were united in marriage

on

at

officiating priest

witnessed by

witnessed by

Births

Child
Mother
Father
Gotra
Nakṣatra
Date
Time
Place

Child
Mother
Father
Gotra
Nakṣatra
Date
Time
Place

Child
Mother
Father
Gotra
Nakṣatra
Date
Time
Place

Child
Mother
Father
Gotra
Nakṣatra
Date
Time
Place

Saṁskāras

Haircutting (*muṇḍana*), Thread Ceremony (*upanayana)*, Houseblessing (*gṛha-praveśa*), etc.

Bhagavad Gītā

Bhagavad Gītā

Translation and Annotations
by
Shukavak N. Dasa

Foundation for Indic Philosophy and Culture
Claremont Graduate University

in cooperation with

Śrī Publications
Los Angeles

Foundation for Indic Philosophy and Culture
Claremont Graduate University

in cooperation with

Śrī Publications
www.sanskrit.org

ISBN 1-889756-32-6 (Paperback)

Library of Congress Cataloging-in-Publication Data

Bhagavadgītā. English & Sanskrit
Bhagavad Gītā/translation and annotations by Shukavak N. Dasa.
p. cm.
Cover title: Srīmadbhagavadgītā.
In English and Sanskrit (also romanized); includes translation from Sanskrit.
Includes bibliographical references and index.
ISBN 1-889756-34-2 (Hardcover) – ISBN 1-889756-32-6 (pbk.)
1. Bhagavadgītā–Commentaries. I. Title: Srīmadbhagavadgītā. II. Dasa, Shukavak, 1953- III. Title.

BL1138.62.E5 2004c
294.5'92404521–dc22
2004057943

Acknowledgements

I thank the following persons who have helped in the preparation of this volume: Sukulina Narayana Dasa, Haricaraṇa Dāsa, Ralph McDowell, Kathleen Marvin, Jerri Marvin and Vikki Truver.

A special thanks to Dr. Vijay and Madhu Arora, Jay and Melanie Arora for their generous financial support.

About the Author

Shukavak N. Dasa received his Ph.D. in South Asian Studies and his Masters degree in Sanskrit grammar from the University of Toronto. He regularly lectures on Hinduism and he has been instrumental in developing Hindu Temples in the United States and Canada. He is the author of *Hindu Encounter with Modernity.*

Contents

Abbreviations

BG	*Bhagavad Gītā*
BU	*Bṛhad-āraṇyaka Upaniṣad*
ChU	*Chāndogya Upaniṣad*
IU	*Īśa Upaniṣad*
KauU	*Kauṣītakī Upaniṣad*
KU	*Kaṭha Upaniṣad*
MB	*Mahābhārata*
MaiU	*Maitrī Upaniṣad*
MS	*Manu-saṁhitā*
R	*Rāmāyaṇa*
RV	*Ṛg Veda*
SK	*Sāṅkhya-kārikā*
ŚU	*Śvetāśvatara Upaniṣad*
TA	*Taitirīya Āranyaka*
TU	*Taitirīya Upaniṣad*
VS	*Vasiṣṭha-smṛti*

Introduction

In my years of teaching Hinduism in temples and other places of learning throughout the United States and Canada, I have often told my students that if they read only one book of Hindu *śāstra*, let that be *Bhagavad Gītā.* I have even encouraged my younger students, who are regularly confronted by their non-Hindu friends, to think of *Bhagavad Gītā* as the "Bible" of Hinduism. While this is not factually correct—there is no single Hindu text which speaks with the same exclusive authority as does the Bible in Judaism or Christianity—it does emphasize the importance and universal recognition of *Bhagavad Gītā.*

The *Gītā,* as it is often called, is a short work of 700 Sanskrit verses known as *ślokas.* Even though it can be read in just a few sessions, it captures the very essence of Hindu thought. In the last two centuries, hundreds of editions have been published in various Western languages. I have before me over forty current English translations. So why publish another edition of the *Gītā*?

I place currently available translations of *Bhagavad Gītā* into three categories: the academic translation, the literary translation, and the devotional translation interpreted within a particular theological tradition. Academic translations of the *Gītā* are useful because they open up to scholars of religion and other disciplines the theological and linguistic dimensions of the work. However, because their language and syntax are often so literal, they are not readable to even the serious student of Hinduism, let alone the general reader. Like much scholarship in the religious field, they are not designed to encourage religious faith. In fact, they may discourage it. The same is true of the purely literary translations of the *Gītā.* Unfortunately, literary translations often avoid or undervalue the religious nature of the work. The *Bhagavad Gītā* is, first and foremost, a living religious work. It stands in parity with the world's greatest scriptures and for this reason it should be presented in a manner that recognizes and gives value to religious faith. Finally, many Hindu religious groups translate the *Gītā* in a manner consistent with their own theological leanings. Their versions of the *Gītā* are designed to imbue the reader with the religious faith of their own particular flavor. While such translations allow an easy interpretation of the *Gītā*, the approach is often overly simplistic. It fails to offer an objective and balanced approach sought by the general student of Hinduism. Undeniably, the *Gītā* speaks and invites understanding on many levels, much of which remains closed to the reader of an unabashedly sectarian translation.

I say this not to disparage the academic, literary, or theological translations of the *Gītā,* but to remind the reader that a translator who opts for one of these approaches necessarily speaks to a limited audience. The *Gītā,* by its nature, speaks to a universal audience, and such translations exclude many readers that a work of this magnitude should include.

The present volume offers an alternative. I have translated *Bhagavad Gītā* in a scholarly way, but not so scholarly that the general reader will find it obscure. Moreover, I have written it from a perspective in which the *Gītā* appears as much more than a work of world-class literature, but as a living religious text meant to inspire faith in the Divine. As far as possible, I have tried to avoid expressing a philosophical bias. In other words, this edition is an attempt to present *Bhagavad Gītā* in a theologically neutral way.

At the outset, however, I must admit that it is virtually impossible to create a theologically neutral translation of *Bhagavad Gītā.* It is the nature and beauty of the Sanskrit language that it invites multiple interpretations. My solution to this problem has been to utilize a system of annotation in the form of footnotes, which allows me to make a particular translation and then to show an alternative translation or interpretation when it is appropriate.

My system of annotation utilizes the commentaries of three classical interpreters of *Bhagavad Gītā*: Śaṅkara, Rāmānuja and Madhva.[1] Of course, the *Gītā* has been interpreted by thousands of commentators over the centuries and the interested reader is encouraged to delve into some of these commentaries. For practical purposes, however, I have chosen to draw from the notes of these three commentators because they represent a balanced cross section of possible interpretations. In fact, the ways these classical theologians have read *Bhagavad Gītā* have so influenced the course of Hindu thought, that a modern student who reads the *Gītā* with an eye to these three commentators will have obtained a balanced exposure to the theological expanse of the work.

This presentation of the *Gītā* is not a literal translation. Had I followed the exact syntax and made a precise word-for-word rendering of the Sanskrit, my translation would be unreadable. Instead, I have attempted to walk a fine line between readability and literal accuracy. I have made full use of my system of annotation to inform the reader where I have stepped over that line in favor of readability. Since I wanted this translation to "talk" to the modern reader as much as possible, if literal accuracy had to be sacrificed, I have willingly made that sacrifice.

I have also made this translation gender neutral. The Sanskrit text of the *Gītā* is decidedly masculine in tone, but I have found in teaching the *Gītā* that many students feel uneasy by this perspective. When it does not seriously affect the meaning of the text, I have changed the masculine form of a noun or pronoun to an appropriate indefinite form. For example, Arjuna asks this

1. The reader may see the website www.sanskrit.org to view a short biographical and theological sketch of each of these commentators.

question: *atha kena prayukto 'yaṁ pāpaṁ carati pūruṣaḥ*. "By what is a **man** forced to perform evil?" My translation reads, "By what is **one** forced to perform evil." Although the Sanskrit noun *puruṣaḥ* is masculine, I have made it gender neutral.

Another feature of this translation is that I include the original Sanskrit *devanāgarī*[2] as well as a Roman transliteration. While I realize that many of my readers may not make use of either the *devanāgarī* or the transliteration, I feel the visual presence of the original text adds authenticity and spiritual weight to the translation. I recognize that as Hinduism expands in the West, the emerging forms of this ancient religious tradition must necessarily be reflected through the medium of the Western languages. While this is a natural thing, it does present the danger that the emerging culture may drift too far afield. The presence of the original Sanskrit becomes a psychological "hitching-post" to remind the reader of the linguistic foundations of *Bhagavad Gītā.* I feel that every Hindu should have at least a rudimentary understanding of Sanskrit and that all Hindu temples and related institutions bear the responsibility to teach it.

One of the great problems in translating or reading a religious work like *Bhagavad Gītā* is that it is all too easy to approach it with foreign concepts of religion in mind. If we live in the West we may unknowingly approach the *Gītā* with Christian, Jewish, or Islamic notions of God, soul, heaven, hell, and sin. We translate *brahman* as God, *ātman* as soul, *pāpam* as sin, *dharma* as religion or duty. However, *brahman* is not the same as God; *ātman* is not equivalent to the soul, *pāpam* is not sin and *dharma* is much more than mere duty or religion. A work like the *Gītā,* therefore, has to be translated and

2. *Devanāgarī* is the script or "alphabet" customarily used in written Sanskrit. A language should not be confused with the script in which it is written. *Devanāgarī* is not exclusive to Sanskrit, since many other ancient languages have also been written using *devanāgarī.* Moreover, the Sanskrit language can be transliterated by using other scripts, including the Latin alphabet with appropriate diacritics.

read on its own terms and not those of another religious tradition. Because the Hinduism now developing in the West is often reflected through the lenses of Christianity, Judaism and Islam, the theological uniqueness of Vedic religion is slowly being eroded.

For these reasons, there are certain Sanskrit terms in the *Gītā* that I have chosen not to translate into English. For example, such terms as *brahman, dharma,* and *yoga* are left untranslated. The reader is thus urged to become comfortable with a lexicon that is essential to an understanding of the *Gītā*, and Hinduism in general. My system of annotation offers an explanation of these terms as they are introduced and these terms are included in the glossary.

Another feature of this work is the adoption of the academic standard of Sanskrit transliteration. I have included a chart of this system at the end of this volume. Sanskrit terms are usually rendered into English by an *ad hoc* phonetic system. This will be familiar to most of my readers. For example, the reader will likely be used to seeing the terms *Ram, Vishnu,* and *Geeta.* Unfortunately, this approach is inadequate to convey the proper pronunciation of the Sanskrit. Instead these terms will appear as *Rāma, Viṣṇu* and *Gītā.* I encourage the reader to study and use the system I have adopted. It provides a precise phonetic rendering of the Sanskrit alphabet.[3]

Finally, many readers may be aware that *Bhagavad Gītā* is part of a much larger work, the *Mahābhārata,* but they may not be aware that there are many divergent editions of the *Mahābhārata.* These include a Kashmiri edition, a Bengali edition, a Maharastrian edition, and three South Indian editions.[4] Unlike most available

3. The reader may go to the website www.sanskrit.org and download an audio file that demonstrates the correct pronunciation of the Sanskrit language and this system of transliteration.

4. In many cases, whole stories or sections are missing, or substantially different, from one edition to the next.

translations of *Bhagavad Gītā,* the present *Gītā* is a translation of the critical edition of the *Mahābhārata.*[5]

Date of Bhagavad Gītā

Since *Bhagavad Gītā* is included within the *Mahābhārata,* the date of the *Gītā* depends on that of the *Mahābhārata.* The problem with dating the *Mahābhārata* and most things of ancient India is that because there are few absolutely fixed dates, any dating must be tentative at best. Starting in the late eighteenth century, throughout the nineteenth and even into the twentieth century, indologists spent a great deal of time attempting to establish the date of the *Vedas* and other related texts including the *Mahābhārata.* Any attempt to discuss in detail their reasoning or offer a verdict on their conclusions would take us well beyond the scope of this introduction. Readers who wish to pursue this discussion are directed to two excellent works that will serve as a starting point for such an inquiry: V. Krishnamacharya's *History of Sanskrit Literature,* and B.B. Majumdar's *Krsna in History and Legend.* In all likelihood we will never know for certain the precise dating of ancient Indian texts. Vedic orthodoxy speaks of a religious tradition that is many thousands of years old. According to this tradition, mankind is currently in the Kali Yuga, an era which began in 3,102 BCE. The *Mahābhārata,* in the orthodox view, has come to us from the beginning of that era, and is therefore over 5,000 years old. However, modern historical and archaeological evidence, and even

5. The critical edition of *Mahābhārata* was compiled by the Bhandarkar Oriental Research Institute in September, 1966. The Institute prepared this recension by collecting segments from sixty source manuscripts written in such diverse scripts as Devanāgarī, Bengali, Telugu, Grantha, and Malayalam. The number of variant readings that affect the *Gītā* are much fewer than those of other parts of *Mahābhārata.* This is probably due to the enduring popularity of the *Gītā.* A few manuscripts do contain additional verses, which amount to an additional nineteen stanzas. However, from the time of Śaṅkara to the present day, most scholars and readers of *Bhagavad Gītā* think of it as comprising 700 verses. The readings accepted by Śaṅkara, Rāmānuja, and Madhva are substantially the same as those of the critical edition.

internal comparative evidence from the *Purāṇas,* suggest a much later date—between 1,000 and 400 BCE. From a strictly religious perspective, however, there is little need to know the chronological history of ancient India. Whether *Bhagavad Gītā* was spoken 2,500 years ago or 5,000 years ago is not relevant. What does matter is whether the *Gītā* has meaning for us today.

Similar questions can be asked about the Great War and about Kṛṣṇa. Did a battle actually take place at Kurukṣetra? Was Kṛṣṇa an actual historical personality? Again, the answers are the same: we do not know, and probably never will. But if our focus is on the spiritual message of *Bhagavad Gītā,* does it matter? To me it does not. Kṛṣṇa's message rings true today, as it has for countless millions of human beings in the past. From a religious perspective, the value of *Bhagavad Gītā* is found in what it has to say today, and not in when it was said.

Teachings of Bhagavad Gītā

The main teachings of *Bhagavad Gītā* include *dharma, karma, yoga,* matter, the soul, and finally God. The method by which these topics are discussed is called *sāṅkhya* or analysis. Using the context of war and Arjuna's indecision to fight, Kṛṣṇa presents Arjuna with an analysis of each of these topics. Here is a summary:

The first two topics, *dharma* and *karma,* are suggested in the first sentence of the *Gītā* "*dharma-kṣetre kuru-kṣetre...*" "on the field of *dharma,* the field of action." The word *dharma* is derived from the Sanskrit root *dhṛ,* meaning to uphold or support. There is a famous dictum, "*dharmo dhārayati prajāḥ,*" "*Dharma* is what upholds all beings." *Dharma* refers to both natural law as well as social law. *Dharma* is what holds the stars and planets in the heavens; *dharma* is liquidity in water and hardness in stone. *Dharma* is what determines the nature of tigers and deer. Similarly, there is a *dharma* by which human society functions in harmony with the universe. Each member of society, man or woman, mother or father, student or worker, priest or warrior, has a certain *dharma* to uphold. *Dharma* is, therefore, what shapes and holds society together. When the members of society perform their *dharma* collectively, the social order is in accord with natural law. Prosperity reigns.

It is also said, "*dharmo rakṣati rakṣitaḥ,*" "Protect *dharma* and *dharma* will protect you." Arjuna is a warrior and so his *dharma* is to protect *dharma,* which, in part, involves maintaining the social order of society. And yet at the very moment when he is to fulfill his *dharma* he breaks down and refuses. He is caught in a bind. On the one hand, his duty is to fight in order to protect *dharma* and yet he knows that fighting will destroy the very fabric of society, to unravel *dharma,* if you will. What is he to do? He turns to Kṛṣṇa and asks the perennial question, "What is the meaning of life? How should I act?" In reality *Bhagavad Gītā* is not about fighting at all. The Great War is simply the context in which the teachings of the *Gītā* occur. The *Gītā* is about action.

The word *kuru* in the opening sentence that I quoted is derived from the root *kṛ,* to act. Therefore, *kuru-kṣetra* means "on the field of action." So at the very beginning the theme of action is introduced. As a military man, Arjuna is obliged to act in order to fulfill his *dharma.* Throughout the *Gītā,* Kṛṣṇa speaks about correct action, forbidden action and even inaction, but mostly he explains how action, if performed improperly, binds the living being to a cycle of repeated birth and death. In other words, action is a source of bondage for the living being in this world. Arjuna is encouraged to act in a way that frees himself from such bondage. But how is this to be done?

The answer to this question is through *yoga.* The word y*oga* is used in many ways in the *Gītā,* but in its most basic form *yoga* simply means to join. In fact, the English word yoke is cognate with the Sanskrit word *yoga*—both being derived from the Indo-European root *yuj,* to join. *Yoga* is, therefore, the joining of the soul with God.

There are many forms of *yoga* mentioned in the *Gītā*: *karma-yoga, jñāna-yoga, bhakti-yoga, dhyāna-yoga, sāṅkhya-yoga,* etc. Each of these forms of *yoga* constitutes a process or action whereby the soul seeks freedom from bondage to action. Therefore, action is not only the source of bondage, but also the source of liberation for the soul. When the performance of one's duty or work becomes the principal means of joining with God, the process is called *karma-yoga.* When the acquisition of knowledge is the principal means, the process is called *jñāna-yoga.* Love, when offered to God for a similar purpose, constitutes *bhakti-yoga,* the *yoga* of devotion. When one sits fixed in meditation for the purpose of attaining union with the divine, the process is known as *dhyāna-yoga.* Kṛṣṇa encourages Arjuna to always act as a *yogī.* Specifically, as a warrior, he is a man of action and must fight according to the principles of *karma-yoga.* For persons with other natures and inclinations, Kṛṣṇa offers the paths of *bhakti-yoga, dhyāna-yoga, sāṅkhya-yoga,* or *jñāna-yoga.*

Bhagavad Gītā also provides a detailed analysis of matter. Matter is said to comprise five primary coarse elements: earth, water, fire, air, and space. In addition, it is made of three subtle elements: mind, intelligence, and sense of self. Everything in this world is a combination of one or more of these eight elements. Inanimate objects like rocks, liquids, or gases are a combination of only the five coarse elements; a living being is composed of all eight elements. Notice that mind, intelligence, and sense of self are here viewed as material things. In much of Western philosophy mind, intelligence and self are not considered material things. In *Bhagavad Gītā* both the physical and psychological makeup of a living being are just forms of matter.

There is another interesting dimension to matter that is unique to the *Gītā.* Matter operates in three phases or modes known as *guṇas.* All of life is conditioned by some combination of these three *guṇas.* The three *guṇas* are *sattva, rajas,* and *tamas*: goodness, passion, and darkness. In *Bhagavad Gītā* everything human, animal, insect, plant, mineral, and even such things as charity, penance, and food are conditioned by some combination of these three *guṇas.* The three *guṇas,* in conjunction with action, are the means by which the living being is bound to matter. One meaning of the word *guṇa* is rope. It is as if the living being is tied or roped to matter by these *guṇas.* Arjuna is told that if he acts according to one of the paths of *yoga* he can transcend these three *guṇas* and thereby free himself from matter.

In *Bhagavad Gītā,* matter is also viewed as forever changing. For this reason it is called *asat*—that which is untrue and temporary. The three commentators whose views are often discussed in the annotations offer strikingly different interpretations of the meaning of *asat,* and thus, of the nature of matter. In contrast to matter, Kṛṣṇa speaks of a higher principle, which he calls *sat.* This is spirit—that which is true and eternal. In English, we can call this spiritual principle, the "soul." So long as this eternal soul resides in matter, it is conditioned by the three *guṇas* and so remains bound to matter. The process or action of *yoga* extracts the soul from matter. Arjuna's lamentation and refusal to fight is based on his inability to perceive this higher principle. He identifies his family members with matter. In other words, he sees them as bodies that can be killed, instead of seeing them as eternal souls that can never be killed. The *Gītā* begins as Kṛṣṇa exhorts Arjuna to understand that the soul is eternal, and to act with this understanding.

Finally, Kṛṣṇa tells Arjuna to look even deeper, to look beyond the soul to see what lies as the foundation of both matter and spirit. This is *brahman.* In English, we sometimes translate *brahman* as God or the Supreme. In Sanskrit *brahman* means "the big" or "the great." *Brahman* is the substratum that supports all things, even *dharma.* Kṛṣṇa repeatedly identifies himself as being non-different from this *brahman.* In other words, Kṛṣṇa is that supreme God.

I am frequently asked what the *Gītā* teaches. This line of

questioning can easily extend beyond the scope of the *Gītā*, to the meaning of religion and ultimately to the meaning of life itself. It is widely accepted nowadays that all religions ultimately teach the same thing. If this is the case, we might reasonably assume that all sacred texts teach the same thing as well. It follows that there is one ultimate teaching in the *Gītā*, which reflects whatever it is that all religions have in common. Many Hindu religious groups in their zeal to find this "one teaching" present or endorse an edition of the *Gītā* that supports a particular theological conclusion which ironically, not all Hindus, let alone all religions, would accept.

However, I have learned that all religions do not teach the same thing, either about God, the soul, an after-life, or even about the nature of this world. The differences between Christian, Buddhist, Islamic, and Hindu views on these matters are striking. Similarly, although the human mind has searched diligently for one final conclusion in *Bhagavad Gītā*, such a conclusion is not forthcoming. This will become clear as the reader sees the divergent points of view expressed by just three of the thousands of commentators on the *Bhagavad Gītā*. Compare the commentaries of Śaṅkara, Rāmānuja and Madhva I have annoted in the text. All three have distinct points of view. Each draws his conclusions from the same sources, the *Gītā* and the *Vedas*. Śaṅkara's theology is called *advaita*, nonduality. It concludes that reality is ultimately just one thing, *brahman*, that there is no separate existence of a soul, and that our physical world is illusory. Rāmānuja's theology is called *viṣiṣṭādvaita*, modified nonduality. It states that reality is ultimately one and yet is modified into many. Madhva's theology is called *dvaita*, duality. It proclaims that reality is not one, that it is diverse, that there are distinct souls and that our physical world is real. Each of these divergent views has evolved over a thousand years and continues to have followers today.

Why such diversity between the different religions and even within the same religion on the same religious text? Diversity is a statement about the beauty and mystery of creation. While each of the world's religions is different, all have at least one common feature. Each is a unique expression of the human attempt to understand and find meaning in life, to reach higher and touch that which transcends the world of mundane affairs. But life is so much more than can be expressed by one religion. Why is there so much diversity of interpretation of the *Bhagavad Gītā*? Simply because the *Gītā* has captured the mystery and diverse nature of life. I am not going to tell the reader how to think about the *Gītā*. That would be like an artist telling someone how to interpret a piece of art. I leave it to the thoughtful judgment of the reader. Instead, I wish to offer a religious model that I think is helpful to understand and interpret, not only Hinduism and *Bhagavad Gītā*, but religion in general. This model is derived from the *Bhāgavata-purāṇa*. There we find a verse:

vadanti tat tattva-vidas tattvaṁ yaj jñānam advayam
brahmeti paramātmeti bhagavān iti śabdyate

> "Those who know the truth speak of this truth as undifferentiated knowledge categorized as *brahman*, *paramātmā* and *bhagavān*." (*Bhāg.* 1.2.11)

The essence of this verse is captured by the single word "*tat*." *Tat* is simply the neuter pronoun "that." We look into a telescope and see the vast array of stars and galaxies and we are struck with wonder. We look into a microscope and see exquisite detail and beauty. Again, we are struck with wonder. In each case we ask, "What are we seeing?" In other words, "what is the *that*, which creates such sense of wonder?" This question about the mystery and wonder of life is the perennial question that has been asked in many forms since human eyes first opened and saw this wonderful and awesome thing called life. "Who are we?" What is the world?" "Is there a purpose?" In other words, "What is the truth?"[6]

6. The pronoun *tat* plus the neuter abstract suffix *tva* creates the word *tattva*, "thatness". *Tattva* is usually translated as "truth."

The *Bhāgavata-purāṇa* says that a human being can never fully grasp this truth because ultimate truth is beyond human comprehension. We reach out and attempt to grasp it just the same. This is what constitutes religion. How this truth is captured and understood in human terms takes three forms: *brahman, paramātmā,* and *bhagavān.* In other words, these are the three basic ways that human beings conceive of ultimate reality. *Brahman* is truth expressed as sheer power. *Paramātmā* is truth expressed as divine immanence, God within all things. *Bhagavān* is truth expressed as divine personality: Kṛṣṇa, Rāma, Jesus. The scientist, who seeks to unravel the laws of nature on the level of the macrocosm or microcosm, pursues truth as *brahman.* The *yogī* who sits in meditation, contemplating God within, pursues truth as *paramātmā.* The worshipper who prays before a sacred image of Śiva or Jesus pursues truth as *bhagavān.* Similarly, each of the world's religions seeks and expresses truth in one or more of these ways. In the *Gītā,* all three of these ways are employed, and depending on which perspective the seekers of truth are naturally inclined, they reach a distinctive conclusion as to the nature of truth and the meaning of *Bhagavad Gītā.* Like the three blind men of Indosthan who try to describe an elephant, we perceive this truth according to our unique perspective, and even then only partially.

It is a great tribute to the depth of the *Gītā's* theology that it is open to such a wide range of interpretation. The great mystery of the *Gītā* is that it has spoken to generations of human beings. In the vast array of Vedic literature it has stood out as *the* book of the Hindus. You are now invited to make *Bhagavad Gītā* your book as well.

Setting of Bhagavad Gītā

One of the great problems one encounters when reading the *Gītā* for the first time is the bewildering number of proper names found in the first chapter. I vividly recall reading the *Gītā* as a teenager for the first time. I almost gave up halfway through Chapter One because of the complexity of names. Admittedly, there is little that can be done to simplify the names, but with some understanding of the *Gītā's* context the reader will be more inclined to make it through the first chapter. The first chapter is one of the most spiritually significant chapters because it reveals Arjuna's humanity. There is much in the later chapters of *Bhagavad Gītā* that takes the reader to dizzying heights of mysticism and divinity. In the first chapter, Arjuna's predicament is everyman's predicament. We can easily identify with Arjuna's struggle because life has taught each of us that we have our own battles to fight.

The setting of the *Gītā* revolves around the rivalry of two opposing cousin families, the Kaurava and the Pāṇḍava. How this rivalry came about requires a brief historical narrative of the *Mahābhārata*. There once was a king, Vicitravīrya by name, who had two queens: Aṁbikā and Aṁbālikā. It so happened that because King Vicitravīrya was unable to father children, according to the custom of levirate[7] his half-brother, Vyāsa, could lie with his two wives. Unfortunately, Vyāsa was of such frightful appearance that both Aṁbikā and Aṁbālikā were totally repulsed by his presence. Aṁbikā, in her terror, closed her eyes as she lay with him and consequently gave birth to a blind son, Dhṛtarāṣṭra. When Aṁbālikā's turn came she turned white from fright and gave birth to the pale son, Pāṇḍu. (The word *pāṇḍu* means pale.) As Dhṛtarāṣṭra was blind, Pāṇḍu ruled the kingdom at Hāstinapura, near present day Delhi. Pāṇḍu had two wives: Kuntī and Mādrī. One day, while hunting, Pāṇḍu mistakenly killed a deer as it was mating. As luck would have it, the deer turned out to be a powerful sage in disguise. This led to the pronouncement of a curse upon Pāṇḍu demanding that he too would die at such a time when he would lie with one of his wives. Consequently, he turned his kingdom over to his blind half brother, Dhṛtarāṣṭra, and left for the forest with his two wives Kuntī and Mādrī to follow a life of celibacy.

---

7. The practice of levirate allows the brother of a deceased or incapacitated husband to father children with the wife.

When Kuntī was a little girl she had the good fortune to receive a special *mantra* or magical prayer from the famous sage Durvāsa. The *mantra* allowed her to invoke any god that she wished and bear a son by him. In an act of childhood curiosity, Kuntī called down the sun god, Sūryadeva, and gave birth to a powerful son, Karṇa. She abandoned Karṇa by setting him afloat on a river as she was not married at the time. Karṇa was later found and raised by a chariot driver. Karṇa is one of the most compelling and tragic figures in the *Mahābhārata*. He was unaware of his divine nature for most of his life. He eventually became allied with the Kaurava against the Pāṇḍava. Kuntī never revealed the secret of Karṇa's birth, not even to her husband.

After her marriage to Pāṇḍu, Kuntī offered to use her *mantra* to bear children for Pāṇḍu. Pāṇḍu had been cursed by a sage and could not have children of his own. Pāṇḍu asked Kuntī to invoke Dharma, the all-powerful god of destiny. This she did, and Yudhiṣṭhira was born. Afterwards she called for the wind, Vāyudeva, and Bhīma was born. Finally, she called Indradeva, the king of the gods, and the famous archer Arjuna was born. Not to be outdone, Mādrī, Pāṇḍu's other wife, received this *mantra* from Kuntī and called the twin Aśvins, who pull the chariot of the dawn. Nakula and Sahadeva were born. Thus Pāṇḍu became the father of five divine sons known as the Pāṇḍava: Yudhiṣṭhira, Bhīma, Arjuna, Nakula and Sahadeva. Not long after this Pāṇḍu fell victim to his human passions and died in the arms of Mādrī. Afterwards Mādrī joined Pāṇḍu on the funeral pyre and left Kuntī alone to raise the five children.

In the meantime, Pāṇḍu's blind older brother, Dhṛtarāṣṭra, had married a beautiful princess named Gāndhārī. When Gāndhārī heard of the sons born to Kuntī and Mādrī, she too desired children and eventually gave birth to one hundred sons, headed by Duryodhana. At the moment of Duryodhana's birth, jackals and mules cried out, the moon turned blood red and the earth shook in fear and disgust. A great evil had come upon the earth. These one hundred sons of Dhṛtarāṣṭra, headed by Duryodhana, are known as the Kaurava.

After the death of Pāṇḍu, the Pāṇḍava were given over to Dhṛtarāṣṭra for care. As a result the Pāṇḍava and the Kaurava grew up together in the city of Hastināpura. Unfortunately these two cousin families became bitter rivals and eventually a terrible war, known as the Battle of Kurukṣetra,[8] took place to determine which family would rule. The famous dialogue between Arjuna and Kṛṣṇa, known as *Bhagavad Gītā*, occurred just as this Great War was about to commence.

The Cast of Characters

Here is a brief summary of the principal names that appear in Chapter One.

Kṛṣṇa–the *Bhāgavata-purāṇa,* one of the principal sources of information about the life of Kṛṣṇa, tells how in the days near the end of the *dvāpara yuga*[9] the earth had been overcome by a multitude of malevolent kings and their armies. To remove the Earth's burden a great incarnation of God appeared in Mathura, just south of the present day city of Delhi. Such forms of God appear in this world from time to time to rectify the affairs of mankind. They are known as *avatāras.* The most famous *avatāra* of Viṣṇu, Śrī Kṛṣṇa, appeared on Earth along with his entourage of family members, the Yādava. Kṛṣṇa's advent on earth at the time of the *Mahābhārata* was a divine intervention in human affairs to relieve the earth of its burden and to reestablish *dharma.* The appearance of Bhagavān Śrī Kṛṣṇa is explained according to this famous dictum of *Bhagavad Gītā*:

8. Kurukṣetra is a large tract of land near the ancient capital city of the Kaurava known as Hastināpura in Northern India. It is near present day Delhi. In ancient times Kurukṣetra was a place of pilgrimage and therefore is called *dharma-kṣetra,* the field of *dharma,* in the *Bhagavad Gītā.*
9. See Fn. under BG 4.8.

yadā yadā hi dharmasya glānir bhavati bhārata
abhyutthānam adharmasya tadātmānaṁ sṛjāmy aham
paritrāṇāya sādhūnāṁ vināśāya ca duṣkṛtām
dharma-saṁsthāpanārthāya sambhavāmi yuge yuge

"Whenever there is a decline in *dharma,* O descendant of Bharata, and an increase of *adharma,* at that time, I manifest Myself. For the protection of the good and for the destruction of those who do evil, as well as to reestablish *dharma,* I appear time and time again."

All of Kṛṣṇa's activities relating to the Kaurava and the Pāṇḍava and the Great War of Kurukṣetra, wherein *Bhagavad Gītā* was spoken, must therefore be seen in this context.

Arjuna–amongst the Pāṇḍava Arjuna, was the third brother and the son of Indradeva. He was known for his skill in archery and great valor on the battlefield. It was Arjuna who won the hand of Draupadī, the collective wife of the Pāṇḍava, in a contest of archery. Arjuna was a close friend of Kṛṣṇa and the one to whom *Bhagavad Gītā* was spoken. During the battle, Arjuna's chariot was driven by Kṛṣṇa and pulled between the two armies. It is Arjuna's despondency upon seeing the people he had to fight that prompted Kṛṣṇa to speak *Bhagavad Gītā.*

Bhīṣma–grandfather to both the Pāṇḍava and the Kaurava. Bhīṣma was the old sage-warrior who raised both Dhṛtarāṣṭra and Pāṇḍu. He had taken a vow of chastity and received a blessing that he could not be killed except at his own will. He was the greatest fighter and teacher of the time. Bhīṣma was actually partial to Kṛṣṇa and the Pāṇḍava, but because of the circumstances of court politics he was forced to take the side of the Kaurava.

Droṇācārya–teacher to both the Pāṇḍava and Kaurava. A *brāhmaṇa* by birth, Droṇācārya became a renowned warrior. Again, due to force of circumstances, Droṇācārya was forced to side with the Kaurava against the Pāṇḍava. It was primarily the presence of both

Bhīṣma and Droṇācārya that caused Arjuna to hesitate and break down on the battlefield just as the fighting was to commence.

Duryodhana–King Dhṛtarāṣṭra's eldest son. Duryodhana was able to exercise great power and influence in the kingdom because of his father's blindness. His purpose was to prevent the Pāṇḍava from taking power and ruling in the place of Yudhiṣṭhira, the first son of Pāṇḍu. Duryodhana was, therefore, the principal cause of all the events that led to the war.

Karṇa–the first son of Kuntī by the sun god. He was, therefore, elder to Yudhiṣṭhira.

Sañjaya–King Dhṛtarāṣṭra's chief minister who witnessed the events of the great battle and related this information to the king including the dialogue between Kṛṣṇa and Arjuna. Sañjaya was known for his great knowledge and saintliness.

Yudhiṣṭhira–the son of Dharma and the head of the Pāṇḍava. Had Yudhiṣṭhira known that Karṇa was actually his senior brother, he immediately would have abdicated his rights to the kingdom and the Great War could have been avoided. Karṇa became a great friend to Duryodhana and a bitter enemy of Arjuna. In the end Arjuna killed Karṇa. It was Yudhiṣṭhira's greatest despair when he finally learned the truth of Karṇa's birth from Kṛṣṇa after the Great War. Yudhiṣṭhira's constant desire to follow the ways of *dharma* is a recurrent theme throughout the *Mahābhārata.*

Apart from these main characters there is a host of minor characters mentioned in the first chapter of the *Gītā.* It is unnecessary to go into the details regarding these characters. I recommend the introduction to *Bhagavad Gītā* by Winthrop Sargeant to my readers who wish to go further into the details of the *Mahābhārata.*

Bhagavad Gītā

धृतराष्ट्र उवाच ।
धर्मक्षेत्रे कुरुक्षेत्रे समवेता युयुत्सवः ।
मामकाः पाण्डवाश्चैव किमकुर्वत संजय ॥ १

dhṛtarāṣṭra uvāca
dharma-kṣetre kuru-kṣetre samavetā yuyutsavaḥ
māmakāḥ pāṇḍavāś caiva kim akurvata sañjaya

संजय उवाच ।
दृष्ट्वा तु पाण्डवानीकं व्यूढं दुर्योधनस्तदा ।
आचार्यमुपसंगम्य राजा वचनमब्रवीत् ॥ २

sañjaya uvāca
dṛṣṭvā tu pāṇḍavānīkaṁ vyūḍhaṁ duryodhanas tadā
ācāryam upasaṅgamya rājā vacanam abravīt

पश्यैतां पाण्डुपुत्राणामाचार्य महतीं चमूम् ।
व्यूढां द्रुपदपुत्रेण तव शिष्येण धीमता ॥ ३

paśyaitāṁ pāṇḍu-putrāṇāṁ ācārya mahatīṁ camūm
vyūḍhāṁ drupada-putreṇa tava śiṣyeṇa dhīmatā

अत्र शूरा महेष्वासा भीमार्जुनसमा युधि ।
युयुधानो विराटश्च द्रुपदश्च महारथः ॥ ४

atra śūrā maheṣv-āsā bhīmārjuna-samā yudhi
yuyudhāno virāṭaś ca drupadaś ca mahā-rathaḥ

Chapter One

Arjuna's Despondency

The Setting

1) Dhṛtarāṣṭra inquired:
O Sañjaya, after assembling at Kurukṣetra on the field of *dharma,*[1] what did my sons and the sons of Pāṇḍu do, being prepared for battle?

2) Sañjaya replied:
Seeing the army of the sons of Pāṇḍu marshalled for war, King Duryodhana approached his teacher[2] and spoke the following words.

3) O master, behold the great army of the sons of Pāṇḍu, arranged by your skillful disciple, the son of Drupada.

4) Observe heroes and great bowmen, peers in battle to Bhīma and Arjuna, such as Yuyudhāna, Virāṭa, and the great chariot fighter[3] Drupada.

Chapter One is traditionally entitled *arjuna-viṣāḍa-yoga,* The *Yoga* of Arjuna's Despondency.

1. *Dharma* derives from *dhṛ* meaning to hold up or to maintain. Thus *dharma* is literally that which sustains and holds the world together. *Dharma* is often translated as divine law, duty or even religion. It is no coincidence that this great battle was fought at a sacred place or that the first word of the *Bhagavad Gītā* is *dharma.* Indeed, the theme of *dharma* constitutes the very essence of *Bhagavad Gītā.*

2. The teacher of Duryodhana was Droṇācārya.

3. A "great chariot fighter" (*mahā-ratha)* is said to be one who can single-handedly fight ten thousand foot soldiers.

धृष्टकेतुश्चेकितानः काशिराजश्च वीर्यवान् ।
पुरुजित्कुन्तिभोजश्च शैब्यश्च नरपुंगवः ॥ ५

dhṛṣṭaketuś cekitānaḥ kāśirājaś ca vīryavān
purujit kuntibhojaś ca śaibyaś ca nara-puṅgavaḥ

युधामन्युश्च विक्रान्त उत्तमौजाश्च वीर्यवान् ।
सौभद्रो द्रौपदेयाश्च सर्व एव महारथाः ॥ ६

yudhāmanyuś ca vikrānta uttamaujāś ca vīryavān
saubhadro draupadeyāś ca sarva eva mahā-rathāḥ

अस्माकं तु विशिष्टा ये तान्निबोध द्विजोत्तम ।
नायका मम सैन्यस्य संज्ञार्थं तान्ब्रवीमि ते ॥ ७

asmākaṁ tu viśiṣṭā ye tān nibodha dvijottama
nāyakā mama sainyasya saṁjñārthaṁ tān bravīmi te

भवान्भीष्मश्च कर्णश्च कृपश्च समितिंजयः ।
अश्वत्थामा विकर्णश्च सौमदत्तिस्तथैव च ॥ ८

bhavān bhīṣmaś ca karṇaś ca kṛpaś ca samitiṁjayaḥ
aśvatthāmā vikarṇaś ca saumadattis tathaiva ca

अन्ये च बहवः शूरा मदर्थे त्यक्तजीविताः ।
नानाशस्त्रप्रहरणाः सर्वे युद्धविशारदाः ॥ ९

anye ca bahavaḥ śūrā mad-arthe tyakta-jīvitāḥ
nānā-śastra-praharaṇāḥ sarve yuddha-viśāradāḥ

अपर्याप्तं तदस्माकं बलं भीष्माभिरक्षितम् ।
पर्याप्तं त्विदमेतेषां बलं भीमाभिरक्षितम् ॥ १०

aparyāptaṁ tad asmākaṁ balaṁ bhīṣmābhirakṣitam
paryāptaṁ tv idam eteṣāṁ balaṁ bhīmābhirakṣitam

5) There is Dhṛṣṭaketu, Cekitāna, and the heroic king of Kāśi, as well as Purujit, Kuntibhoja, and the foremost of men, Śaibya.

6) There is the bold Yudhāmanyu, the heroic Uttamaujas, and the son of Subhadrā, as well as the sons of Draupadī—all great chariot fighters.

7) O best of the twice-born,[4] I will now describe the most distinguished commanders of our army.

8) There is your good self, there is Bhīṣma, Karṇa and the battle winning Kṛpa, as well as Aśvatthāmā, Vikarṇa, and the son of Somadatta.

9) And there are many other heroes ready to give up their lives for my sake, all skilled in battle with various throwing weapons.

10) Protected by Bhīṣma our strength is unbounded[5] whereas the strength of the Pāṇḍava, protected by Bhīma, is limited.

---

4. "Twice-born" refers to members of the three higher *varṇas* in the system of *varṇāśrama*: *brāhmaṇas, kṣatriyas* and *vaiśyas.* One's first birth takes place from the mother. One's second birth is a spiritual birth through the father or spiritual teacher (*guru*). In the system of *varṇāśrama* only members of the higher *varṇas* mentioned above receive this second birth. In other words, Kṛṣṇa is reminding Arjuna of his high social and spiritual position.

5. What is here translated as "unbounded" is a rendering of *aparyāptam.* But *aparyāptam* literally means limited or insufficient. This, however, does not seem to make sense given the boastful nature of Duryodhana in that he is supposed to be inspiring his forces. Some manuscripts reverse the names of Bhīṣma and Bhīma in order to give what appears to be the required meaning. The critical edition, however, does not switch the

अयनेषु च सर्वेषु यथाभागमवस्थिताः ।
भीष्ममेवाभिरक्षन्तु भवन्तः सर्व एव हि ॥ ११

ayaneṣu ca sarveṣu yathā-bhāgam avasthitāḥ
bhīṣmam evābhirakṣantu bhavantaḥ sarva eva hi

तस्य संजनयन्हर्षं कुरुवृद्धः पितामहः ।
सिंहनादं विनद्योच्चैः शङ्खं दध्मौ प्रतापवान् ॥ १२

tasya sañjanayan harṣaṁ kuru-vṛddhaḥ pitāmahaḥ
siṁha-nādaṁ vinadyoccaiḥ śaṅkhaṁ dadhmau pratāpavān

ततः शङ्खाश्च भेर्यश्च पणवानकगोमुखाः ।
सहसैवाभ्यहन्यन्त स शब्दस्तुमुलोऽभवत् ॥ १३

tataḥ śaṅkhāś ca bheryaś ca paṇavānaka-gomukhāḥ
sahasaivābhyahanyanta sa śabdas tumulo 'bhavat

ततः श्वेतैर्हयैर्युक्ते महति स्यन्दने स्थितौ ।
माधवः पाण्डवश्चैव दिव्यौ शङ्खौ प्रदध्मतुः ॥ १४

tataḥ śvetair hayair yukte mahati syandane sthitau
mādhavaḥ pāṇḍavaś caiva divyau śaṅkhau pradadhmatuḥ

पाञ्चजन्यं हृषीकेशो देवदत्तं धनंजयः ।
पौण्ड्रं दध्मौ महाशङ्खं भीमकर्मा वृकोदरः ॥ १५

pāñcajanyaṁ hṛṣīkeśo devadattaṁ dhanañjayaḥ
pauṇḍraṁ dadhmau mahā-śaṅkhaṁ bhīma-karmā vṛkodaraḥ

अनन्तविजयं राजा कुन्तीपुत्रो युधिष्ठिरः ।
नकुलः सहदेवश्च सुघोषमणिपुष्पकौ ॥ १६

anantavijayaṁ rājā kuntī-putro yudhiṣṭhiraḥ
nakulaḥ sahadevaś ca sughoṣa-maṇipuṣpakau

11) On all fronts, each of you must stand firm in your positions, and above all, protect Grandfather Bhīṣma.

12) Bhīṣma, the aged grandfather of the Kurus, then roared like a lion on high and blew his powerful conch, bringing joy to Duryodhana.

13) Conchshells, kettledrums, cymbals, large battle drums and horns all at once blared forth, making a sound that was tumultuous.

14) Standing in the great war chariot drawn by white horses, Kṛṣṇa and Arjuna, the son of Pāṇḍu, then sounded their divine conchshells.[6]

15) Kṛṣṇa sounded his conch, Pāñcajanya.[7] Arjuna, conqueror of wealth, blew the conch Devadatta,[8] and Bhīma of terrible deeds[9] sounded his great conch, Pauṇḍra.

16) King Yudhiṣṭhira, the son of Kuntī, sounded Anantavijaya. Nakula and Sahadeva blew Sughoṣa and Maṇipuṣpaka.

---

names and so leaves us with the problem. Commentators often explain Duryodhana's degradation of his own strength as a comment on Bhīṣma's partiality towards Kṛṣṇa and the Pāṇḍava.

6. The conches of Kṛṣṇa and Arjuna are described as "divine" (*divya*), whereas the conches of the others are not called "divine."

7. During the time that Kṛṣṇa lived with his teacher, Sāndīpani, Kṛṣṇa acquired the great conch named Pāñcajanya. An aquatic demon named Pañcajana, who had taken the form of a conch, kidnapped Sāndīpani's son. Kṛṣṇa entered the water and rescued the boy by killing Pañcajana. Thereafter, Kṛṣṇa used the great conch Pāñcajanya.

8. The conch Devadatta was given to Arjuna by his divine father, Indra.

9. Here Bhīma is literally called *vṛkodara,* wolf-belly, due to his famed voracious appetite.

काश्यश्च परमेष्वासः शिखण्डी च महारथः ।
धृष्टद्युम्नो विराटश्च सात्यकिश्चापराजितः ॥ १७

kāśyaś ca parameṣv-āsaḥ śikhaṇḍī ca mahā-rathaḥ
dhṛṣṭadyumno virāṭaś ca sātyakiś cāparājitaḥ

द्रुपदो द्रौपदेयाश्च सर्वशः पृथिवीपते ।
सौभद्रश्च महाबाहुः शङ्खान्दध्मुः पृथक्पृथक् ॥ १८

drupado draupadeyāś ca sarvaśaḥ pṛthivī-pate
saubhadraś ca mahā-bāhuḥ śāṅkhān dadhmuḥ pṛthak pṛthak

स घोषो धार्तराष्ट्राणां हृदयानि व्यदारयत् ।
नभश्च पृथिवीं चैव तुमुलो व्यनुनादयन् ॥ १९

sa ghoṣo dhārtarāṣṭrāṇāṁ hṛdayāni vyadārayat
nabhaś ca pṛthivīṁ caiva tumulo vyanunādayan

अथ व्यवस्थितान्दृष्ट्वा धार्तराष्ट्रान्कपिध्वजः ।
प्रवृत्ते शस्त्रसंपाते धनुरुद्यम्य पाण्डवः ॥ २०

atha vyavasthitān dṛṣṭvā dhārtarāṣṭrān kapi-dhvajaḥ
pravṛtte śastra-sampāte dhanur udyamya pāṇḍavaḥ

हृषीकेशं तदा वाक्यमिदमाह महीपते ।
सेनयोरुभयोर्मध्ये रथं स्थापय मेऽच्युत ॥ २१

hṛṣīkeśaṁ tadā vākyam idam āha mahī-pate
senayor ubhayor madhye rathaṁ sthāpaya me 'cyuta

यावदेतान्निरीक्षेऽहं योद्धुकामानवस्थितान् ।
कैर्मया सह योद्धव्यमस्मिन्रणसमुद्यमे ॥ २२

yāvad etān nirīkṣe 'haṁ yoddhu-kāmān avasthitān
kair mayā saha yoddhavyam asmin raṇa-samudyame

17-18) The great archer the King of Kāśi, and the great charioteer Śikhaṇḍī, as well as Dhṛṣṭadyumna, Virāṭa, and the unconquerable Sātyaki, Drupada, and the sons of Draupadī, along with the great-armed son of Subhadrā, altogether sounded their respective conchshells.

19) That tumultuous sound pierced the hearts of the sons of Dhṛtarāṣṭra and caused heaven and earth to resound.

20) Then Arjuna, the son of Pāṇḍu, whose flag is marked with the emblem of Hanumān,[10] seeing the sons of Dhṛtarāṣṭra prepared for battle, took up his bow as the clash of arms was about to commence.

21-22) Arjuna spoke the following words to Hṛṣīkeśa, Kṛṣṇa, "O Lord of the earth, O Acyuta,[11] place my chariot between the two armies, that I might see those who desire to fight and with whom I must engage in this enterprise of war.

---

10. The epithet "emblem of Hanumān" is literally *kapi-dhvaja*, the flag of the monkey. The epithet is meant to remind Dhṛtarāṣṭra of Hanumān sitting on the banner of Arjuna's chariot.
11. In this verse Kṛṣṇa is addressed as Hṛṣīkeśa, master of the senses, and Acyuta, one who is firm and who does not yield to passions.

योत्स्यमानानवेक्षेऽहं य एतेऽत्र समागताः ।
धार्तराष्ट्रस्य दुर्बुद्धेर्युद्धे प्रियचिकीर्षवः ॥ २३

yotsyamānān avekṣe 'haṁ ya ete 'tra samāgatāḥ
dhārtarāṣṭrasya durbuddher yuddhe priya-cikīrṣavaḥ

एवमुक्तो हृषीकेशो गुडाकेशेन भारत ।
सेनयोरुभयोर्मध्ये स्थापयित्वा रथोत्तमम् ॥ २४

evam ukto hṛṣīkeśo guḍākeśena bhārata
senayor ubhayor madhye sthāpayitvā rathottamam

भीष्मद्रोणप्रमुखतः सर्वेषां च महीक्षिताम् ।
उवाच पार्थ पश्यैतान्समवेतान्कुरूनिति ॥ २५

bhīṣma-droṇa-pramukhataḥ sarveṣāṁ ca mahī-kṣitām
uvāca pārtha paśyaitān samavetān kurūn iti

तत्रापश्यत्स्थितान्पार्थः पितॄनथ पितामहान् ।
आचार्यान्मातुलान्भ्रातॄन्पुत्रान्पौत्रान्सखींस्तथा ॥ २६

tatrāpaśyat sthitān pārthaḥ pitṝn atha pitāmahān
ācāryān mātulān brātṝn putrān pautrān sakhīṁs tathā

श्वशुरान्सुहृदश्चैव सेनयोरुभयोरपि ।
तान्समीक्ष्य स कौन्तेयः सर्वान्बन्धूनवस्थितान् ॥ २७

śvaśurān suhṛdaś caiva senayor ubhayor api
tān samīkṣya sa kaunteyaḥ sarvān bandhūn avasthitān

23) "I wish to see those who have assembled here desiring to satisfy the evil minded son of Dhṛtarāṣṭra in battle."

24) O Dhṛtarāṣṭra, Arjuna, conqueror of sleep,[12] thus spoke to Kṛṣṇa, who placed that finest of chariots between the two armies.

25) Kṛṣṇa then spoke as follows before Bhīṣma and Droṇa and all the chiefs of the earth: "O Pārtha,[13] behold the assembled Kurus."

26-27) There Arjuna saw fathers, grandfathers, teachers, uncles, brothers, sons, grandsons, companions, as well as fathers-in-laws and close friends standing before him. In both armies the son of Kuntī saw all his kinsmen arrayed for battle.

---

12. Here Arjuna is called Guḍākeśa, conqueror of sleep. This is in contrast to Dhṛtarāṣṭra who is blind. The metaphor suggests that Arjuna is spiritually awake whereas Dhṛtarāṣṭra lives in spiritual darkness.
13. Being the son of Pṛthā, Arjuna is called "Pārtha." Throughout the *Gītā* this name is used 38 times, more than any other address. The second place goes to Kaunteya, which has been used 24 times. The use of "Pārtha" shows intimacy between Kṛṣṇa and Arjuna. When Kṛṣṇa wants to say something special or give Arjuna assurance he calls Arjuna Pārtha.

कृपया परयाविष्टो विषीदन्निदमब्रवीत् ।
दृष्ट्वेमान्स्वजनान्कृष्ण युयुत्सून्समवस्थितान् ॥ २८

kṛpayā parayāviṣṭo viṣīdann idam abravīt
dṛṣṭvemān sva-janān kṛṣṇa yuyutsūn samupasthitān

सीदन्ति मम गात्राणि मुखं च परिशुष्यति ।
वेपथुश्च शरीरे मे रोमहर्षश्च जायते ॥ २९

sīdanti mama gātrāṇi mukhaṁ ca pariśuṣyati
vepathuś ca śarīre me roma-harṣaś ca jāyate

गाण्डीवं स्रंसते हस्तात्त्वक्चैव परिदह्यते ।
न च शक्नोम्यवस्थातुं भ्रमतीव च मे मनः ॥ ३०

gāṇḍīvaṁ sraṁsate hastāt tvak caiva paridahyate
na ca śaknomy avasthātuṁ bhramatīva ca me manaḥ

निमित्तानि च पश्यामि विपरीतानि केशव ।
न च श्रेयोऽनुपश्यामि हत्वा स्वजनमाहवे ॥ ३१

nimittāni ca paśyāmi viparītāni keśava
na ca śreyo 'nupaśyāmi hatvā sva-janam āhave

28-29) Overcome with profound compassion and lamentation, Arjuna spoke the following words: O Kṛṣṇa, seeing my kinsmen standing before me desiring to fight, the limbs of my body sink down in despair and my mouth dries up. My body trembles and my hair bristles on end.

30) My bow, Gāṇḍīva,[14] slips from my hand and my skin is burning. My mind is reeling and I unable to stand.

31) O Kṛṣṇa, killer of the Keśī demon,[15] I see only evil omens. I see no good in killing my kinsmen in battle.

---

14. The bow Gāṇḍīva was presented to Arjuna by the fire god, Agnideva, in exchange for assistance provided by Arjuna to exstinguish the burning of the Khāṇḍava forest.
15. Kṛṣṇa is here called Keśava, killer of the Keśī demon. Indirectly Arjuna is asking Kṛṣṇa to kill his demons of doubt. In verses 31 – 44 Arjuna intenifies his plea for help by addressing Kṛṣṇa with names meant to invoke Kṛṣṇa's various qualities.

न काङ्क्षे विजयं कृष्ण न च राज्यं सुखानि च ।
किं नो राज्येन गोविन्द किं भोगैर्जीवितेन वा ॥ ३२

na kāṅkṣe vijayaṁ kṛṣṇa na ca rājyaṁ sukhāni ca
kiṁ no rājyena govinda kiṁ bhogair jīvitena vā

येषामर्थे काङ्क्षितं नो राज्यं भोगाः सुखानि च ।
त इमेऽवस्थिता युद्धे प्राणांस्त्यक्त्वा धनानि च ॥ ३३

yeṣām arthe kāṅkṣitaṁ no rājyaṁ bhogāḥ sukhāni ca
ta ime 'vasthitā yuddhe prāṇāṁs tyaktvā dhanāni ca

आचार्याः पितरः पुत्रास्तथैव च पितामहाः ।
मातुलाः श्वशुराः पौत्राः स्यालाः संबन्धिनस्तथा ॥ ३४

ācāryāḥ pitaraḥ putrās tathaiva ca pitāmahāḥ
mātulāḥ śvaśurāḥ pautrāḥ syālāḥ sambandhinas tathā

एतान्न हन्तुमिच्छामि घ्नतोऽपि मधुसूदन ।
अपि त्रैलोक्यराज्यस्य हेतोः किं नु महीकृते ॥ ३५

etān na hantum icchāmi ghnato 'pi madhusūdana
api trailokya-rājyasya hetoḥ kiṁ nu mahī-kṛte

निहत्य धार्तराष्ट्रान्नः का प्रीतिः स्याज्जनार्दन ।
पापमेवाश्रयेदस्मान्हत्वैतानाततायिनः ॥ ३६

nihatya dhārtarāṣṭrān naḥ kā prītiḥ syāj janārdana
pāpam evāśrayed asmān hatvaitān ātatāyinaḥ

32-34) O Kṛṣṇa, Govinda,[16] I do not desire victory, kingdom or happiness. What use is a kingdom or enjoyments or even life itself, when teachers, fathers, sons, as well as grandfathers, uncles, fathers-in-law, grandsons, brothers-in-law–all kinsmen, are prepared to sacrifice life and wealth in battle?

35) O Madhusūdana,[17] though they are prepared to kill me, I do not desire to kill them even for dominion over the three worlds, what to speak of this earth.

36) O Janārdana,[18] what joy could we find in killing the sons of Dhṛtarāṣṭra? Only evil can befall us in killing such aggressors.[19]

---

16. Kṛṣṇa is called Govinda, one who gives pleasure and calms the senses.
17. Here Kṛṣṇa is called Madhusūdana, killer of the Madhu demon.
18. Another name for Kṛṣṇa is Janārdana, one who gives prosperity to the people.
19. The word *ātatāyinaḥ,* translated as aggressors, refers to persons guilty of six kinds of crimes: arson, poisoning, murder by offensive weapon, robbery with violence, forcible seizure of lands and kidnapping of married women. According to *smṛti-śāstra* such aggressors are to be killed. (VS 3/19, MS 8/351).

तस्मान्नार्हा वयं हन्तुं धार्तराष्ट्रान्सबान्धवान् ।
स्वजनं हि कथं हत्वा सुखिनः स्याम माधव ॥ ३७

tasmān nārhā vayaṁ hantuṁ dhārtarāṣṭrān sa-bāndhavān
sva-janaṁ hi kathaṁ hatvā sukhinaḥ syāma mādhava

यद्यप्येते न पश्यन्ति लोभोपहतचेतसः ।
कुलक्षयकृतं दोषं मित्रद्रोहे च पातकम् ॥ ३८

yady apy ete na paśyanti lobhopahata-cetasaḥ
kula-kṣaya-kṛtaṁ doṣaṁ mitra-drohe ca pātakam

कथं न ज्ञेयमस्माभिः पापादस्मान्निवर्तितुम् ।
कुलक्षयकृतं दोषं प्रपश्यद्भिर्जनार्दन ॥ ३९

kathaṁ na jñeyam asmābhiḥ pāpād asmān nivartitum
kula-kṣaya-kṛtaṁ doṣaṁ prapaśyadbhir janārdana

कुलक्षये प्रणश्यन्ति कुलधर्माः सनातनाः ।
धर्मे नष्टे कुलं कृत्स्नमधर्मोऽभिभवत्युत ॥ ४०

kula-kṣaye praṇaśyanti kula-dharmāḥ sanātanāḥ
dharme naṣṭe kulaṁ kṛtsnam adharmo 'bhibhavaty uta

अधर्माभिभवात्कृष्ण प्रदुष्यन्ति कुलस्त्रियः ।
स्त्रीषु दुष्टासु वार्ष्णेय जायते वर्णसंकरः ॥ ४१

adharmābhibhavāt kṛṣṇa praduṣyanti kula-striyaḥ
strīṣu duṣṭāsu vārṣṇeya jāyate varṇa-saṅkaraḥ

संकरो नरकायैव कुलघ्नानां कुलस्य च ।
पतन्ति पितरो ह्येषां लुप्तपिण्डोदकक्रियाः ॥ ४२

saṅkaro narakāyaiva kula-ghnānāṁ kulasya ca
patanti pitaro hy eṣāṁ lupta-piṇḍodaka-kriyāḥ

37) Therefore, we should not kill the sons of Dhṛtarāṣṭra who are our kinsmen. O Mādhava,[20] how can there be happiness in killing one's own family?

38-39) Even if those whose hearts are overtaken by greed do not see the evil in destroying the family or the crime of treachery against a friend, how can we, O Janārdana, who can see this wrong, not turn away from this evil?

40) When the family is destroyed, the ancient and sacred traditions are destroyed, and when sacred traditions are destroyed, *adharma*[21] certainly overtakes the entire family.

41) O Kṛṣṇa, descendant of Vṛṣṇi, when *adharma* prevails, the women of the family become spoiled, and when the women become spoiled, unwanted population[22] arises.

42) Unwanted population leads to hell for both those who destroy the family and the family itself. When the rites of ceremonial food and water offerings[23] are interrupted, the ancestors fall.

---

20. Now Arjuna is addressing Kṛṣṇa as Mādhava, husband of the goddess of fortune.
21. Adharma is the opposite of *dharma.* See BG 1.1 fn.1.
22. "Unwanted population" is a gloss of the Sanskrit term *varṇa-saṅkara,* which literally refers to the intermingling of caste. Such intermingling of caste leads to unwanted population.
23. "The rites of ceremonial food and water offerings" refers to the rituals of *śrāddha* and *tarpaṇa.* The belief is that departed souls, called *pitṛs,* are sustained by regular offerings of food and water by living relatives. Nourished by such relatives the *pitṛs* are sustained in a heavenly realm known as *pitṛ-loka.* In turn, they help the family living in this world. Consequently, there is a mutual exchange of help between the departed ancestors and their relatives in this world. Stopping these rites would interfere with this mutual process and thus both parties would suffer.

दोषैरेतैः कुलघ्नानां वर्णसंकरकारकैः ।
उत्साद्यन्ते जातिधर्माः कुलधर्माश्च शाश्वताः ॥ ४३

doṣair etaiḥ kula-ghnānāṁ varṇa-saṅkara-kārakaiḥ
utsādyante jāti-dharmāḥ kula-dharmāś ca śāśvatāḥ

उत्सन्नकुलधर्माणां मनुष्याणां जनार्दन ।
नरके नियतं वासो भवतीत्यनुशुश्रुम ॥ ४४

utsanna-kula-dharmāṇāṁ manuṣyāṇāṁ janārdana
narake niyataṁ vāso bhavatīty anuśuśruma

अहो बत महत्पापं कर्तुं व्यवसिता वयम् ।
यद्राज्यसुखलोभेन हन्तुं स्वजनमुद्यताः ॥ ४५

aho bata mahat pāpaṁ kartuṁ vyavasitā vayam
yad rājya-sukha-lobhena hantuṁ svajanam udyatāḥ

यदि मामप्रतीकारमशस्त्रं शस्त्रपाणयः ।
धार्तराष्ट्रा रणे हन्युस्तन्मे क्षेमतरं भवेत् ॥ ४६

yadi mām apratīkāram aśastraṁ śastra-pāṇayaḥ
dhārtarāṣṭrā raṇe hanyus tan me kṣemataraṁ bhavet

एवमुक्त्वार्जुनः संख्ये रथोपस्थ उपाविशत् ।
विसृज्य सशरं चापं शोकसंविग्नमानसः ॥ ४७

evam uktvārjunaḥ saṅkhye rathopastha upāviśat
visṛjya saśaraṁ cāpaṁ śoka-saṁvigna-mānasaḥ

43) Those who destroy the family and create unwanted population destroy both the laws that regulate society and the ancient family traditions.

44) O Janārdana, those whose family traditions have been destroyed certainly dwell in hell. This we have heard.

45) Alas, how sad it is that we are determined to commit such great evil. We are prepared to kill our own kinsmen out of greed for royal happiness.

46) It would be better if the sons of Dhṛtarāṣṭra, weapons in hand, should kill me, unresisting and without weapons in battle.

47) Speaking in this way, his mind overcome with grief, Arjuna sank down on the seat of his chariot. In the midst of both armies he cast aside his bow and arrows.[24]

---

24. Some texts begin this verse with *sanjaya uvāca*, "Sanjaya said."

संजय उवाच ।

तं तथा कृपयाविष्टमश्रुपूर्णाकुलेक्षणम् ।
विषीदन्तमिदं वाक्यमुवाच मधुसूदनः ॥ १

sañjaya uvāca
taṁ tathā kṛpayāviṣṭam aśru-pūrṇākulekṣaṇam
viṣīdantam idaṁ vākyam uvāca madhusūdanaḥ

श्रीभगवानुवाच ।

कुतस्त्वा कश्मलमिदं विषमे समुपस्थितम् ।
अनार्यजुष्टमस्वर्ग्यमकीर्तिकरमर्जुन ॥ २

śrī-bhagavān uvāca
kutas tvā kaśmalam idaṁ viṣame samupasthitam
anārya-juṣṭam asvargyam akīrti-karam arjuna

क्लैब्यं मा स्म गमः पार्थ नैतत्त्वय्युपपद्यते ।
क्षुद्रं हृदयदौर्बल्यं त्यक्त्वोत्तिष्ठ परंतप ॥ ३

klaibyaṁ mā sma gamaḥ pārtha naitat tvayy upapadyate
kṣudraṁ hṛdaya-daurbalyaṁ tyaktvottiṣṭha parantapa

Chapter Two

Sāṅkhya Yoga

Kṛṣṇa Protests

1) Sañjaya said:
Seeing Arjuna tearful and overwhelmed with compassion and despair, Madhusūdana[1] spoke the following words.

2) Kṛṣṇa Bhagavān[2] said:
O Arjuna,[3] how has such faintheartedness come upon you at this time of crisis? It does not befit a person of character[4] nor does it lead to heaven. It is the cause of infamy alone.

3) O Pārtha, scorcher of the enemy, do not give into such unmanliness, it does not become you. Give up this petty weakness of heart and arise.

Chapter Two is traditionally entitled *sāṅkhya-yoga,* The *Yoga* of Discrimination.

1. Here Kṛṣṇa is called Madhusūdana, killer of the Madhu demon, because He will now kill the demon of doubt that has entered the heart of Arjuna.

2. *Bhagavān* literally means one possessed of *bhaga. Bhaga* means the sun, the moon, or any positive attribute such as luster, fame, etc. Sometimes six *bhagas* are identified as wealth, virtue, glory, greatness, knowledge and renunciation. Kṛṣṇa, as *bhagavān,* possesses all six of these *bhagas* or attributes.

3. In this verse Kṛṣṇa addresses Arjuna by his direct name. The word "arjuna" means "one who is pure or white." The use of this form of address suggests that what is naturally pure has become stained by the impurity of ignorance.

4. "Does not befit a person of character" (*anārya-juṣṭam*) is literally "not suitable for an Aryan." Aryan means a noble one or person of distinction.

अर्जुन उवाच ।
कथं भीष्ममहं संख्ये द्रोणं च मधुसूदन ।
इषुभिः प्रतियोत्स्यामि पूजार्हावरिसूदन ॥ ४

arjuna uvāca
kathaṁ bhīṣmam ahaṁ saṅkhye droṇaṁ ca madhusūdana
iṣubhiḥ pratiyotsyāmi pūjārhāv ari-sūdana

गुरूनहत्वा हि महानुभावा-
ञ्श्रेयो भोक्तुं भैक्ष्यमपीह लोके ।
हत्वार्थकामांस्तु गुरूनिहैव
भुञ्जीय भोगान्रुधिरप्रदिग्धान् ॥ ५

gurūn ahatvā hi mahānubhāvāñ śreyo bhoktuṁ bhaikṣyam apīha loke
hatvārtha-kāmāṁs tu gurūn ihaiva bhuñjīya bhogān rudhira-pradigdhān

न चैतद्विद्मः कतरन्नो गरीयो
यद्वा जयेम यदि वा नो जयेयुः ।
यानेव हत्वा न जिजीविषाम-
स्तेऽवस्थिताः प्रमुखे धार्तराष्ट्राः ॥ ६

na caitad vidmaḥ kataran no garīyo yad vā jayema yadī vā no jayeyuḥ
yān eva hatvā na jijīviṣāmas te 'vasthitāḥ pramukhe dhārtarāṣṭrāḥ

कार्पण्यदोषोपहतस्वभावः
पृच्छामि त्वा धर्मसंमूढचेताः ।
यच्छ्रेयः स्यान्निश्चितं ब्रूहि तन्मे
शिष्यस्तेऽहं शाधि मां त्वां प्रपन्नम् ॥ ७

kārpaṇya-doṣopahata-svabhāvaḥ pṛcchāmi tvā dharma-sammūḍha-cetāḥ
yac chreyaḥ syān niścitaṁ brūhi tan me śiṣyas te 'haṁ śādhi māṁ tvāṁ prapannam

Arjuna's Response: I shall not Fight

4) Arjuna replied:
O Madhusūdana, O slayer of the foe, how shall I fight Bhīṣma and Droṇa with arrows in battle? They are worthy of my worship.

5) Better to live in this world eating the food of beggars than by killing my esteemed teachers. Though they desire worldly gain, I would only enjoy the spoils of war tainted with their blood if they met death at my hands.

Please Instruct Me

6) And neither do we know which is better—whether we should kill the sons of Dhṛtarāṣṭra, or whether they should kill us. For if we kill those who now stand before us, our lives would not be worth living.

7) My very being is overpowered by weakness. I am bewildered about my duty. What is best for me? I am your student surrendered unto you. Please instruct me.

न हि प्रपश्यामि ममापनुद्या-
द्यच्छोकमुच्छोषणमिन्द्रियाणाम् ।
अवाप्य भूमावसपत्नमृद्धं
राज्यं सुराणामपि चाधिपत्यम् ॥ ८

na hi prapaśyāmi mamāpanudyād yac chokam ucchoṣaṇam indriyāṇām
avāpya bhūmāv asapatnam ṛddhaṁ rājyaṁ surāṇām api cādhipatyam

संजय उवाच ।
एवमुक्त्वा हृषीकेशं गुडाकेशः परंतप ।
न योत्स्य इति गोविन्दमुक्त्वा तूष्णीं बभूव ह ॥ ९

sañjaya uvāca
evam uktvā hṛṣīkeśaṁ guḍākeśaḥ parantapaḥ
na yotsya iti govindam uktvā tūṣṇīṁ babhūva ha

तमुवाच हृषीकेशः प्रहसन्निव भारत ।
सेनयोरुभयोर्मध्ये विषीदन्तमिदं वचः ॥ १०

tam uvāca hṛṣīkeśaḥ prahasann iva bhārata
senayor ubhayor madhye viṣīdantam idaṁ vacaḥ

श्रीभगवानुवाच ।
अशोच्यानन्वशोचस्त्वं प्रज्ञावादांश्च भाषसे ।
गतासूनगतासूंश्च नानुशोचन्ति पण्डिताः ॥ ११

śrī-bhagavān uvāca
aśocyān anvaśocas tvaṁ prajñā-vādāṁś ca bhāṣase
gatāsūn agatāsūṁś ca nānuśocanti paṇḍitāḥ

8) Though I may obtain an unrivalled kingdom on earth with dominion over the gods, I am unable to remove this grief, which is afflicting my senses.

9) Sañjaya said:
Speaking to Kṛṣṇa[5] in this way, Arjuna,[6] scorcher of the enemy, declared, "I shall not fight," and fell silent.

10) O Dhṛtarāṣṭra, smiling faintly amidst the two armies, Kṛṣṇa spoke these words to the despondent Arjuna.

Kṛṣṇa Begins to Instruct Arjuna

11) Kṛṣṇa Bhagavān said:
My dear Arjuna, you speak words of learning and yet you are mourning for what is not worthy of grief. The truly learned lament neither for the living nor for the dead.

---

5. Here the actual address to Kṛṣṇa is Hṛṣīkeśa and Govinda. Hṛṣīkeśa means master of the senses. Arjuna is asking Kṛṣṇa to take charge of his senses that are out of control. Govinda means one who can give pleasure and calm the senses.
6. Here Arjuna is addressed as Guḍākeśa "conqueror of sleep" and Parantapa "scorcher of the enemy." The use of these forms of address suggest that Arjuna is being asked to wake up from his despondency and allow God to take charge of his disturbed mind and senses. Only in this way can he overcome his enemies.

न त्वेवाहं जातु नासं न त्वं नेमे जनाधिपाः ।
न चैव न भविष्यामः सर्वे वयमतः परम् ॥ १२
na tv evāhaṁ jātu nāsaṁ na tvaṁ neme janādhipāḥ
na caiva na bhaviṣyāmaḥ sarve vayam ataḥ param

देहिनोऽस्मिन्यथा देहे कौमारं यौवनं जरा ।
तथा देहान्तरप्राप्तिर्धीरस्तत्र न मुह्यति ॥ १३
dehino 'smin yathā dehe kaumāraṁ yauvanaṁ jarā
tathā dehāntara-prāptir dhīras tatra na muhyati

मात्रास्पर्शास्तु कौन्तेय शीतोष्णसुखदुःखदाः ।
आगमापायिनोऽनित्यास्तांस्तितिक्षस्व भारत ॥ १४
mātrā-sparśās tu kaunteya śītoṣṇa-sukha-duḥkha-dāḥ
āgamāpāyino 'nityās tāṁs titikṣasva bhārata

यं हि न व्यथयन्त्येते पुरुषं पुरुषर्षभ ।
समदुःखसुखं धीरं सोऽमृतत्वाय कल्पते ॥ १५
yaṁ hi na vyathayanty ete puruṣaṁ puruṣarṣabha
sama-duḥkha-sukhaṁ dhīraṁ so 'mṛtatvāya kalpate

नासतो विद्यते भावो नाभावो विद्यते सतः ।
उभयोरपि दृष्टोऽन्तस्त्वनयोस्तत्त्वदर्शिभिः ॥ १६
nāsato vidyate bhāvo nābhāvo vidyate sataḥ
ubhayor api dṛṣṭo 'ntas tv anayos tattva-darśibhiḥ

12) Never was there a time when I did not exist, nor you, nor these kings, nor in the future will you or any of these kings cease to exist.[7]

13) As the embodied soul experiences childhood, youth and old age, similarly the soul obtains another body at the time of death. The learned are not bewildered by such a change.

14) O son of Kuntī, contact with matter produces the sensations of heat and cold, happiness and distress. They come and go. O descendant of Bharata, you must tolerate them.

15) O bull amongst men, such contact does not lead to suffering for the learned person who is equal in happiness and distress. Indeed, such a person is fit for immortality.

This Eternal Soul

16) There is no permanence to that which is *asat*; there is no cessation to that which is *sat*.[8] Those who have seen the truth understand the difference between the two.

---

7. This verse illustrates the theological distinction between dualism and monism. On the side of dualism, Rāmānuja argues that the clear distinction between "I," "you" and "these kings" proves the existence of a plurality of souls (*ātman*) that are subject to rebirth until liberation is achieved. Śaṅkara, on the side of monism, says that the distinction is simply conventional. The plural number is used with reference to the bodies of the kings, etc. and not to the soul, which is without distinction.
8. Here, for the first time, the words *sat* and *asat* are introduced. *Sat* refers to things that are real and true, while *asat* refers to those things that are unreal and untrue. Śaṅkara, Rāmānuja and Madhva all agree that *asat* refers to the body and by extension, matter (*prakṛti*). By contrast, *sat*, refers to spirit. Rāmānuja states that the difference between matter and spirit is that matter is changeable whereas spirit is unchangeable. For this reason, matter is called *asat* while spirit is called *sat*. Similarly, Madhva

अविनाशि तु तद्विद्धि येन सर्वमिदं ततम् ।
विनाशमव्ययस्यास्य न कश्चित्कर्तुमर्हति ॥ १७

avināśi tu tad viddhi yena sarvam idaṁ tatam
vināśam avyayasyāsya na kaścit kartum arhati

अन्तवन्त इमे देहा नित्यस्योक्ताः शरीरिणः ।
अनाशिनोऽप्रमेयस्य तस्माद्युध्यस्व भारत ॥ १८

antavanta ime dehā nityasyoktāḥ śarīriṇaḥ
anāśino 'prameyasya tasmād yuddhyasva bhārata

य एनं वेत्ति हन्तारं यश्चैनं मन्यते हतम् ।
उभौ तौ न विजानीतो नायं हन्ति न हन्यते ॥ १९

ya enaṁ vetti hantāraṁ yaś cainaṁ manyate hatam
ubhau tau na vijānīto nāyaṁ hanti na hanyate

न जायते म्रियते वा कदाचि-
न्नायं भूत्वा भविता वा न भूयः ।
अजो नित्यः शाश्वतोऽयं पुराणो
न हन्यते हन्यमाने शरीरे ॥ २०

na jāyate mriyate vā kadācin nāyaṁ bhūtvā bhavitā vā na bhūyaḥ
ajo nityaḥ śāśvato 'yaṁ purāṇo na hanyate hanyamāne śarīre

वेदाविनाशिनं नित्यं य एनमजमव्ययम् ।
कथं स पुरुषः पार्थ कं घातयति हन्ति कम् ॥ २१

vedāvināśinaṁ nityaṁ ya enam ajam avyayam
kathaṁ sa puruṣaḥ pārtha kaṁ ghātayati hanti kam

17) That which pervades this[9] entire world is indestructible. No one is able to destroy what is imperishable.

18) These bodies of the eternal, indestructible and indefinable soul are said to possess an end. Therefore, O descendant of Bharata, fight.

19) One who thinks the soul[10] can kill or can be killed, does not understand, for the soul never kills nor is killed.

20) The soul is never born, nor does it ever die, nor having once been does it ever cease to be. Unborn, eternal and everlasting, this ancient one is not killed when the body is slain.

21) O Pārtha, how can a person who knows the soul to be indestructible, eternal, unborn and imperishable, kill anyone or cause anyone to kill?

---

points out that matter is never unreal at any time. It exists eternally. The difference between matter and spirit is that matter is a temporary and gross manifestation of reality. It is therefore is called *asat.* On the other hand, spirit, being an unchanging manifestation of reality, is called *sat.* Rāmānuja and Madhva appear to be in aggreement. In contrast, Śaṅkara says that what is *asat* does not in fact exist. In other words, matter is unreal. Spirit, on the other hand, is real. That most people perceive matter as real, according to Śaṅkara, is the result of faulty consciousness. For further uses of *sat* and *asat* see BG 11.37, 13.12, 17.23 and 17.26-28.

9. The word "this" (*idam*) can refer either to the world, as Śaṅkara and Rāmānuja take it, or to the body as others take it.

10. From verse 19 to verse 30 a description of the eternal principle of *sat* is given. This is the soul. In all cases the pronouns *enam* and *ayam* (it/this) are used to denote it. Nowhere are the words soul or self (*ātman*) actually employed.

वासांसि जीर्णानि यथा विहाय
नवानि गृह्णाति नरोऽपराणि ।
तथा शरीराणि विहाय जीर्णा-
न्यन्यानि संयाति नवानि देही ॥ २२

vāsāṁsi jīrṇāni yathā vihāya navāni gṛhṇāti naro 'parāṇi
tathā śarīrāṇi vihāya jīrṇāny anyāni saṁyāti navāni dehī

नैनं छिन्दन्ति शस्त्राणि नैनं दहति पावकः ।
न चैनं क्लेदयन्त्यापो न शोषयति मारुतः ॥ २३

nainaṁ chindanti śastrāṇi nainaṁ dahati pāvakaḥ
na cainaṁ kledayanty āpo na śoṣayati mārutaḥ

अच्छेद्योऽयमदाह्योऽयमक्लेद्योऽशोष्य एव च ।
नित्यः सर्वगतः स्थाणुरचलोऽयं सनातनः ॥ २४

acchedyo 'yam adāhyo 'yam akledyo 'śoṣya eva ca
nityaḥ sarva-gataḥ sthāṇur acalo 'yaṁ sanātanaḥ

अव्यक्तोऽयमचिन्त्योऽयमविकार्योऽयमुच्यते ।
तस्मादेवं विदित्वैनं नानुशोचितुमर्हसि ॥ २५

avyakto 'yam acintyo 'yam avikāryo 'yam ucyate
tasmād evaṁ viditvainaṁ nānuśocitum arhasi

अथ चैनं नित्यजातं नित्यं वा मन्यसे मृतम् ।
तथापि त्वं महाबाहो नैनं शोचितुमर्हसि ॥ २६

atha cainaṁ nitya-jātaṁ nityaṁ vā manyase mṛtam
tathāpi tvaṁ mahā-bāho nainaṁ śocitum arhasi

जातस्य हि ध्रुवो मृत्युर्ध्रुवं जन्म मृतस्य च ।
तस्मादपरिहार्येऽर्थे न त्वं शोचितुमर्हसि ॥ २७

jātasya hi dhruvo mṛtyur dhruvaṁ janma mṛtasya ca
tasmād aparihārye 'rthe na tvaṁ śocitum arhasi

22) As a person gives up an old garment and puts on one that is new, similarly the soul gives up the material body and accepts a body that is new.

23) Weapons can never cut the soul, nor can fire scorch it. Waters cannot moisten it, nor can the wind dry it.

24) The soul can neither be divided nor burned. It is insoluble and inextinguishable. It is eternal, all pervading, fixed, unshakable, and everlasting.

25) It is unmanifest, inconceivable and unchangeable. Knowing this you should not grieve.

Another Point of View

26) If, on the other hand, you think that the soul is constantly born and constantly dies, then again, O great-armed one, you should not grieve.

27) Death is certain for one who has been born, and birth is certain for one who has died, therefore you should not grieve for what is inevitable.

अव्यक्तादीनि भूतानि व्यक्तमध्यानि भारत ।
अव्यक्तनिधनान्येव तत्र का परिदेवना ॥ २८

avyaktādīni bhūtāni vyakta-madhyāni bhārata
avyakta-nidhanāny eva tatra kā paridevanā

आश्चर्यवत्पश्यति कश्चिदेन-
माश्चर्यवद्वदति तथैव चान्यः ।
आश्चर्यवच्चैनमन्यः शृणोति
श्रुत्वाप्येनं वेद न चैव कश्चित् ॥ २९

āścarya-vat paśyati kaścid enam āścarya-vad vadati tathaiva cānyaḥ
āścarya-vac cainam anyaḥ śṛṇoti śrutvāpy enaṁ veda na caiva kaścit

देही नित्यमवध्योऽयं देहे सर्वस्य भारत ।
तस्मात्सर्वाणि भूतानि न त्वं शोचितुमर्हसि ॥ ३०

dehī nityam avadhyo 'yaṁ dehe sarvasya bhārata
tasmāt sarvāṇi bhūtāni na tvaṁ śocitum arhasi

स्वधर्ममपि चावेक्ष्य न विकम्पितुमर्हसि ।
धर्म्याद्धि युद्धाच्छ्रेयोऽन्यत्क्षत्रियस्य न विद्यते ॥ ३१

sva-dharmam api cāvekṣya na vikampitum arhasi
dharmyād dhi yuddhāc chreyo 'nyat kṣatriyasya na vidyate

यदृच्छया चोपपन्नं स्वर्गद्वारमपावृतम् ।
सुखिनः क्षत्रियाः पार्थ लभन्ते युद्धमीदृशम् ॥ ३२

yadṛcchayā copapannaṁ svarga-dvāram apāvṛtam
sukhinaḥ kṣatriyāḥ pārtha labhante yuddham īdṛśam

अथ चेत्त्वमिमं धर्म्यं संग्रामं न करिष्यसि ।
ततः स्वधर्मं कीर्तिं च हित्वा पापमवाप्स्यसि ॥ ३३

atha cet tvam imaṁ dharmyaṁ saṅgrāmaṁ na kariṣyasi
tataḥ sva-dharmaṁ kīrtiṁ ca hitvā pāpam avāpsyasi

28) A living being is unmanifest in the beginning, manifest in the middle and again unmanifest at the end. O descendant of Bharata, why should you grieve about this?

29) By a rare chance[11] someone may see this soul; by a rare chance another may speak of this soul. Still another may hear of this soul, but even after seeing, speaking and hearing no one can truely know the soul.

30) O descendant of Bharata, that which is situated within the body of every being can never be killed. Therefore, you should grieve for no living being.

A Warrior's Duty

31) Considering your duty as a warrior, again you should not hesitate, for nothing is better for a warrior than to fight a battle for the sake of *dharma.*

32) Happy are those warriors, O son of Pṛthā, who obtain the opportunity to fight in a battle that opens the doorway to heaven.

33) But if you abandon your duty and fail to engage in this warfare, you will incur sin and lose your reputation.

---

11. "By a rare chance" (*āścaryavat*) is literally "by a great wonder" or "by a marvel."

अकीर्तिं चापि भूतानि कथयिष्यन्ति तेऽव्ययाम् ।
संभावितस्य चाकीर्तिर्मरणादतिरिच्यते ॥ ३४

akīrtiṁ cāpi bhūtāni kathayiṣyanti te 'vyayām
sambhāvitasya cākīrtir maraṇād atiricyate

भयाद्रणादुपरतं मंस्यन्ते त्वां महारथाः ।
येषां च त्वं बहुमतो भूत्वा यास्यसि लाघवम् ॥ ३५

bhayād raṇād uparataṁ maṁsyante tvāṁ mahā-rathāḥ
yeṣāṁ ca tvaṁ bahu-mato bhūtvā yāsyasi lāghavam

अवाच्यवादांश्च बहून्वदिष्यन्ति तवाहिताः ।
निन्दन्तस्तव सामर्थ्यं ततो दुःखतरं नु किम् ॥ ३६

avācya-vādāṁś ca bahūn vadiṣyanti tavāhitāḥ
nindantas tava sāmarthyaṁ tato duḥkhataraṁ nu kim

हतो वा प्राप्स्यसि स्वर्गं जित्वा वा भोक्ष्यसे महीम् ।
तस्मादुत्तिष्ठ कौन्तेय युद्धाय कृतनिश्चयः ॥ ३७

hato vā prāpsyasi svargaṁ jitvā vā bhokṣyase mahīm
tasmād uttiṣṭha kaunteya yuddhāya kṛta-niścayaḥ

सुखदुःखे समे कृत्वा लाभालाभौ जयाजयौ ।
ततो युद्धाय युज्यस्व नैवं पापमवाप्स्यसि ॥ ३८

sukha-duḥkhe same kṛtvā lābhālābhau jayājayau
tato yuddhāya yujyasva naivaṁ pāpam avāpsyasi

एषा तेऽभिहिता सांख्ये बुद्धिर्योगे त्विमां शृणु ।
बुद्ध्या युक्तो यया पार्थ कर्मबन्धं प्रहास्यसि ॥ ३९

eṣā te 'bhihitā sāṅkhye buddhir yoge tv imāṁ śṛṇu
buddhyā yukto yayā pārtha karma-bandhaṁ prahāsyasi

34) People will speak of your disgrace, and for one who has been honored, disgrace is worse than death.

35) The great fighters, who now praise you, will think that you have left the battle out of fear. They will hold you in contempt.

36) Your rivals will utter harsh words and criticize your abilities. What could be more distressing?

37) Either you will be killed here and attain heaven, or you will conquer and enjoy the earth. O son of Kuntī, arise and prepare to fight.

38) You must fight this battle and treat happiness and distress, gain and loss, victory and defeat as equal. In this way, you will never incur sin.

The Practice of Yoga

39) O son of Pṛthā, I have thus declared to you an understanding that is based on *sāṅkhya*;[12] now listen to it in terms of *yoga*.[13] Disciplined by this understanding you will be freed from the bondage of action.

---

12. The word *sāṅkhya* literally means enumeration or analysis, but it may also refer to the formal system of philosophy that enumerates or analyses the constituents of matter (*prakṛti*) and spirit (*puruṣa*). Since the preceding conversation has little to do with this kind of formal analysis I take *sāṅkhya* in its non-technical sense as a general analysis of Arjuna's situation. Some traditional commentators, (Rāmānuja, for example) equate *sāṅkhya* with *jñāna-yoga*.

13. The word *yoga* has many uses in the *Bhagavad Gītā*. In general it refers to any path or method to attain liberation. Many forms of *yoga* will subsequently be discussed: *karma-yoga, bhakti-yoga, dhyāna-yoga,* etc. In this case, *yoga* likely refers to *karma-yoga*, the path of spiritual action. See BG 3.3.

नेहाभिक्रमनाशोऽस्ति प्रत्यवायो न विद्यते ।
स्वल्पमप्यस्य धर्मस्य त्रायते महतो भयात् ॥ ४०
nehābhikrama-nāśo 'sti pratyavāyo na vidyate
sv-alpam apy asya dharmasya trāyate mahato bhayāt

व्यवसायात्मिका बुद्धिरेकेह कुरुनन्दन ।
बहुशाखा ह्यनन्ताश्च बुद्धयोऽव्यवसायिनाम् ॥ ४१
vyavasāyātmikā buddhir ekeha kuru-nandana
bahu-śākhā hy anantāś ca buddhayo 'vyavasāyinām

यामिमां पुष्पितां वाचं प्रवदन्त्यविपश्चितः ।
वेदवादरताः पार्थ नान्यदस्तीति वादिनः ॥ ४२
yām imāṁ puṣpitāṁ vācaṁ pravadanty avipaścitaḥ
veda-vāda-ratāḥ pārtha nānyad astīti vādinaḥ

कामात्मानः स्वर्गपरा जन्मकर्मफलप्रदाम् ।
क्रियाविशेषबहुलां भोगैश्वर्यगतिं प्रति ॥ ४३
kāmātmānaḥ svarga-parā janma-karma-phala-pradām
kriyā-viśeṣa-bahulāṁ bhogaiśvarya-gatiṁ prati

भोगैश्वर्यप्रसक्तानां तयापहृतचेतसाम् ।
व्यवसायात्मिका बुद्धिः समाधौ न विधीयते ॥ ४४
bhogaiśvarya-prasaktānāṁ tayāpahṛta-cetasām
vyavasāyātmikā buddhiḥ samādhau na vidhīyate

त्रैगुण्यविषया वेदा निस्त्रैगुण्यो भवार्जुन ।
निर्द्वंद्वो नित्यसत्त्वस्थो निर्योगक्षेम आत्मवान् ॥ ४५
trai-guṇya-viṣayā vedā nistrai-guṇyo bhavārjuna
nirdvandvo nitya-sattva-stho niryoga-kṣema ātmavān

40) There is no loss or decrease in this undertaking. Even a little of this *dharma* saves one from great danger.[14]

41) O beloved son of the Kurus, the intelligence of those who are determined is fixed, but the intelligence of those who lack determination is many-branched.

Vedic Religion

42-43) O Pārtha, the ignorant who delight in the mere words of the *Vedas* contend that there is nothing more than this. They speak flowery words and perform rituals for enjoyment and power, which simply lead to rebirth. Such fools are full of desires and are intent on heaven alone.

44) Those whose hearts have been stolen by such speech, who are attached to enjoyment and power, fail to develop a determined intellect or even concentration of mind.

45) The subject matter of the *Vedas* relates to the three *guṇas*.[15] O Arjuna, transcend these *guṇas*. Rise above duality. Fix yourself in goodness. Become free from striving and possession and focus on the soul alone.

---

14. Both Śaṅkara and Rāmānuja describe "great danger" as the cycle of rebirth, *saṁsāra*. Other commentators take it as the loss of human birth and subsequent rebirth in a lower species of life.

15. "The three qualities of matter" (*trai-guṇya*) refers to the three *guṇas*: *sattva* (goodness), *rajas* (passion) and *tamas* (darkness). The word *guṇa* has many meanings in Sanskrit, the most primary of which is quality. The three *guṇas* are sometimes called "the three strands of matter," "the three constituents of matter," or "the three modes of material nature." The subject matter of the three *guṇas* is central to the *Gītā*. These terms are first mentioned by name in BG 7.12 and described in greater detail in Chapter 14 and elsewhere. For more information about the specific nature of each *guṇa* see BG 14.5-20. In a related issue, Madhva says that the subject mat-

यावानर्थ उदपाने सर्वतः संप्लुतोदके ।
तावान्सर्वेषु वेदेषु ब्राह्मणस्य विजानतः ॥ ४६

yāvān artha udapāne sarvataḥ samplutodake
tāvān sarveṣu vedeṣu brāhmaṇasya vijānataḥ

कर्मण्येवाधिकारस्ते मा फलेषु कदाचन ।
मा कर्मफलहेतुर्भूर्मा ते सङ्गोऽस्त्वकर्मणि ॥ ४७

karmaṇy evādhikāras te mā phaleṣu kadācana
mā karma-phala-hetur bhūr mā te saṅgo 'stv akarmaṇi

योगस्थः कुरु कर्माणि सङ्गं त्यक्त्वा धनंजय ।
सिद्ध्यसिद्ध्योः समो भूत्वा समत्वं योग उच्यते ॥ ४८

yoga-sthaḥ kuru karmāṇi saṅgaṁ tyaktvā dhanañjaya
siddhy-asiddhyoḥ samo bhūtvā samatvaṁ yoga ucyate

दूरेण ह्यवरं कर्म बुद्धियोगाद्धनंजय ।
बुद्धौ शरणमन्विच्छ कृपणाः फलहेतवः ॥ ४९

dūreṇa hy avaraṁ karma buddhi-yogād dhanañjaya
buddhau śaraṇam anviccha kṛpaṇāḥ phala-hetavaḥ

बुद्धियुक्तो जहातीह उभे सुकृतदुष्कृते ।
तस्माद्योगाय युज्यस्व योगः कर्मसु कौशलम् ॥ ५०

buddhi-yukto jahātīha ubhe sukṛta-duṣkṛte
tasmād yogāya yujyasva yogaḥ karmasu kauśalam

कर्मजं बुद्धियुक्ता हि फलं त्यक्त्वा मनीषिणः ।
जन्मबन्धविनिर्मुक्ताः पदं गच्छन्त्यनामयम् ॥ ५१

karma-jaṁ buddhi-yuktā hi phalaṁ tyaktvā manīṣiṇaḥ
janma-bandha-vinirmuktāḥ padaṁ gacchanty anāmayam

46) What is the use for small pools of water when pure water flows from every direction? Similarly, what is the use of the *Vedas* for the learned person who knows *brahman*.[16]

Arjuna's Duty to Act

47) You have a right to perform your duty, but you are not entitled[17] to the results. Never allow the fruits of an action to be your motivation and never be attached to inaction.[18]

48) Become fixed in the discipline of *yoga* and perform your duty. Abandon attachment and become equal in success or failure. O conqueror of wealth, such balance is called *yoga*.

49) O Dhanañjaya, action performed with discipline of intellect is far superior to ordinary action. Seek shelter in enlightenment. Wretched are those who are motivated by results alone.

50) Those whose intellects are disciplined rid themselves of both good and evil actions in this world. Therefore, strive for the discipline of *yoga*, which is the perfection of all work.

51) The wise, whose intellects are disciplined and who are freed from the bonds of birth, give up attachment to the fruits of work and attain to that state which is free of all suffering.

---

ter of the *Vedas* only *appears* to relate to the three qualities of matter, but in truth the *Vedas* contain deeper meanings that should not be confused with the outward appearance that relates only to these qualities of matter.

16. "The learned person who knows *brahman*" (*brāhmaṇasya vijānataḥ*) is literally "to the learned *brāhmaṇa*." In the system of *varṇāśrama-dharma* a *brāhmaṇa* is a priest and teacher.

17. Here the word "right" and "entitled" are a translation of *adhikāra*. Literally, *adhikāra* means jurisdiction, claim, authority, duty, etc. It implies both the obligation to act as well as the freedom to choose actions. This verse is saying that Arjuna has jurisdiction over his actions, but not over the results of his actions.

18. "Never be attached to inaction" means always perform your duty.

यदा ते मोहकलिलं बुद्धिर्व्यतितरिष्यति ।
तदा गन्तासि निर्वेदं श्रोतव्यस्य श्रुतस्य च ॥ ५२

yadā te moha-kalilaṁ buddhir vyatitariṣyati
tadā gantāsi nirvedaṁ śrotavyasya śrutasya ca

श्रुतिविप्रतिपन्ना ते यदा स्थास्यति निश्चला ।
समाधावचला बुद्धिस्तदा योगमवाप्स्यसि ॥ ५३

śruti-vipratipannā te yadā sthāsyati niścalā
samādhāv acalā buddhis tadā yogam avāpsyasi

अर्जुन उवाच ।
स्थितप्रज्ञस्य का भाषा समाधिस्थस्य केशव ।
स्थितधीः किं प्रभाषेत किमासीत व्रजेत किम् ॥ ५४

arjuna uvāca
sthita-prajñasya kā bhāṣā samādhi-sthasya keśava
sthita-dhīḥ kiṁ prabhāṣeta kim āsīta vrajeta kim

श्रीभगवानुवाच ।
प्रजहाति यदा कामान्सर्वान्पार्थ मनोगतान् ।
आत्मन्येवात्मना तुष्टः स्थितप्रज्ञस्तदोच्यते ॥ ५५

śrī-bhagavān uvāca
prajahāti yadā kāmān sarvān pārtha mano-gatān
ātmany evātmanā tuṣṭaḥ sthita-prajñas tadocyate

दुःखेष्वनुद्विग्नमनाः सुखेषु विगतस्पृहः ।
वीतरागभयक्रोधः स्थितधीर्मुनिरुच्यते ॥ ५६

duḥkheṣv anudvigna-manāḥ sukheṣu vigata-spṛhaḥ
vīta-rāga-bhaya-krodhaḥ sthita-dhīr munir ucyate

52) When your intelligence has crossed beyond the tangle of delusion, you will become indifferent to all that has been heard and all that is to be heard.

53) When your intelligence stands firm, opposed to what has been heard, you will attain the discipline of *yoga*.

A Person of Mature Understanding

54) Arjuna inquired:
O Keśava, what are the characteristics of one whose understanding is mature, who is fixed in concentration and whose thoughts are focused. How does that person speak? How does that person sit and walk?

55) Kṛṣṇa Bhagavān said:
O Pārtha, when one has given up all desires that originate within the mind, and has found contentment within, one is said to be of mature understanding.

56) One whose mind is free of anxiety during times of trouble, and who is without the desire for happiness, whose passions, fears and anger have departed, is called a sage of steady mind.

यः सर्वत्रानभिस्नेहस्तत्तत्प्राप्य शुभाशुभम् ।
नाभिनन्दति न द्वेष्टि तस्य प्रज्ञा प्रतिष्ठिता ॥ ५७

yaḥ sarvatrānabhisnehas tat tat prāpya śubhāśubham
nābhinandati na dveṣṭi tasya prajñā pratiṣṭhitā

यदा संहरते चायं कूर्मोऽङ्गानीव सर्वशः ।
इन्द्रियाणीन्द्रियार्थेभ्यस्तस्य प्रज्ञा प्रतिष्ठिता ॥ ५८

yadā saṁharate cāyaṁ kūrmo 'ṅgānīva sarvaśaḥ
indriyāṇīndriyārthebhyas tasya prajñā pratiṣṭhitā

विषया विनिवर्तन्ते निराहारस्य देहिनः ।
रसवर्जं रसोऽप्यस्य परं दृष्ट्वा निवर्तते ॥ ५९

viṣayā vinivartante nirāhārasya dehinaḥ
rasa-varjaṁ raso 'py asya paraṁ dṛṣṭvā nivartate

यततो ह्यपि कौन्तेय पुरुषस्य विपश्चितः ।
इन्द्रियाणि प्रमाथीनि हरन्ति प्रसभं मनः ॥ ६०

yatato hy api kaunteya puruṣasya vipaścitaḥ
indriyāṇi pramāthīni haranti prasabhaṁ manaḥ

तानि सर्वाणि संयम्य युक्त आसीत मत्परः ।
वशे हि यस्येन्द्रियाणि तस्य प्रज्ञा प्रतिष्ठिता ॥ ६१

tāni sarvāṇi saṁyamya yukta āsīta mat-paraḥ
vaśe hi yasyendriyāṇi tasya prajñā pratiṣṭhitā

ध्यायतो विषयान्पुंसः सङ्गस्तेषूपजायते ।
सङ्गात्संजायते कामः कामात्क्रोधोऽभिजायते ॥ ६२

dhyāyato viṣayān puṁsaḥ saṅgas teṣūpajāyate
saṅgāt sañjāyate kāmaḥ kāmāt krodho 'bhijāyate

57) One who is free of desire, whether good or evil, and who neither rejoices nor hates, is a person of mature understanding.

58) As the tortoise withdraws its limbs on all sides, so a person of mature understanding is able to withdraw the senses from the sense objects.

59) Although the taste for enjoyment remains, the learned person ceases to engage the senses.[19] However, when one experiences the Supreme, even the taste for sense enjoyment vanishes.

60) O son of Kuntī, the churning senses forcibly carry away the mind of even a learned person who strives for *yoga.*

61) The disciplined person should remain intent on Me while controlling the senses. The intelligence of one whose senses are under control stands firm.

62) While contemplating the objects of the senses, attachment to them arises; from such attachment desire develops, and from desire a person experiences anger.

---

19. Literally, this line reads: The sense objects turn away for the embodied soul who abstains from food, although the taste remains.

क्रोधाद्भवति संमोहः संमोहात्स्मृतिविभ्रमः ।
स्मृतिभ्रंशाद्बुद्धिनाशो बुद्धिनाशात्प्रणश्यति ॥ ६३

krodhād bhavati sammohaḥ sammohāt smṛti-vibhramaḥ
smṛti-bhraṁśād buddhi-nāśo buddhi-nāśāt praṇaśyati

रागद्वेषवियुक्तैस्तु विषयानिन्द्रियैश्चरन् ।
आत्मवश्यैर्विधेयात्मा प्रसादमधिगच्छति ॥ ६४

rāga-dveṣa-viyuktais tu viṣayān indriyaiś caran
ātma-vaśyair vidheyātmā prasādam adhigacchati

प्रसादे सर्वदुःखानां हानिरस्योपजायते ।
प्रसन्नचेतसो ह्याशु बुद्धिः पर्यवतिष्ठते ॥ ६५

prasāde sarva-duḥkhānāṁ hānir asyopajāyate
prasanna-cetaso hy āśu buddhiḥ paryavatiṣṭhate

नास्ति बुद्धिरयुक्तस्य न चायुक्तस्य भावना ।
न चाभावयतः शान्तिरशान्तस्य कुतः सुखम् ॥ ६६

nāsti buddhir ayuktasya na cāyuktasya bhāvanā
na cābhāvayataḥ śāntir aśāntasya kutaḥ sukham

इन्द्रियाणां हि चरतां यन्मनोऽनुविधीयते ।
तदस्य हरति प्रज्ञां वायुर्नावमिवाम्भसि ॥ ६७

indriyāṇāṁ hi caratāṁ yan mano 'nuvidhīyate
tad asya harati prajñāṁ vāyur nāvam ivāmbhasi

तस्माद्यस्य महाबाहो निगृहीतानि सर्वशः ।
इन्द्रियाणीन्द्रियार्थेभ्यस्तस्य प्रज्ञा प्रतिष्ठिता ॥ ६८

tasmād yasya mahā-bāho nigṛhītāni sarvaśaḥ
indriyāṇīndriyārthebhyas tasya prajñā pratiṣṭhitā

63) From anger, delusion arises and from delusion comes the bewilderment of memory. When memory is bewildered, intelligence is lost and when intelligence is lost, one is destroyed.

64) But when passion and hatred are eliminated, the disciplined soul attains serenity through self-control even though the senses remain engaged with their sense objects.

65) All sufferings cease for one who has attained serenity. Once the mind is tranquil, intelligence quickly becomes steady.

66) There can be no understanding for one who is without discipline, nor can there be any development of mind.[20] One who has failed to develop the mind can find no peace. How can there be happiness without peace?

67) As the wind carries away a boat on water, so the mind that focuses on the wandering senses carries away a person's discrimination.

68) O great-armed Arjuna, one whose senses are withdrawn from the objects of the senses is a person of steady intelligence.

20. The word *bhāvanā* that is here translated as "development of mind" is literally "coming to be." Śaṅkara takes it as "meditation." Rāmānuja takes it as "right disposition of mind." Madhva takes it as "concentration of mind."

या निशा सर्वभूतानां तस्यां जागर्ति संयमी ।
यस्यां जाग्रति भूतानि सा निशा पश्यतो मुनेः ॥ ६९

yā niśā sarva-bhūtānāṁ tasyāṁ jāgarti saṁyamī
yasyāṁ jāgrati bhūtāni sā niśā paśyato muneḥ

आपूर्यमाणमचलप्रतिष्ठं
समुद्रमापः प्रविशन्ति यद्वत् ।
तद्वत्कामा यं प्रविशन्ति सर्वे
स शान्तिमाप्नोति न कामकामी ॥ ७०

āpūryamāṇam acala-pratiṣṭhaṁ samudram āpaḥ praviśanti yadvat
tadvat kāmā yaṁ praviśanti sarve sa śāntim āpnoti na kāma-kāmī

विहाय कामान्यः सर्वान्पुमांश्चरति निःस्पृहः ।
निर्ममो निरहंकारः स शान्तिमधिगच्छति ॥ ७१

vihāya kāmān yaḥ sarvān pumāṁś carati niḥspṛhaḥ
nirmamo nirahaṅkāraḥ sa śāntim adhigacchati

एषा ब्राह्मी स्थितिः पार्थ नैनां प्राप्य विमुह्यति ।
स्थित्वास्यामन्तकालेऽपि ब्रह्मनिर्वाणमृच्छति ॥ ७२

eṣā brāhmī sthitiḥ pārtha naināṁ prāpya vimuhyati
sthitvāsyām anta-kāle 'pi brahma-nirvāṇam ṛcchati

69) What is night for all beings is a time of awakening for one who is self-controlled. What is the time of awakening for all beings is night for the sage of vision.

70) As the ocean remains ever still, even though water constantly flows into it, so the sage of steady intelligence remains at peace in spite of the constant flow of desire. This is not the case for one who seeks to satisfy such desires.

71) A person who lives without longing, letting go of all desires, and who is free from worldly ties and egotism, attains peace.

72) O Pārtha, such is the divine life. One who achieves this state is no longer deluded, and at the time of death attains union with *brahman.*[21]

---

21. What is here translated as "union with *brahman*" is *brahma-nirvāṇa. Nirvāṇa* means "blown out" or "extinguished" and so it refers to the extinguishing of material existence and thereby the attainment of *brahman*, the Supreme. For a similar usuage see BG 5.24.

अर्जुन उवाच ।
ज्यायसी चेत्कर्मणस्ते मता बुद्धिर्जनार्दन ।
तत्किं कर्मणि घोरे मां नियोजयसि केशव ॥ १

arjuna uvāca
jyāyasī cet karmaṇas te matā buddhir janārdana
tat kiṁ karmaṇi ghore māṁ niyojayasi keśava

व्यामिश्रेणेव वाक्येन बुद्धिं मोहयसीव मे ।
तदेकं वद निश्चित्य येन श्रेयोऽहमाप्नुयाम् ॥ २

vyāmiśreṇaiva vākyena buddhiṁ mohayasīva me
tad ekaṁ vada niścitya yena śreyo 'ham āpnuyām

श्रीभगवानुवाच ।
लोकेऽस्मिन्द्विविधा निष्ठा पुरा प्रोक्ता मयानघ ।
ज्ञानयोगेन सांख्यानां कर्मयोगेन योगिनाम् ॥ ३

śrī-bhagavān uvāca
loke 'smin dvi-vidhā niṣṭhā purā proktā mayānagha
jñāna-yogena sāṅkhyānāṁ karma-yogena yoginām

न कर्मणामनारम्भान्नैष्कर्म्यं पुरुषोऽश्नुते ।
न च संन्यसनादेव सिद्धिं समधिगच्छति ॥ ४

na karmaṇām anārambhān naiṣkarmyaṁ puruṣo 'śnute
na ca sannyasanād eva siddhiṁ samadhigacchati

Chapter Three

Karma Yoga

A Contemplative Life Versus A Life of Action

1) Arjuna inquired:
O Janārdana, Keśava, if you think a contemplative life[1] is superior to a life of action, why do you urge me to engage in this terrible warfare?

2) I am bewildered by your words, which seem contradictory. Please tell me with certainty what is best for me.

3) Kṛṣṇa Bhagavān said:
O sinless Arjuna, in the past I have described two paths of faith: the discipline of knowledge for those who follow the path of *sāṅkhya,* and the discipline of action for those who follow the path of *yoga.*[2]

4) A person cannot attain freedom from the bonds of action by simply not undertaking action, nor can one attain perfection by the mere renunciation of worldly affairs.

Chapter Three is traditionally entitled, *karma-yoga,* The Yoga of Action.
1. What is translated as "a contemplative life" is *buddhi.* The word *buddhi* has many uses in the *Gītā.* Literally, it means intellect, intelligence or reason. Here Śaṅkara takes it as "divine knowledge." Rāmānuja takes it as "mental disposition."
2. Compare this verse with BG 2.39. The followers of *sāṅkhya* take the path of knowledge (*jñāna-yoga*) and the followers of yoga take the path of action (*karma-yoga*).

न हि कश्चित्क्षणमपि जातु तिष्ठत्यकर्मकृत् ।
कार्यते ह्यवशः कर्म सर्वः प्रकृतिजैर्गुणैः ॥ ५

na hi kaścit kṣaṇam api jātu tiṣṭhaty akarma-kṛt
kāryate hy avaśaḥ karma sarvaḥ prakṛti-jair guṇaiḥ

कर्मेन्द्रियाणि संयम्य य आस्ते मनसा स्मरन् ।
इन्द्रियार्थान्विमूढात्मा मिथ्याचारः स उच्यते ॥ ६

karmendriyāṇi saṁyamya ya āste manasā smaran
indriyārthān vimūḍhātmā mithyācāraḥ sa ucyate

यस्त्विन्द्रियाणि मनसा नियम्यारभतेऽर्जुन ।
कर्मेन्द्रियैः कर्मयोगमसक्तः स विशिष्यते ॥ ७

yas tv indriyāṇi manasā niyamyārabhate 'rjuna
karmendriyaiḥ karma-yogam asaktaḥ sa viśiṣyate

नियतं कुरु कर्म त्वं कर्म ज्यायो ह्यकर्मणः ।
शरीरयात्रापि च ते न प्रसिध्येदकर्मणः ॥ ८

niyataṁ kuru karma tvaṁ karma jyāyo hy akarmaṇaḥ
śarīra-yātrāpi ca te na prasiddhyed akarmaṇaḥ

यज्ञार्थात्कर्मणोऽन्यत्र लोकोऽयं कर्मबन्धनः ।
तदर्थं कर्म कौन्तेय मुक्तसङ्गः समाचर ॥ ९

yajñārthāt karmaṇo 'nyatra loko 'yaṁ karma-bandhanaḥ
tad-arthaṁ karma kaunteya mukta-saṅgaḥ samācara

सहयज्ञाः प्रजाः सृष्ट्वा पुरोवाच प्रजापतिः ।
अनेन प्रसविष्यध्वमेष वोऽस्त्विष्टकामधुक् ॥ १०

saha-yajñāḥ prajāḥ sṛṣṭvā purovāca prajāpatiḥ
anena prasaviṣyadhvam eṣa vo 'stv iṣṭa-kāma-dhuk

5) One cannot exist for even a moment without acting, for all beings are forced to act according to the impulses born of material nature.[3]

6) One who controls the active senses, and yet mentally contemplates the objects of the senses, is a deluded soul and is called an impostor.

7) O Arjuna, one who controls the active senses by the mind, and who undertakes *karma-yoga* without attachment is best.

8) You must perform your required duty, for action is better than inaction. Even for the maintenance of your body you cannot exist without acting.

9) O son of Kuntī, except for action performed as sacrifice,[4] this world is bound by action. Therefore, without attachment, perform your duty as an act of sacrifice.

The Wheel of Sacrifice

10) In ancient times, Prajāpati, the lord of creatures, created all beings along with sacrifice. He declared, "Become prosperous by the performance of sacrifice. Let this be your means to attain all desirable things."[5]

---

3. "The impulses born of material nature" *(prakṛti-jair guṇaiḥ)* refers to the three qualities of material nature called *guṇas*. See BG fn. 2.45.
4. Śaṅkara and Madhva both point out that the word "sacrifice" *(yajña)* used here means Viṣṇu. The implied meaning is that action must be performed as a sacrifice to God.
5. The expression "means to attain all desirable things" is derived from the compound *iṣṭa-kāma-dhuk* "wish-yielding cow of desire." The *kāma-dhuk* is a celestial cow possessed by Indra said to provide not just milk, but whatever its owner desires.

देवान्भावयतानेन ते देवा भावयन्तु वः ।
परस्परं भावयन्तः श्रेयः परमवाप्स्यथ ॥ ११

devān bhāvayatānena te devā bhāvayantu vaḥ
parasparaṁ bhāvayantaḥ śreyaḥ param avāpsyatha

इष्टान्भोगान्हि वो देवा दास्यन्ते यज्ञभाविताः ।
तैर्दत्तानप्रदायैभ्यो यो भुङ्क्ते स्तेन एव सः ॥ १२

iṣṭān bhogān hi vo devā dāsyante yajña-bhāvitāḥ
tair dattān apradāyaibhyo yo bhuṅkte stena eva saḥ

यज्ञशिष्टाशिनः सन्तो मुच्यन्ते सर्वकिल्बिषैः ।
भुञ्जते ते त्वघं पापा ये पचन्त्यात्मकारणात् ॥ १३

yajña-śiṣṭāśinaḥ santo mucyante sarva-kilbiṣaiḥ
bhuñjate te tv aghaṁ pāpā ye pacanty ātma-kāraṇāt

अन्नाद्भवन्ति भूतानि पर्जन्यादन्नसंभवः ।
यज्ञाद्भवति पर्जन्यो यज्ञः कर्मसमुद्भवः ॥ १४

annād bhavanti bhūtāni parjanyād anna-sambhavaḥ
yajñād bhavati parjanyo yajñaḥ karma-samudbhavaḥ

11) Therefore, through acts of sacrifice nourish the gods and let the gods nourish you.[6] Helping each other in this way you will attain the highest good.[7]

12) Being nourished by sacrifice, the gods will provide you with all desirable things. One who enjoys the things of this world, however, without acknowledging the source is a thief.

13) The pious, who eat the remnants of sacrifice are freed from all sins, but the impious, who cook solely for their own sake, eat only sin.[8]

14) All creatures arise from food.[9] Food springs from the rain.[10] Rain arises from sacrifice, and sacrifice is brought about by action.[11]

---

6. The literal sense of this line is: cause the gods to be and the gods will cause you to be. This reflects a metaphysical relationship between the divine beings and mankind; each creates and sustains the existence of the other.
7. In this context Śaṅkara says that the highest good is *svarga*, heaven. Others suggest it means *mokṣa*. Śaṅkara's interpretation is consistent with the teachings of the *Gītā*. See BG 7.20-23. Worship of gods leads to the fulfillment of human desire in this world and not to *mokṣa,* liberation.
8. The understanding behind this verse is as follows: foods offered to God through the performance of sacrifice become sanctified and cleansed of sin (*karma*). Such foods are commonly called *prasāda,* which literally means "divine mercy." These foods are able to purify those who partake of them.
9. The *Manu-saṁhita* (MS 3.76) describes how creatures arise from food: An oblation properly offered into the fire reaches the sun. From the sun rain is born, from rain food is created, and from food creatures arise. Also see TU 2.2 and 3.7.
10. Here the word *parjanya* means both rain and the rain god.
11. The word action as it is used in this verse means sacrificial action and not action in general.

कर्म ब्रह्मोद्भवं विद्धि ब्रह्माक्षरसमुद्भवम् ।
तस्मात्सर्वगतं ब्रह्म नित्यं यज्ञे प्रतिष्ठितम् ॥ १५

karma brahmodbhavaṁ viddhi brahmākṣara-samudbhavam
tasmāt sarva-gataṁ brahma nityaṁ yajñe pratiṣṭhitam

एवं प्रवर्तितं चक्रं नानुवर्तयतीह यः ।
अघायुरिन्द्रियारामो मोघं पार्थ स जीवति ॥ १६

evaṁ pravartitaṁ cakraṁ nānuvartayatīha yaḥ
aghāyur indriyārāmo moghaṁ pārtha sa jīvati

यस्त्वात्मरतिरेव स्यादात्मतृप्तश्च मानवः ।
आत्मन्येव च संतुष्टस्तस्य कार्यं न विद्यते ॥ १७

yas tv ātma-ratir eva syād ātma-tṛptaś ca mānavaḥ
ātmany eva ca santuṣṭas tasya kāryaṁ na vidyate

15) Know that sacrificial action arises from *brahman* and that *brahman* arises from the Imperishable. Therefore, the all-pervading *brahman* is eternally situated in acts of sacrifice.[12]

16) O son of Pṛthā, one who exists only to enjoy the senses and who fails to maintain this cycle of action[13] is sinful and lives in vain.

Satisfaction in the Soul

17) But for the person who takes pleasure in the soul,[14] who is self-content and who rejoices in the soul alone, there is no obligation to perform such action.

---

12. There is a wide variation of interpretation in this verse according to how the word *brahman* is translated. The word *brahman* is used three times. Śaṅkara says that *brahman* has two meanings in this verse: the *Vedas* and the Supreme. According to Śaṅkara the verse could be translated as follows: "Know that sacrificial action arises from the *Vedas* and that the *Vedas* arise from the Supreme. Therefore, the all pervading Supreme is eternally situated in acts of sacrifice." Rāmānuja, on the other hand, says that *brahman* means the body as well as the living being. A translation according to Rāmānuja reads: "Know that action arises from the *body* and that the body arises from the *living being*. Therefore, everyone's body is eternally situated in acts of sacrifice." Madhva, in another interpretation, says that *brahman* here means the Supreme as well as the *Vedas* (but in the reverse order of Śaṅkara). Thus his translation would read, "Know that sacrificial action arises from the *Supreme* and that the Supreme is revealed by the imperishable *Vedas*. Therefore, the all pervading Supreme is eternally situated in acts of sacrifice."

13. Reference to the cycle of action (*cakra*) can also be found in the ŚU 1.4-6.

14. Here the word used for "soul" is *ātman*. Some commentators translate *ātman* as self. I use the word soul because self suggests the total being of a person including the emotional and intellectual aspects of personality. But here only the immaterial essence that animates the living being is indicated. Consequently, soul better captures the meaning of *ātman*.

नैव तस्य कृतेनार्थो नाकृतेनेह कश्चन ।
न चास्य सर्वभूतेषु कश्चिदर्थव्यपाश्रयः ॥ १८

naiva tasya kṛtenārtho nākṛteneha kaścana
na cāsya sarva-bhūteṣu kaścid artha-vyapāśrayaḥ

तस्मादसक्तः सततं कार्यं कर्म समाचर ।
असक्तो ह्याचरन्कर्म परमाप्नोति पूरुषः ॥ १९

tasmād asaktaḥ satataṁ kāryaṁ karma samācara
asakto hy ācaran karma param āpnoti pūruṣaḥ

कर्मणैव हि संसिद्धिमास्थिता जनकादयः ।
लोकसंग्रहमेवापि संपश्यन्कर्तुमर्हसि ॥ २०

karmaṇaiva hi saṁsiddhim āsthitā janakādayaḥ
loka-saṅgraham evāpi sampaśyan kartum arhasi

यद्यदाचरति श्रेष्ठस्तत्तदेवेतरो जनः ।
स यत्प्रमाणं कुरुते लोकस्तदनुवर्तते ॥ २१

yad yad ācarati śreṣṭhas tat tad evetaro janaḥ
sa yat pramāṇaṁ kurute lokas tad anuvartate

न मे पार्थास्ति कर्तव्यं त्रिषु लोकेषु किंचन ।
नानवाप्तमवाप्तव्यं वर्त एव च कर्मणि ॥ २२

na me pārthāsti kartavyaṁ triṣu lokeṣu kiñcana
nānavāptam avāptavyaṁ varta eva ca karmaṇi

यदि ह्यहं न वर्तेयं जातु कर्मण्यतन्द्रितः ।
मम वर्त्मानुवर्तन्ते मनुष्याः पार्थ सर्वशः ॥ २३

yadi hy ahaṁ na varteyaṁ jātu karmaṇy atandritaḥ
mama vartmānuvartante manuṣyāḥ pārtha sarvaśaḥ

18) Such a person has no vested interest[15] in what is done or what is not done in this world, nor is this person dependent on any living being.

Act without Attachment

19) Therefore, you must always perform your duty without attachment, for by acting without attachment one attains the Supreme.

20) By action alone King Janaka[16] and others attained perfection. Considering the welfare of all beings you must perform your prescribed duties.

21) Whatever action is performed by a great person all of mankind follows. Whatever example such a person sets the whole world pursues.

22) O son of Pṛthā, in all the three worlds there is nothing that I must do, nor is there anything that I have not attained, and still I engage in work.

23) For if I ceased to work, O Pārtha, all of mankind would surely follow my path.[17]

---

15. What is here translated as "vested interest" is a rendering of the word *artha*, which literally means purpose or interest.
16. King Janaka, ruler of Videha, is the philosopher king famous in the *Upaniṣads* for his charity and learned conversations with the sage Yājñāvalkya. See BṛU 2.1-1, 4.1-4 and KauU 4.1. In the *Rāmāyāṇa* Janaka is the father of Sītā.
17. "O Pārtha, all of mankind would surely follow my path" (*mama vartmānuvartante manuṣyāḥ pārtha sarvaśaḥ*): The identical passage is used in BG 4.11.

उत्सीदेयुरिमे लोका न कुर्यां कर्म चेदहम् ।
संकरस्य च कर्ता स्यामुपहन्यामिमाः प्रजाः ॥ २४

utsīdeyur ime lokā na kuryāṁ karma ced aham
saṅkarasya ca kartā syām upahanyām imāḥ prajāḥ

सक्ताः कर्मण्यविद्वांसो यथा कुर्वन्ति भारत ।
कुर्याद्विद्वांस्तथासक्तश्चिकीर्षुर्लोकसंग्रहम् ॥ २५

saktāḥ karmaṇy avidvāṁso yathā kurvanti bhārata
kuryād vidvāṁs tathāsaktaś cikīrṣur loka-saṅgraham

न बुद्धिभेदं जनयेदज्ञानां कर्मसङ्गिनाम् ।
जोषयेत्सर्वकर्माणि विद्वान्युक्तः समाचरन् ॥ २६

na buddhi-bhedaṁ janayed ajñānāṁ karma-saṅginām
joṣayet sarva-karmāṇi vidvān yuktaḥ samācaran

प्रकृतेः क्रियमाणानि गुणैः कर्माणि सर्वशः ।
अहंकारविमूढात्मा कर्ताहमिति मन्यते ॥ २७

prakṛteḥ kriyamāṇāni guṇaiḥ karmāṇi sarvaśaḥ
ahaṅkāra-vimūḍhātmā kartāham iti manyate

तत्त्ववित्तु महाबाहो गुणकर्मविभागयोः ।
गुणा गुणेषु वर्तन्त इति मत्वा न सज्जते ॥ २८

tattva-vit tu mahā-bāho guṇa-karma-vibhāgayoḥ
guṇā guṇeṣu vartanta iti matvā na sajjate

24) All these worlds would perish if I did not work. I would be the cause of unwanted population[18] and the destruction of all creatures.

25) O descendent of Bharata, as an ignorant person works with attachment, so a learned person should act without attachment and for the welfare of the world.

26) One should not disturb the understanding[19] of the ignorant who are attached to action. Instead, acting with discipline, the learned should engage them in beneficial works.

Material Nature is the Agent

27) In all respects actions are carried out by the qualities of material nature,[20] but the soul deluded by ego thinks, "I am the doer."

28) But the learned person, O great-armed one, who knows the distinction between the qualities of material nature and action, and who understands, "The senses are simply interacting with the sense objects,"[21] is not attached.[22]

---

18. For a note on "unwanted population" see fn. BG 1.41.

19. The expression, "disturb the understanding" (*buddhi-bheda*) is literally, "split the intellect."

20 "The *guṇas* of material nature" (*prakṛteḥ...guṇaiḥ*) refers to the three *guṇas*: *sattva, rajas* and *tamas.* See fn. under BG 2.45.

21. "The senses are simply interacting with the sense objects," (*guṇā guṇeṣu vartanta iti*). Here the word *guṇa* is used twice. Both Śaṅkara and Madhva interpret the first use of the word *guṇa* as "the senses" and the second *guṇa* as "the sense objects."

22. Compare this verse to BG 5.14, 13.20 and 13.29.

प्रकृतेर्गुणसंमूढाः सज्जन्ते गुणकर्मसु ।
तानकृत्स्नविदो मन्दान्कृत्स्नविन्न विचालयेत् ॥ २९

prakṛter guṇa-sammūḍhāḥ sajjante guṇa-karmasu
tān akṛtsna-vido mandān kṛtsna-vin na vicālayet

मयि सर्वाणि कर्माणि संन्यस्याध्यात्मचेतसा ।
निराशीर्निर्ममो भूत्वा युध्यस्व विगतज्वरः ॥ ३०

mayi sarvāṇi karmāṇi sannyasyādhyātma-cetasā
nirāśīr nirmamo bhūtvā yudhyasva vigata-jvaraḥ

ये मे मतमिदं नित्यमनुतिष्ठन्ति मानवाः ।
श्रद्धावन्तोऽनसूयन्तो मुच्यन्ते तेऽपि कर्मभिः ॥ ३१

ye me matam idaṁ nityam anutiṣṭhanti mānavāḥ
śraddhāvanto 'nasūyanto mucyante te 'pi karmabhiḥ

ये त्वेतदभ्यसूयन्तो नानुतिष्ठन्ति मे मतम् ।
सर्वज्ञानविमूढांस्तान्विद्धि नष्टानचेतसः ॥ ३२

ye tv etad abhyasūyanto nānutiṣṭhanti me matam
sarva-jñāna-vimūḍhāṁs tān viddhi naṣṭān acetasaḥ

सदृशं चेष्टते स्वस्याः प्रकृतेर्ज्ञानवानपि ।
प्रकृतिं यान्ति भूतानि निग्रहः किं करिष्यति ॥ ३३

sadṛśaṁ ceṣṭate svasyāḥ prakṛter jñānavān api
prakṛtiṁ yānti bhūtāni nigrahaḥ kiṁ kariṣyati

इन्द्रियस्येन्द्रियस्यार्थे रागद्वेषौ व्यवस्थितौ ।
तयोर्न वशमागच्छेत्तौ ह्यस्य परिपन्थिनौ ॥ ३४

indriyasyendriyasyārthe rāga-dveṣau vyavasthitau
tayor na vaśam āgacchet tau hy asya paripanthinau

29) Those who are bewildered by the qualities of material nature are attached to the actions induced by these qualities. However, those whose knowledge is complete should not disturb the foolish whose knowledge is incomplete.

30) Dedicate all your actions to Me. Fix your mind on the Supreme.[23] Give up this affliction and without desire or egotism, fight.

31) Those who follow My eternal teachings with full faith, and who are without envy, are freed from the bondage of action.

32) But those who, out of envy, fail to follow My teachings are bereft of knowledge. Know them to be lost and without sensitivity.

33) All beings follow their own nature; therefore, even persons of learning act according to their nature. What can suppression accomplish?

34) Passion and hatred rest in each of the senses along with the sense objects. One must not come under their control, for they are one's enemies.

---

23. "Fix your mind on the Supreme" (*adhyātma-cetasā*) is literally, "with thoughts pertaining to the *ātman*." For notes on *adhyātman* see BG 7.29-30 and BG 8.1.

श्रेयान्स्वधर्मो विगुणः परधर्मात्स्वनुष्ठितात् ।
स्वधर्मे निधनं श्रेयः परधर्मो भयावहः ॥ ३५

śreyān sva-dharmo viguṇaḥ para-dharmāt sv-anuṣṭhitāt
sva-dharme nidhanaṁ śreyaḥ para-dharmo bhayāvahaḥ

अर्जुन उवाच ।
अथ केन प्रयुक्तोऽयं पापं चरति पूरुषः ।
अनिच्छन्नपि वार्ष्णेय बलादिव नियोजितः ॥ ३६

arjuna uvāca
atha kena prayukto 'yaṁ pāpaṁ carati pūruṣaḥ
anicchann api vārṣṇeya balād iva niyojitaḥ

श्रीभगवानुवाच ।
काम एष क्रोध एष रजोगुणसमुद्भवः ।
महाशनो महापाप्मा विद्ध्येनमिह वैरिणम् ॥ ३७

śrī-bhagavān uvāca
kāma eṣa krodha eṣa rajo-guṇa-samudbhavaḥ
mahāśano mahā-pāpmā viddhy enam iha vairiṇam

धूमेनाव्रियते वह्निर्यथादर्शो मलेन च ।
यथोल्बेनावृतो गर्भस्तथा तेनेदमावृतम् ॥ ३८

dhūmenāvriyate vahnir yathādarśo malena ca
yatholbenāvṛto garbhas tathā tenedam āvṛtam

आवृतं ज्ञानमेतेन ज्ञानिनो नित्यवैरिणा ।
कामरूपेण कौन्तेय दुष्पूरेणानलेन च ॥ ३९

āvṛtaṁ jñānam etena jñānino nitya-vairiṇā
kāma-rūpeṇa kaunteya duṣpūreṇānalena ca

35) Better to perform one's own duty imperfectly than to perform another's duty perfectly. Destruction in the performance of one's own duty is preferable. To follow another's duty invites danger.[24]

Desire: The Enemy of this World

Arjuna inquired:
36) O Kṛṣṇa, descendent of Vṛṣṇi, by what force are men drawn to perform evil deeds even against their will?

37) Kṛṣṇa Bhagavān said:
It is desire, it is anger, born from the quality of *rajas*. Know this to be the all devouring, sinful enemy of this world.

38) As fire is covered by smoke, as a mirror is covered by dust, or as the embryo is covered by the membrane, so this[25] living being is covered by desire.

39) O son of Kuntī, even the knowledge of a learned person is covered by this eternal enemy in the form of desire, which burns like an insatiable fire.

---

24. "One's own duty" refers to one's position within the social order of *varṇāśrama-dharma* as *brāhmaṇa, kṣatriya, vaiśya* or *śūdra*. It was considered an act of *adharma* to work outside of one's social position. A similar version of this verse is repeated in BG 18.47.
25. The word used here is simply *idam*, meaning "this." The question arises what is meant by "this?" Śaṅkara says it is knowledge. Rāmānuja and Madhva say it is the living beings. Others say it is the world.

इन्द्रियाणि मनो बुद्धिरस्याधिष्ठानमुच्यते ।
एतैर्विमोहयत्येष ज्ञानमावृत्य देहिनम् ॥ ४०

indriyāṇi mano buddhir asyādhiṣṭhānam ucyate
etair vimohayaty eṣa jñānam āvṛtya dehinam

तस्मात्त्वमिन्द्रियाण्यादौ नियम्य भरतर्षभ ।
पाप्मानं प्रजहिह्येनं ज्ञानविज्ञाननाशनम् ॥ ४१

tasmāt tvam indriyāṇy ādau niyamya bharatarṣabha
pāpmānaṁ prajahi hy enaṁ jñāna-vijñāna-nāśanam

इन्द्रियाणि पराण्याहुरिन्द्रियेभ्यः परं मनः ।
मनसस्तु परा बुद्धिर्यो बुद्धेः परतस्तु सः ॥ ४२

indriyāṇi parāṇy āhur indriyebhyaḥ paraṁ manaḥ
manasas tu parā buddhir yo buddheḥ paratas tu saḥ

एवं बुद्धेः परं बुद्ध्वा संस्तभ्यात्मानमात्मना ।
जहि शत्रुं महाबाहो कामरूपं दुरासदम् ॥ ४३

evaṁ buddheḥ paraṁ buddhvā saṁstabhyātmānam ātmanā
jahi śatruṁ mahā-bāho kāma-rūpaṁ durāsadam

40) The senses, the mind, and the intellect are said to be the resting place of this desire, which deludes and obscures knowledge of this embodied one.

41) Therefore, O bull of the Bharatas, in the very beginning, curb the senses and kill this evil one who is the destroyer of both knowledge and wisdom.[26]

42) The senses, they say, are exalted. Higher than the senses is the mind. Higher still is the intellect. Beyond the intellect, however, is the soul.[27]

43) O mighty-armed Arjuna, knowing the soul to be higher than the intellect, you must control the mind through the use of intelligence[28] and slay this enemy in the form of insurmountable desire.

---

26. "The destroyer of both knowledge and wisdom" is a translation of *jñāna-vijñāna-nāśanam.* Knowledge (*jñāna*) means knowledge that is acquired through books. It could be called theoretical knowledge. Wisdom (*vijñāna*) is realized knowledge gained through practical life experience and inner realization. For other uses of these terms see BG 6.8, 7.2 and 9.1.

27. Literally, the Sanskrit says "beyond the intellect, however, is he" (*yo buddheḥ paratas tu saḥ).*" Śaṅkara interprets "he" as the *ātman,* the Self. See BG 6.5 fn 5. Rāmānuja takes it as desire and Madhva says it is God (*paramātman).*

28. The expression "controlling the mind through the use of intelligence" is literally "supporting the *ātman* by the *ātman*" (*saṁstabhyātmānam ātmanā).* For an explanation of the use of *ātman* see BG 6.5 fn 5. A translation based on Śaṅkara reads: "controlling the self by the Self." Rāmānuja and Madhva, on the other hand, interpret the first *ātman* as the mind and the second *ātman* as the intelligence. This is the interpretation that I have followed. A similar interpretation of *ātman* is seen in BG 6. 5-6 and elsewhere.

श्रीभगवानुवाच ।
इमं विवस्वते योगं प्रोक्तवानहमव्ययम् ।
विवस्वान्मनवे प्राह मनुरिक्ष्वाकवेऽब्रवीत् ॥ १

śrī-bhagavān uvāca
imaṁ vivasvate yogaṁ proktavān aham avyayam
vivasvān manave prāha manur ikṣvākave 'bravīt

एवं परंपराप्राप्तमिमं राजर्षयो विदुः ।
स कालेनेह महता योगो नष्टः परंतप ॥ २

evaṁ paramparā-prāptam imaṁ rājarṣayo viduḥ
sa kāleneha mahatā yogo naṣṭaḥ parantapa

Chapter Four

Knowledge and Renunciation

A History of Kṛṣṇa's Teachings

1) Kṛṣṇa Bhagavān said:
In the beginning I spoke this eternal discipline to Vivasvān,[1] Vivasvān spoke it to Manu[2] and Manu in turn spoke it to Ikṣvāku.[3]

2) O scorcher of the enemy, the saintly kings[4] thus understood this discipline through a line of succession,[5] but with the passing of time, these teachings became lost.

Chapter Four is traditionally entitled *jñāna-karma-sannyāsa-yoga,* The *Yoga* of Renunciation of Action in Knowledge.

1. The creator god, Brahmā, had a spiritual son named Marīci, who had a son, Prajāpati Kaśyapa. Kaśyapa married the twelve daughters of Dakṣa, who in turn gave birth to the gods, demons, and many other beings. One of these daughters named Dākṣāyaṇī was the mother of the sun god, Vivasvān.

2. Vivasvān became the father of the Manu known as Vaivasvata. A day of Brahmā is called a *kalpa* and is equal to 4,320,000,000 years. This day is divided into 14 equal periods called *manvantaras,* each presided over by a Manu. Vaivasvata Manu is the seventh Manu in the present *kalpa* cycle and the source of the solar line of kings known as the *sūrya-vaṁśa.*

3. One of Vaivasvata's sons through Ilā was known as Ikṣvāku. Ikṣvāku became the progenitor of the *sūrya-vaṁśa* on earth from which the sage-kings Janaka (BG 3.20), Sagara, and Raghu Rāma, the grandfather of Rāma descended.

4. The saintly kings include such personalities as Aśvapati, Ambarīṣa and Janaka, all mentioned in the *Upaniṣads.*

5. "A line of succession" (*paramparā*) is literally, "one after another." It is a chain of teachers and disciples.

स एवायं मया तेऽद्य योगः प्रोक्तः पुरातनः
भक्तोऽसि मे सखा चेति रहस्यं ह्येतदुत्तमम् । ३

sa evāyaṁ mayā te 'dya yogaḥ proktaḥ purātanaḥ
bhakto 'si me sakhā ceti rahasyaṁ hy etad uttamam

अर्जुन उवाच ।
अपरं भवतो जन्म परं जन्म विवस्वतः ।
कथमेतद्विजानीयां त्वमादौ प्रोक्तवानिति ।। ४

arjuna uvāca
aparaṁ bhavato janma paraṁ janma vivasvataḥ
kathaṁ etad vijānīyāṁ tvam ādau proktavān iti

श्रीभगवानुवाच ।
बहूनि मे व्यतीतानि जन्मानि तव चार्जुन ।
तान्यहं वेद सर्वाणि न त्वं वेत्थ परंतप ।। ५

śrī-bhagavān uvāca
bahūni me vyatītāni janmāni tava cārjuna
tāny ahaṁ veda sarvāṇi na tvaṁ vettha parantapa

अजोऽपि सन्नव्ययात्मा भूतानामीश्वरोऽपि सन् ।
प्रकृतिं स्वामधिष्ठाय संभवाम्यात्ममायया ।। ६

ajo 'pi sann avyayātmā bhūtānām īśvaro 'pi san
prakṛtiṁ svām adhiṣṭhāya sambhavāmy ātma-māyayā

3) Because you are My devotee as well as My friend, I now declare this ancient discipline of *yoga* to you. Indeed, this is a supreme secret.

4) Arjuna inquired:
How can I understand that you spoke these teachings in the beginning, since your birth comes after the birth of Vivasvān?

5) Kṛṣṇa Bhagavān said:
O Arjuna, scorcher of the enemy, both you and I have passed many births. I know them all, whereas you do not.

6) Even though I am unborn and imperishable and I am the lord of all beings, I take control of My material energy[6] and appear through the agency of My creative power.[7]

---

6. The expression "I take control of My material energy" (*prakṛtiṁ svām adhiṣṭhāya)* is open to a wide variation of interpretation. *Adhiṣṭhāya* is taken by Śaṅkara to mean, "brings under power" and *prakṛti* is taken to refer to material energy. In other words, God takes charge of matter. Madhva takes the expression to mean that God establishes himself in matter, which he alone owns and controls. He makes it clear that the Lord is not born from matter and is, therefore, not subject to the dictates of this phenomenal world like ordinary beings. Rāmānuja, on the other hand, handles the expression in another way. He takes *prakṛtiṁ svām* to mean God's divine nature instead of material nature. So that when Kṛṣṇa appears in this world he does so in his original "divine nature."
7. Both Rāmānuja and Madhva take the words, "through the agency of My creative power" (*ātma-māyayā*) to mean by "My free will." They take the word *māyā* as synonymous with *prajñā* or volition. According to this interpretation, the latter half of the verse could be rendered: "My divine form nonetheless appears in matter through the agency of My *free will.*" The word "*māyā*" is often used to mean "illusion" or "trick." In the RV it is used to mean "uncanny power" or "deceit." In the *Upaṇiṣads* (ŚU 4.10) it is used only once to mean *prakṛti*, material energy. In the *Gītā māyā* is that form of *prakṛti* that depends on God and therefore is called "divine energy" *daivī māyā* (BG 7.14), but at the same time it distracts man's attention from God. (BG 7.15, 7.25).

यदा यदा हि धर्मस्य ग्लानिर्भवति भारत ।
अभ्युत्थानमधर्मस्य तदात्मानं सृजाम्यहम् ॥ ७

yadā yadā hi dharmasya glānir bhavati bhārata
abhyutthānam adharmasya tadātmānaṁ sṛjāmy aham

परित्राणाय साधूनां विनाशाय च दुष्कृताम् ।
धर्मसंस्थापनार्थाय संभवामि युगे युगे ॥ ८

paritrāṇāya sādhūnāṁ vināśāya ca duṣkṛtām
dharma-saṁsthāpanārthāya sambhavāmi yuge yuge

जन्म कर्म च मे दिव्यमेवं यो वेत्ति तत्त्वतः ।
त्यक्त्वा देहं पुनर्जन्म नैति मामेति सोऽर्जुन ॥ ९

janma karma ca me divyam evaṁ yo vetti tattvataḥ
tyaktvā dehaṁ punar janma naiti mām eti so 'rjuna

वीतरागभयक्रोधा मन्मया मामुपाश्रिताः ।
बहवो ज्ञानतपसा पूता मद्भावमागताः ॥ १०

vīta-rāga-bhaya-krodhā man-mayā mām upāśritāḥ
bahavo jñāna-tapasā pūtā mad-bhāvam āgatāḥ

7) For whenever there is a decline in *dharma*, O descendant of Bhārata, and an increase of *adharma*,[8] at that time, I manifest Myself.

8) For the protection of the good and for the destruction of those who do evil, as well as to reestablish *dharma*, I appear time and time again.[9]

Knowledge of God

9) O Arjuna, one who truly understands the divine nature of my birth and activities, upon quitting this body, is not reborn into this world. Instead, such a person comes to Me.[10]

10) Taking shelter of Me alone, many in the past, whose passions, fears and anger have been quieted by the austerity of knowledge, have attained to My nature.[11]

---

8. *Adharma* is the opposite of *dharma*. See fn. BG 1.1. In this verse both Śaṅkara and Rāmānuja take *dharma* in a very specific sense, namely the system of *varṇāśrama-dharma*. This is the system of four divisions of human population and four stages of life. See fn. BG 4.13.
9. In the expression "time and time again" (*yuge yuge*) the word *yuga* has a specific meaning. There are four *yugas* or ages: *satya* (*kṛta*), *tretā*, *dvāpara* and *kali*. The combined time period of one *yuga* cycle (these four *yugas* combined) is 4,320,000 years. The implied meaning is that God appears at various times during these *yuga* periods. See BG 8.17.
10. The expression "comes to Me" (*mām eti*) is based on the principle that whatever one meditates upon or worships, one attains. See BG 8.6 and 9.25. Śaṅkara says *mām eti* means attains liberation (*mokṣa*). Rāmānuja says it means that one's sins are destroyed and one is able to take shelter of God.
11. "My nature" (*mad-bhāva*) is a reoccurring phrase. See BG 8.5, 13.18 and 14.19.

ये यथा मां प्रपद्यन्ते तांस्तथैव भजाम्यहम् ।
मम वर्त्मानुवर्तन्ते मनुष्याः पार्थ सर्वशः ॥ ११

ye yathā māṁ prapadyante tāṁs tathaiva bhajāmy aham
mama vartmānuvartante manuṣyāḥ pārtha sarvaśaḥ

काङ्क्षन्तः कर्मणां सिद्धिं यजन्त इह देवताः ।
क्षिप्रं हि मानुषे लोके सिद्धिर्भवति कर्मजा ॥ १२

kāṅkṣantaḥ karmaṇāṁ siddhiṁ yajanta iha devatāḥ
kṣipraṁ hi mānuṣe loke siddhir bhavati karma-jā

चातुर्वर्ण्यं मया सृष्टं गुणकर्मविभागशः ।
तस्य कर्तारमपि मां विद्ध्यकर्तारमव्ययम् ॥ १३

cātur-varṇyaṁ mayā sṛṣṭaṁ guṇa-karma-vibhāgaśaḥ
tasya kartāram api māṁ viddhy akartāram avyayam

न मां कर्माणि लिम्पन्ति न मे कर्मफले स्पृहा ।
इति मां योऽभिजानाति कर्मभिर्न स बध्यते ॥ १४

na māṁ karmāṇi limpanti na me karma-phale spṛhā
iti māṁ yo 'bhijānāti karmabhir na sa badhyate

एवं ज्ञात्वा कृतं कर्म पूर्वैरपि मुमुक्षुभिः ।
कुरु कर्मैव तस्मात्त्वं पूर्वैः पूर्वतरं कृतम् ॥ १५

evaṁ jñātvā kṛtaṁ karma pūrvair api mumukṣubhiḥ
kuru karmaiva tasmāt tvaṁ pūrvaiḥ pūrvataraṁ kṛtam

किं कर्म किमकर्मेति कवयोऽप्यत्र मोहिताः ।
तत्ते कर्म प्रवक्ष्यामि यज्ज्ञात्वा मोक्ष्यसेऽशुभात् ॥ १६

kiṁ karma kim akarmeti kavayo 'py atra mohitāḥ
tat te karma pravakṣyāmi yaj jñātvā mokṣyase 'śubhāt

11) O son of Pṛthā, in whatever way they approach Me I reward them accordingly. For in all respects, mankind follows My path.[12]

Action and Nonaction

12) In this world mankind desires success and therefore sacrifices to various deities. Success quickly arises from the performance of such action in this world.

13) The four divisions of human society[13] were created by Me according to quality and action. Although I am the creator of this system, know that I am changeless and that I perform no action.

14) Actions do not affect me, nor do I desire the results of action. One who thus knows My nature is not bound by actions.

15) Understanding action in this way, those in the past who desired liberation performed their duty. Therefore, you must perform your duty as the ancients have done.

16) Even the learned are bewildered by action and nonaction. Therefore, I will declare to you what action is. Knowing this, you will be freed from evil.[14]

---

12. The second line of this verse, "for in all respects, mankind follows My path" (*mama vartmānuvartante manuṣyāḥ pārtha sarvaśaḥ*), is identical with the second line of BG 3.23.
13. "The four divisions of human society" (*cātur-varṇyam*) refers to the system of four *varṇas* and four *āśramas*, i.e. the four classes of society: priests (*brāhmaṇas*), warriors (*kṣatriyas*), merchants (*vaiśyas*) and workers (*śūdras*) and the four stages of life: studentship (*brahmacārī*), householder (*gṛhastha*), retired (*vānaprastha*) and renounced (*sannyāsī*).
14. Both Śaṅkara and Rāmānuja describe "freed from evil" (*mokṣyase aśubhāt*) as the cycle of rebirth (*saṁsāra*).

कर्मणो ह्यपि बोद्धव्यं बोद्धव्यं च विकर्मणः ।
अकर्मणश्च बोद्धव्यं गहना कर्मणो गतिः ॥ १७

karmaṇo hy api boddhavyaṁ boddhavyaṁ ca vikarmaṇaḥ
akarmaṇaś ca boddhavyaṁ gahanā karmaṇo gatiḥ

कर्मण्यकर्म यः पश्येदकर्मणि च कर्म यः ।
स बुद्धिमान्मनुष्येषु स युक्तः कृत्स्नकर्मकृत् ॥ १८

karmaṇy akarma yaḥ paśyed akarmaṇi ca karma yaḥ
sa buddhimān manuṣyeṣu sa yuktaḥ kṛtsna-karma-kṛt

यस्य सर्वे समारम्भाः कामसंकल्पवर्जिताः ।
ज्ञानाग्निदग्धकर्माणं तमाहुः पण्डितं बुधाः ॥ १९

yasya sarve samārambhāḥ kāma-saṅkalpa-varjitāḥ
jñānāgni-dagdha-karmāṇaṁ tam āhuḥ paṇḍitaṁ budhāḥ

त्यक्त्वा कर्मफलासङ्गं नित्यतृप्तो निराश्रयः ।
कर्मण्यभिप्रवृत्तोऽपि नैव किंचित्करोति सः ॥ २०

tyaktvā karma-phalāsaṅgaṁ nitya-tṛpto nirāśrayaḥ
karmaṇy abhipravṛtto 'pi naiva kiñcit karoti saḥ

निराशीर्यतचित्तात्मा त्यक्तसर्वपरिग्रहः ।
शारीरं केवलं कर्म कुर्वन्नाप्नोति किल्बिषम् ॥ २१

nirāśīr yata-cittātmā tyakta-sarva-parigrahaḥ
śārīraṁ kevalaṁ karma kurvan nāpnoti kilbiṣam

17) The ways of action are mysterious. Therefore, action, forbidden action, and nonaction must be understood.

18) One is enlightened among mankind who sees nonaction in action[15] and action in nonaction.[16] Such a disciplined person works in all kinds of ways.

19) A person is called truly learned whose actions are without desire and motive, and whose deeds have been consumed in the fire of knowledge.

20) Even though engaged in action, one who is without attachment to the result of action, who is ever satisfied[17] and who is independent,[18] performs no action.

21) One who is without aspirations and whose intellect and mind are restrained, who is free of possessions and who acts with body alone, incurs no sin.

---

15. Nonaction (*akarma*) refers to those "activities" that are performed without ego and without attachment. Such actions produce no binding result. By contrast, ordinary action (*karma*) is activity performed out of ego and with attachment. This kind of activity necessarily produces a result. Thus, to see nonaction in action means to know how to act with a spiritual purpose and without ego or attachment.
16. One who sees action in nonaction means to realize that simply ceasing to act in this world does not necessarily release one from the result. It is better to engage in activity in this world, but in a manner that is without ego and attachment.
17. "Ever satisfied" (*nitya-tṛptaḥ*) means satisfied with the soul within.
18. "Independent" (*nirāśrayaḥ*) means not relying on material nature (*prakṛti*).

यदृच्छालाभसंतुष्टो द्वंद्वातीतो विमत्सरः ।
समः सिद्धावसिद्धौ च कृत्वापि न निबध्यते ॥ २२

yadṛcchā-lābha-santuṣṭo dvandvātīto vimatsaraḥ
samaḥ siddhāv asiddhau ca kṛtvāpi na nibadhyate

गतसङ्गस्य मुक्तस्य ज्ञानावस्थितचेतसः ।
यज्ञायाचरतः कर्म समग्रं प्रविलीयते ॥ २३

gata-saṅgasya muktasya jñānāvasthita-cetasaḥ
yajñāyācarataḥ karma samagraṁ pravilīyate

ब्रह्मार्पणं ब्रह्महविर्ब्रह्माग्नौ ब्रह्मणा हुतम् ।
ब्रह्मैव तेन गन्तव्यं ब्रह्मकर्मसमाधिना ॥ २४

brahmārpaṇaṁ brahma havir brahmāgnau brahmaṇā hutam
brahmaiva tena gantavyaṁ brahma-karma-samādhinā

22) One who is satisfied with what comes of its own accord, who has transcended duality,[19] who is without envy, and is equal in success and failure, is never bound by action even though performing action.

23) The results of action entirely melt away for one who acts solely for the sake of sacrifice, whose attachments are gone, who is liberated, and whose heart and mind are situated in knowledge.

Sacrifice as Brahman

24) The sacrificial act is *brahman*; the sacrificial oblation is *brahman*; into the fire, *brahman* is poured by *brahman*. Indeed, one who is absorbed in this action of *brahman* attains *brahman*.[20]

---

19. "Who has transcended duality" (*dvandvātītaḥ*) refers to one who is no longer attached to the pairs of opposites: heat and cold, pleasure and pain, success and failure, happiness and suffering, etc. The idea of duality (*dvandva*) and the need to transcend it is a recurrent theme in the *Gītā*. Life may be compared to a pendulum constantly swinging to and fro, between the duality of the opposite poles. The *yogī* endeavors to remain centered, neither attached to one side or the other. See BG 5.3 for a similar usage.

20. Here the Vedic sacrifice or *yajña* is interpreted in a metaphysical way, namely all aspects of the sacrifice–the performer, the oblation and the act itself–are viewed as *brahman,* the Supreme. By extension, not only are ritual acts to be viewed as acts pertaining to the Supreme, but all actions become acts of sacrifice if performed with the proper understanding. The performer is thus not bound by such actions.

दैवमेवापरे यज्ञं योगिनः पर्युपासते ।
ब्रह्माग्नावपरे यज्ञं यज्ञेनैवोपजुह्वति ॥ २५
daivam evāpare yajñaṁ yoginaḥ paryupāsate
brahmāgnāv apare yajñaṁ yajñenaivopajuhvati

श्रोत्रादीनीन्द्रियाण्यन्ये संयमाग्निषु जुह्वति ।
शब्दादीन्विषयानन्य इन्द्रियाग्निषु जुह्वति ॥ २६
śrotrādinīndriyāṇy anye saṁyamāgniṣu juhvati
śabdādīn viṣayān anya indriyāgniṣu juhvati

सर्वाणीन्द्रियकर्माणि प्राणकर्माणि चापरे ।
आत्मसंयमयोगाग्नौ जुह्वति ज्ञानदीपिते ॥ २७
sarvāṇīndriya-karmāṇi prāṇa-karmāṇi cāpare
ātma-saṁyama-yogāgnau juhvati jñāna-dīpite

द्रव्ययज्ञास्तपोयज्ञा योगयज्ञास्तथापरे ।
स्वाध्यायज्ञानयज्ञाश्च यतयः संशितव्रताः ॥ २८
dravya-yajñās tapo-yajñā yoga-yajñās tathāpare
svādhyāya-jñāna-yajñāś ca yatayaḥ saṁśita-vratāḥ

25) Some *yogīs* offer sacrifice to the gods,[21] while others offer sacrifice into the fire of *brahman* for the sake of sacrifice itself.[22]

26) Some offer the senses, such as hearing, into the fire of self-restraint, while others offer the sense objects, such as sound, into the fire of the senses.[23]

27) Still others offer the actions of all the senses and the actions of the vital breaths into the fire of self-restraint kindled by knowledge.[24]

28) There are many sages of strict vows. Some sacrifice material possessions, others sacrifice through austerities,[25] others sacrifice through discipline,[26] and still others sacrifice through Vedic recitation and knowledge.

---

21. That is to say they employ the sacrifice in order to appease the gods and thereby attain material benefit.
22. Others cease to perform ritual sacrifice for material gain, but instead perform all actions as acts of sacrifice to the Supreme.
23. To offer the senses as well as their sense objects into the fire of self-restraint means to practice sense control as an act of sacrifice.
24. There are five vital breaths or life-airs: *prāṇa*, in-breath; *apāṇa*, out-breath; *vyāna*, diffused-breath; *udāna*, upper-breath; and *samāna*, concentrated-breath. By the control of the breath one can obtain mastery over the senses and the mind. This too becomes an act of sacrifice to the Supreme.
25. "The practice of austerities" according to Rāmānuja means such austerities that involve fasting. He mentions the fast of *cāndrāyaṇa*, which requires the gradual diminution of food during the waning moon and corresponding increase in food during the waxing moon.
26. "Sacrifice through discipline (*yoga*)" according to Śaṅkara means breath-control. According to Rāmānuja it means staying at places of pilgrimage.

अपाने जुह्वति प्राणं प्राणेऽपानं तथापरे ।
प्राणापानगती रुद्ध्वा प्राणायामपरायणाः ॥ २९

apāne juhvati prāṇaṁ prāṇe 'pānaṁ tathāpare
prāṇāpāna-gatī ruddhvā prāṇāyāma-parāyaṇāḥ

अपरे नियताहाराः प्राणान्प्राणेषु जुह्वति ।
सर्वेऽप्येते यज्ञविदो यज्ञक्षपितकल्मषाः ॥ ३०

apare niyatāhārāḥ prāṇān prāṇeṣu juhvati
sarve 'py ete yajña-vido yajña-kṣapita-kalmaṣāḥ

यज्ञशिष्टामृतभुजो यान्ति ब्रह्म सनातनम् ।
नायं लोकोऽस्त्ययज्ञस्य कुतोऽन्यः कुरुसत्तम ॥ ३१

yajña-śiṣṭāmṛta-bhujo yānti brahma sanātanam
nāyaṁ loko 'sty ayajñasya kuto 'nyaḥ kurusattama

एवं बहुविधा यज्ञा वितता ब्रह्मणो मुखे ।
कर्मजान्विद्धि तान्सर्वानेवं ज्ञात्वा विमोक्ष्यसे ॥ ३२

evaṁ bahu-vidhā yajñā vitatā brahmaṇo mukhe
karma-jān viddhi tān sarvān evaṁ jñātvā vimokṣyase

29) Some offer the in-coming breath into the out-going breath, while others offer the out-going breath into the in-coming breath. Restraining the movements of both the in-breath and out-breath, they are intent upon vital breath control.[27]

30) Others restrain their eating, as well as the control of their life breaths.[28] Indeed, they are all knowers of sacrifice whose sins are destroyed by sacrifice.[29]

31) Those who enjoy the ambrosia of immortality, which consists of the remnants of sacrifice, reach everlasting *brahman.* O best of the Kurus, one who performs no sacrifice has no place in this world, what to speak of the next.

32) Many kinds of sacrifice have thus been declared to be the means to attain *brahman.*[30] Know them all to be born of action and you will become free.

---

27. Inhalation (*pūraka*) is a breathing exercise in which the lungs are filled with as much air as possible by a prolonged act of inspiration. Exhalation (*recaka*) is another exercise in which the lungs are emptied of as much air as possible by a prolonged act of expiration. Stoppage of breath (*kumbhaka*) is the retention of breath for a specific length of time after successively performing a *recaka* and *pūraka.*
28. Literally, they "offer the in-coming breaths into the in-coming breaths" (*prāṇān prāṇeṣu juhvati*).
29. This verse refers to the control of the senses through fasting and regulated diet.
30. "The means to attain *brahman*" (*vitatā brahmaṇo mukhe*) is literally, "spread out in the face of *brahman.*" The expression may also mean, "are offered to *brahman*" or "are performed before *brahman.*" Śaṅkara takes *brahman* to be the *Vedas* and not the Supreme. Thus the expression may simply mean "declared in the *Vedas.*"

श्रेयान्द्रव्यमयाद्यज्ञाज्ज्ञानयज्ञः परंतप ।
सर्वं कर्माखिलं पार्थ ज्ञाने परिसमाप्यते ॥ ३३

śreyān dravya-mayād yajñāj jñāna-yajñaḥ parantapa
sarvaṁ karmākhilaṁ pārtha jñāne parisamāpyate

तद्विद्धि प्रणिपातेन परिप्रश्नेन सेवया ।
उपदेक्ष्यन्ति ते ज्ञानं ज्ञानिनस्तत्त्वदर्शिनः ॥ ३४

tad viddhi praṇipātena paripraśnena sevayā
upadekṣyanti te jñānaṁ jñāninas tattva-darśinaḥ

यज्ज्ञात्वा न पुनर्मोहमेवं यास्यसि पाण्डव ।
येन भूतान्यशेषेण द्रक्ष्यस्यात्मन्यथो मयि ॥ ३५

yaj jñātvā na punar moham evaṁ yāsyasi pāṇḍava
yena bhūtāny aśeṣeṇa drakṣyasy ātmany atho mayi

अपि चेदसि पापेभ्यः सर्वेभ्यः पापकृत्तमः ।
सर्वं ज्ञानप्लवेनैव वृजिनं संतरिष्यसि ॥ ३६

api ced asi pāpebhyaḥ sarvebhyaḥ pāpa-kṛt-tamaḥ
sarvaṁ jñāna-plavenaiva vṛjinaṁ santariṣyasi

यथैधांसि समिद्धोऽग्निर्भस्मसात्कुरुतेऽर्जुन ।
ज्ञानाग्निः सर्वकर्माणि भस्मसात्कुरुते तथा ॥ ३७

yathaidhāṁsi samiddho 'gnir bhasmasāt kurute 'rjuna
jñānāgniḥ sarva-karmāṇi bhasmasāt kurute tathā

33) O Pārtha, scorcher of the enemy, better the sacrifice of knowledge than the sacrifice of material possessions, for without exception all action culminates in the attainment of knowledge.

Transcendent Knowledge

34) By humble submission, intensive inquiry and service, you can know the truth. The self-realized, who have seen this truth, can impart such knowledge to you.

35) O son of Pāṇḍu, when you have thus understood this truth you shall no longer be subject to delusion. You will recognize that all beings are both in yourself and in Me.[31]

36) Even if you are the greatest of all sinners, this boat of knowledge will allow you to transcend all evil.

37) O Arjuna, as fire burns kindling wood to ashes, so the fire of knowledge burns to ashes the results of all actions.

---

31. "You will recognize that all beings are both in yourself and in Me" (*yena bhūtāny aśeṣeṇa drakṣyasy ātmany atho mayi)* is pivotal in the interpretation of the *Gītā* for it touches upon the relationship between God and the individual soul. Śaṅkara states that this verse teaches the identity of the individual soul and God. He writes, "(With this knowledge) you will perceive all beings, from Brahmā down to the grass, in your own Self. You will also see them all in Me. And so you will realize that unity of the soul and God, which is clearly taught in all the *Upaniṣads.*" Rāmānuja, on the other hand, says that these teachings describe the common qualitative relationship between God and the individual soul and not a quantitative relationship. He writes, "By this wisdom you will see all beings in your own self, not characterized as gods, men and other beings, but when dissociated from matter you will see the sameness between you and other beings in that you all share the same form of wisdom."

न हि ज्ञानेन सदृशं पवित्रमिह विद्यते ।
तत्स्वयं योगसंसिद्धः कालेनात्मनि विन्दति ॥ ३८

na hi jñānena sadṛśaṁ pavitram iha vidyate
tat svayaṁ yoga-saṁsiddhaḥ kālenātmani vindati

श्रद्धावाँल्लभते ज्ञानं तत्परः संयतेन्द्रियः ।
ज्ञानं लब्ध्वा परां शान्तिमचिरेणाधिगच्छति ॥ ३९

śraddhāvāl̐ labhate jñānaṁ tat-paraḥ saṁyatendriyaḥ
jñānaṁ labdhvā parāṁ śāntim acireṇādhigacchati

अज्ञश्चाश्रद्दधानश्च संशयात्मा विनश्यति ।
नायं लोकोऽस्ति न परो न सुखं संशयात्मनः ॥ ४०

ajñaś cāśraddadhānaś ca saṁśayātmā vinaśyati
nāyaṁ loko 'sti na paro na sukhaṁ saṁśayātmanaḥ

योगसंन्यस्तकर्माणं ज्ञानसंछिन्नसंशयम् ।
आत्मवन्तं न कर्माणि निबध्नन्ति धनंजय ॥ ४१

yoga-sannyasta-karmāṇaṁ jñāna-sañchinna-saṁśayam
ātmavantaṁ na karmāṇi nibadhnanti dhanañjaya

तस्मादज्ञानसंभूतं हृत्स्थं ज्ञानासिनात्मनः ।
छित्त्वैनं संशयं योगमातिष्ठोत्तिष्ठ भारत ॥ ४२

tasmād ajñāna-sambhūtaṁ hṛt-sthaṁ jñānāsinātmanaḥ
chittvainaṁ saṁśayaṁ yogam ātiṣṭhottiṣṭha bhārata

38) In this world nothing purifies more than knowledge. One whose knowledge is perfected by *yoga* realizes this truth.

39) Intent upon truth and full of faith, one who disciplines the senses acquires wisdom, and having acquired wisdom, quickly attains the supreme spiritual peace.

40) Those who are ignorant, without faith, and who are overcome by doubts, perish. For the doubting soul there is happiness neither in this world nor in the next.

41) O conqueror of wealth, action no longer binds one who is intent upon the soul, whose fruitive actions have been renounced through *yoga*, and whose doubts have been cut down by knowledge.

42) Therefore, with the sword of knowledge cut down the ignorance that has arisen in your heart. O descendant of Bharata, arise and take to the discipline of *yoga*.

अर्जुन उवाच ।
संन्यासं कर्मणां कृष्ण पुनर्योगं च शंससि ।
यच्छ्रेय एतयोरेकं तन्मे ब्रूहि सुनिश्चितम् ॥ १

arjuna uvāca
sannyāsaṁ karmaṇāṁ kṛṣṇa punar yogaṁ ca śaṁsasi
yac chreya etayor ekaṁ tan me brūhi su-niścitam

श्रीभगवानुवाच ।
संन्यासः कर्मयोगश्च निःश्रेयसकरावुभौ ।
तयोस्तु कर्मसंन्यासात्कर्मयोगो विशिष्यते ॥ २

śrī-bhagavān uvāca
sannyāsaḥ karma-yogaś ca niḥśreyasa-karāv ubhau
tayos tu karma-sannyāsāt karma-yogo viśiṣyate

ज्ञेयः स नित्यसंन्यासी यो न द्वेष्टि न काङ्क्षति ।
निर्द्वंद्वो हि महाबाहो सुखं बन्धात्प्रमुच्यते ॥ ३

jñeyaḥ sa nitya-sannyāsī yo na dveṣṭi na kāṅkṣati
nirdvandvo hi mahā-bāho sukhaṁ bandhāt pramucyate

सांख्ययोगौ पृथग्बालाः प्रवदन्ति न पण्डिताः ।
एकमप्यास्थितः सम्यगुभयोर्विन्दते फलम् ॥ ४

sāṅkhya-yogau pṛthag bālāḥ pravadanti na paṇḍitāḥ
ekam apy āsthitaḥ samyag ubhayor vindate phalam

यत्सांख्यैः प्राप्यते स्थानं तद्योगैरपि गम्यते ।
एकं सांख्यं च योगं च यः पश्यति स पश्यति ॥ ५

yat sāṅkhyaiḥ prāpyate sthānaṁ tad yogair api gamyate
ekaṁ sāṅkhyaṁ ca yogaṁ ca yaḥ paśyati sa paśyati

Chapter Five

Renunciation and Action

Renunciation and Yoga

1) Arjuna inquired:
O Kṛṣṇa, you have praised both the renunciation of action as well as *yoga*, please tell me which is better?

2) Kṛṣṇa Bhagavān said:
Both renunciation and *karma-yoga* lead to the highest good, but of the two, *karma-yoga* is better than the renunciation of action.

3) One who neither hates nor desires and who is without duality[1] is known to be ever renounced. Such a person, O great-armed one, is easily freed from bondage.

4) Only the immature speak of the distinction between *sāṅkhya*[2] and *yoga*; not the wise. By properly following either, a person attains the results of both.

5) The position obtained by the followers of *sāṅkhya* is also achieved by the followers of *yoga*. One, truly sees, who knows that *sāṅkhya* and *yoga* are identical.

Chapter Five is traditionally entitled *karma-sannyāsa-yoga*, The *Yoga* of Renunciation and Action.

1. "Without duality" (*nirdvandva*): see fn. under BG 4.22.
2. Both Śaṅkara and Madhva take *sāṅkhya* here to mean renunciation. This seems to fit the context. Rāmānuja, on the other hand, takes *sāṅkhya* to mean knowledge (*jñāna*). This is patterned after the earlier usage where *sāṅkhya* and *yoga* have been used together. See BG 2.39 and 3.3.

संन्यासस्तु महाबाहो दुःखमाप्तुमयोगतः ।
योगयुक्तो मुनिर्ब्रह्म नचिरेणाधिगच्छति ॥ ६

sannyāsas tu mahā-bāho duḥkham āptum ayogataḥ
yoga-yukto munir brahma na cireṇādhigacchati

योगयुक्तो विशुद्धात्मा विजितात्मा जितेन्द्रियः ।
सर्वभूतात्मभूतात्मा कुर्वन्नपि न लिप्यते ॥ ७

yoga-yukto viśuddhātmā vijitātmā jitendriyaḥ
sarva-bhūtātma-bhūtātmā kurvann api na lipyate

नैव किंचित्करोमीति युक्तो मन्येत तत्त्ववित् ।
पश्यञ्शृण्वन्स्पृशञ्जिघ्रन्नश्नन्गच्छन्स्वपञ्श्वसन् ॥ ८

naiva kiñcit karomīti yukto manyeta tattva-vit
paśyañ śṛṇvan spṛśañ jighrann aśnan gacchan svapan śvasan

प्रलपन्विसृजन्गृह्णन्नुन्मिषन्निमिषन्नपि ।
इन्द्रियाणीन्द्रियार्थेषु वर्तन्त इति धारयन् ॥ ९

pralapan visṛjan gṛhṇann unmiṣan nimiṣann api
indriyāṇīndriyārtheṣu vartanta iti dhārayan

ब्रह्मण्याधाय कर्माणि सङ्गं त्यक्त्वा करोति यः ।
लिप्यते न स पापेन पद्मपत्रमिवाम्भसा ॥ १०

brahmaṇy ādhāya karmāṇi saṅgaṁ tyaktvā karoti yaḥ
lipyate na sa pāpena padma-patram ivāmbhasā

कायेन मनसा बुद्ध्या केवलैरिन्द्रियैरपि ।
योगिनः कर्म कुर्वन्ति सङ्गं त्यक्त्वात्मशुद्धये ॥ ११

kāyena manasā buddhyā kevalair indriyair api
yoginaḥ karma kurvanti saṅgaṁ tyaktvātma-śuddhaye

6) But renunciation[3] without *yoga* discipline, O great-armed one, is difficult to achieve. The silent sage, who engages in *yoga*, quickly reaches *brahman.*

7) One engaged in *yoga*, with mind purified, who is self-controlled and has subdued the senses, whose soul has become the soul in all beings,[4] even though performing action, is never bound.

8-9) The learned person who is engaged in *yoga* thinks, "I do nothing at all." Such a person knows that while seeing, hearing, touching, smelling, eating, going about, sleeping, breathing, talking, eliminating, grasping, and opening and closing the eyes: "Only the senses are engaged with their objects."

10) One who acts without attachment, offering all actions to *brahman*, is not tainted by evil, as the lotus leaf is untouched by water.

11) Those who are *yogīs* perform all action with the body, mind, intellect and the senses without attachment and for self-purification.

---

3. Here the word *sannyāsa*, renunciation, is reintroduced. This seems to give justification for interpreting *sāṅkhya* as renunciation in verses four and five.

4. Rāmānuja says the expression: *sarva-bhūtātma-bhūtātmā* (whose soul has become the soul of all beings) means that the *yogī* has realized that all souls have the same form and that the perceived differences are only due to *prakṛti*, material nature.

युक्तः कर्मफलं त्यक्त्वा शान्तिमाप्नोति नैष्ठिकीम् ।
अयुक्तः कामकारेण फले सक्तो निबध्यते ॥ १२

yuktaḥ karma-phalaṁ tyaktvā śāntim āpnoti naiṣṭhikīm
ayuktaḥ kāma-kāreṇa phale sakto nibadhyate

सर्वकर्माणि मनसा संन्यस्यास्ते सुखं वशी ।
नवद्वारे पुरे देही नैव कुर्वन्न कारयन् ॥ १३

sarva-karmāṇi manasā sannyasyāste sukhaṁ vaśī
nava-dvāre pure dehī naiva kurvan na kārayan

न कर्तृत्वं न कर्माणि लोकस्य सृजति प्रभुः ।
न कर्मफलसंयोगं स्वभावस्तु प्रवर्तते ॥ १४

na kartṛtvaṁ na karmāṇi lokasya sṛjati prabhuḥ
na karma-phala-saṁyogaṁ svabhāvas tu pravartate

नादत्ते कस्यचित्पापं न चैव सुकृतं विभुः ।
अज्ञानेनावृतं ज्ञानं तेन मुह्यन्ति जन्तवः ॥ १५

nādatte kasyacit pāpaṁ na caiva sukṛtaṁ vibhuḥ
ajñānenāvṛtaṁ jñānaṁ tena muhyanti jantavaḥ

12) A person who is engaged in this way gives up the results of action and attains lasting peace. But one not following this path becomes attached to the results of action and is bound by desire.

The Soul as Separate from Matter

13) Mentally renouncing all actions, the embodied one, who is in control, dwells happily in the city of nine gates[5] while neither performing action, nor causing any action to be performed.

14) This lord[6] neither creates the means of action, the actions of the world, nor even the relationship between action and its result. This is carried on automatically by the nature of matter.[7]

15) This Lord[8] does not accept the result of anyone's good or evil deeds. In this world knowledge is covered by ignorance that bewilders the living beings.

---

5. The city of nine gates is the human body, which includes nine pathways: two eyes, the mouth, two ears, two nostrils, and two organs of excretion. (KU 5.1) makes the pathways eleven: those listed above plus the fontanel and the navel.
6. Here the expression "this lord," (*prabhu*), is taken by Śaṅkara and Rāmānuja to be the embodied being, the soul, and not God. Madhva takes *prabhu* to be God as well as the individual soul.
7. "The nature of matter" (*svabhāvas*) is literally, "inherent nature."
8. In this verse the expression "this Lord" is derived from the word *vibhu*. Śaṅkara takes *vibhu* to be God, while Rāmānuja continues the idea that it is the individual soul. Madhva agrees with Śaṅkara and takes *vibhu* as the Supreme Lord, Viṣṇu.

ज्ञानेन तु तदज्ञानं येषां नाशितमात्मनः ।
तेषामादित्यवज्ज्ञानं प्रकाशयति तत्परम् ॥ १६

jñānena tu tad ajñānaṁ yeṣāṁ nāśitam ātmanaḥ
teṣām āditya-vaj jñānaṁ prakāśayati tat param

तद्बुद्धयस्तदात्मानस्तन्निष्ठास्तत्परायणाः ।
गच्छन्त्यपुनरावृत्तिं ज्ञाननिर्धूतकल्मषाः ॥ १७

tad-buddhayas tad-ātmānas tan-niṣṭhās tat-parāyaṇāḥ
gacchanty apunar-āvṛttiṁ jñāna-nirdhūta-kalmaṣāḥ

विद्याविनयसंपन्ने ब्राह्मणे गवि हस्तिनि ।
शुनि चैव श्वपाके च पण्डिताः समदर्शिनः ॥ १८

vidyā-vinaya-sampanne brāhmaṇe gavi hastini
śuni caiva śva-pāke ca paṇḍitāḥ sama-darśinaḥ

इहैव तैर्जितः सर्गो येषां साम्ये स्थितं मनः ।
निर्दोषं हि समं ब्रह्म तस्माद्ब्रह्मणि ते स्थिताः ॥ १९

ihaiva tair jitaḥ sargo yeṣāṁ sāmye sthitaṁ manaḥ
nirdoṣaṁ hi samaṁ brahma tasmād brahmaṇi te sthitāḥ

The Light of Knowledge

16) The Supreme[9] shines like the sun for those whose ignorance has been destroyed by knowledge of the soul.

17) Those whose intellect, mind and very foundation are focused on the Supreme, and whose sins are dispelled by knowledge, never again return to this world.

18) The wise see with equal vision a learned and gentle person, a *brāhmaṇa*, a cow, an elephant, a dog and even an outcaste.[10]

19) Those whose minds are situated in serenity have overcome birth in this world. Like *brahman*[11] they are faultless and serene. Consequently, they are situated in *brahman*.

---

9. Rāmānuja reads this verse in another way: "But for those whose ignorance is destroyed by knowledge of the soul, that supreme knowledge shines like the sun." He takes supreme (*param*) as an adjective of knowledge (*jñānam*) instead of a separate noun meaning "the Supreme." Both Śaṅkara and Madhva take *param* as a separate noun meaning the Supreme.
10. Śaṅkara construes "learned and gentle" (*vidyā-vinaya-sampanne)* with "*brāhmaṇa*" *(brāhmaṇe*) making it read "in a learned and gentle *brāhmaṇa*." Rāmānuja, on the other hand, takes them as independent nominal phrases. As the cow and elephant, and the dog and dog-eater seems to constitute pairs, the person of learning and gentleness, and the *brāhmaṇa* must form another pair. I have followed Rāmānuja in this regard.
11. Here Rāmānuja interprets *brahman* as the soul because in its pure state, unfettered by matter, the soul is of the same quality as the Supreme *brahman*.

न प्रहृष्येत्प्रियं प्राप्य नोद्विजेत्प्राप्य चाप्रियम् ।
स्थिरबुद्धिरसंमूढो ब्रह्मविद्ब्रह्मणि स्थितः ॥ २०

na prahṛṣyet priyaṁ prāpya nodvijet prāpya cāpriyam
sthira-buddhir asammūḍho brahma-vid brahmaṇi sthitaḥ

बाह्यस्पर्शेष्वसक्तात्मा विन्दत्यात्मनि यत्सुखम् ।
स ब्रह्मयोगयुक्तात्मा सुखमक्षयमश्नुते ॥ २१

bāhya-sparśeṣv asaktātmā vindaty ātmani yat sukham
sa brahma-yoga-yuktātmā sukham akṣayam aśnute

ये हि संस्पर्शजा भोगा दुःखयोनय एव ते ।
आद्यन्तवन्तः कौन्तेय न तेषु रमते बुधः ॥ २२

ye hi saṁsparśa-jā bhogā duḥkha-yonaya eva te
ādy-antavantaḥ kaunteya na teṣu ramate budhaḥ

शक्नोतीहैव यः सोढुं प्राक्शरीरविमोक्षणात् ।
कामक्रोधोद्भवं वेगं स युक्तः स सुखी नरः ॥ २३

śaknotīhaiva yaḥ soḍhuṁ prāk śarīra-vimokṣaṇāt
kāma-krodhodbhavaṁ vegaṁ sa yuktaḥ sa sukhī naraḥ

योऽन्तःसुखोऽन्तरारामस्तथान्तर्ज्योतिरेव यः ।
स योगी ब्रह्मनिर्वाणं ब्रह्मभूतोऽधिगच्छति ॥ २४

yo 'ntaḥ-sukho 'ntar-ārāmas tathāntar-jyotir eva yaḥ
sa yogī brahma-nirvāṇaṁ brahma-bhūto 'dhigacchati

The Knower of Brahman

20) One thus situated does not rejoice upon obtaining what is desired, nor does such a person lament upon receiving what is undesired. With intelligence fixed and without bewilderment, the knower of *brahman*[12] becomes established in *brahman*.

21) One whose mind is unattached to external objects, who finds happiness within, and who is in union with *brahman*, enjoys unbounded happiness.

22) O son of Kuntī, those pleasures that arise from contact of the senses with their objects[13] are sources of misery, for they have a beginning and an end. One who is wise does not take pleasure in them.

23) Before leaving this body, one who is able to tolerate the urges that arise from desire and anger is a disciplined person and is happy in this world.

Liberation in Brahman

24) A *yogī* whose happiness is within, whose enjoyment is within, and who is illuminated within and who is absorbed in *brahman* attains liberation in *brahman*.[14]

---

12. Here the expression "knower of *brahman*" (*brahma-vit*), can be taken in two ways, as the knower of God or as the knower of the soul. Rāmānuja takes the latter view whereas Śaṅkara takes the former.
13. "Those pleasures that arise from contact of the senses with their objects (*ye hi saṁsparśajā bhogā*) is literally, "those pleasures that arise from contact." Contact means contact between the senses and their objects.
14. For an explanation of "liberation in *brahman*" (*brahma-nirvāṇa*) see fn. BG 2.72.

लभन्ते ब्रह्मनिर्वाणमृषयः क्षीणकल्मषाः ।
छिन्नद्वैधा यतात्मानः सर्वभूतहिते रताः ॥ २५

labhante brahma-nirvāṇam ṛṣayaḥ kṣīṇa-kalmaṣāḥ
chinna-dvaidhā yatātmānaḥ sarva-bhūta-hite ratāḥ

कामक्रोधवियुक्तानां यतीनां यतचेतसाम् ।
अभितो ब्रह्मनिर्वाणं वर्तते विदितात्मनाम् ॥ २६

kāma-krodha-vimuktānāṁ yatīnāṁ yata-cetasām
abhito brahma-nirvāṇaṁ vartate viditātmanām

स्पर्शान्कृत्वा बहिर्बाह्यांश्चक्षुश्चैवान्तरे भ्रुवोः ।
प्राणापानौ समौ कृत्वा नासाभ्यन्तरचारिणौ ॥ २७

sparśan kṛtvā bahir bāhyāṁś cakṣuś caivāntare bhruvoḥ
prāṇāpānau samau kṛtvā nāsābhyantara-cāriṇau

यतेन्द्रियमनोबुद्धिर्मुनिर्मोक्षपरायणः ।
विगतेच्छाभयक्रोधो यः सदा मुक्त एव सः ॥ २८

yatendriya-mano-buddhir munir mokṣa-parāyaṇaḥ
vigatecchā-bhaya-krodho yaḥ sadā mukta eva saḥ

भोक्तारं यज्ञतपसां सर्वलोकमहेश्वरम् ।
सुहृदं सर्वभूतानां ज्ञात्वा मां शान्तिमृच्छति ॥ २९

bhoktāraṁ yajña-tapasāṁ sarva-loka-maheśvaram
suhṛdaṁ sarva-bhūtānāṁ jñātvā māṁ śāntim ṛcchati

25) Seers whose sins are destroyed, whose doubts are removed, who are self-controlled and who rejoice in the welfare of all beings attain liberation in *brahman.*

26) For the self-realized sage, who is freed from desire and anger and whose thoughts are controlled, liberation in *brahman* is close at hand.

27-28) Shutting out external objects, fixing the vision between the eyebrows, balancing the incoming and outgoing breaths[15], the silent sage whose senses, mind and intellect are controlled, who is intent on liberation and who has given up desire, fear and anger is ever liberated.

29) The one who knows Me to be the recipient of all sacrifice and austerities, as the Great Lord of the world and as the friend of all beings attains peace.

---

15. For a note on the in-coming and out-going breaths see fn. under BG 4.29.

श्रीभगवानुवाच ।
अनाश्रितः कर्मफलं कार्यं कर्म करोति यः ।
स संन्यासी च योगी च न निरग्निर्न चाक्रियः ॥ १

śrī-bhagavān uvāca
anāśritaḥ karma-phalaṁ kāryaṁ karma karoti yaḥ
sa sannyāsī ca yogī ca na niragnir na cākriyaḥ

यं संन्यासमिति प्राहुर्योगं तं विद्धि पाण्डव ।
न ह्यसंन्यस्तसंकल्पो योगी भवति कश्चन ॥ २

yaṁ sannyāsam iti prāhur yogaṁ tam viddhi pāṇḍava
na hy asannyasta-saṅkalpo yogī bhavati kaścana

आरुरुक्षोर्मुनेर्योगं कर्म कारणमुच्यते ।
योगारूढस्य तस्यैव शमः कारणमुच्यते ॥ ३

ārurukṣor muner yogaṁ karma kāraṇam ucyate
yogārūḍhasya tasyaiva śamaḥ kāraṇam ucyate

यदा हि नेन्द्रियार्थेषु न कर्मस्वनुषज्जते ।
सर्वसंकल्पसंन्यासी योगारूढस्तदोच्यते ॥ ४

yadā hi nendriyārtheṣu na karmasv anuṣajjate
sarva-saṅkalpa-sannyāsī yogārūḍhas tadocyate

Chapter Six

Dhyāna-yoga

Yoga *and Renunciation*

1) Kṛṣṇa Bhagavān said:
Those who perform their duty without seeking the results are truly renounced and are *yogīs,* and not those who light no fire or perform no work.[1]

2) O son of Pāṇḍu, understand that *yoga* and renunciation are the same, for no one can become a *yogī* without giving up the conception of oneself as the enjoyer.[2]

3) Activity is said to be the means for the sage who undertakes the discipline of *yoga.* But meditation[3] is the means for the one who has attained such *yoga.*

4) When a person no longer clings to the objects of the senses or to actions, having renounced all conception of oneself as the enjoyer,[4] one is said to have attained to *yoga.*

Chapter Six is traditionally entitled *dhyāna-yoga,* The *Yoga* of Meditation.

1. "Light no fire and perform no work" (*na niragnir na cākriyaḥ*) can be taken in two ways. It can refer to the performance of daily rituals such as the fire sacrifice (*agni-hotrā*) and daily prayers (*sandhya-vandana*), or to general worldly engagement.

2. "The conception of oneself as the enjoyer" is a gloss on the word *saṅkalpa. Saṅkalpa* is a very complex word in Sanskrit. It literally means conception, but also includes such meanings as imagination, mental resolve, will or even mental construct. Here Śaṅkara takes it as "attachment to the results of action." Rāmānuja takes it as "false identification of the soul with the body."

3. "Meditation" is a translation of the word *śama. Śama* literally means to become quiet or tranquil as well as to restrain the passions.

4. See fn. to BG 6.2 above.

उद्धरेदात्मनात्मानं नात्मानमवसादयेत् ।
आत्मैव ह्यात्मनो बन्धुरात्मैव रिपुरात्मनः ॥ ५
uddhared ātmanātmānaṁ nātmānam avasādayet
ātmaiva hy ātmano bandhur ātmaiva ripur ātmanaḥ

बन्धुरात्मात्मनस्तस्य येनात्मैवात्मना जितः ।
अनात्मनस्तु शत्रुत्वे वर्तेतात्मैव शत्रुवत् ॥ ६
bandhur ātmātmanas tasya yenātmaivātmanā jitaḥ
anātmanas tu śatrutve vartetātmaiva śatru-vat

जितात्मनः प्रशान्तस्य परमात्मा समाहितः ।
शीतोष्णसुखदुःखेषु तथा मानावमानयोः ॥ ७
jitātmanaḥ praśāntasya paramātmā samāhitaḥ
śītoṣṇa-sukha-duḥkheṣu tathā mānāvamānayoḥ

The Mind as Friend or Enemy

5) A person must elevate oneself by the mind and never allow oneself to be degraded, for the mind is both one's friend as well as one's enemy.[5]

6) The mind that has been conquered becomes a friend, but for one who has failed to subdue the mind that very mind becomes one's enemy.[6]

7) In all circumstances–heat and cold, happiness and distress as well as in honor and dishonor–one who has subdued the mind[7] and achieved peace has become united with the Supreme soul.

---

5. This verse and the following verse illustrate both the beauty and complexity of translating Sanskrit. Between these two verses the word *ātman* has been used thirteen times! The word *ātman* has many meanings in Sanskrit: soul, breath, the Self, one's self (as a reflexive pronoun), mind, intellect, body, the Supreme Soul, *brahman* and so on. The applied meaning is therefore both contextual and dependent on one's underlying theology. Literally, this verse reads "a person must elevate the *ātman* by the *ātman* and not degrade the *ātman*, for the *ātman* is the only friend of the *ātman* as well as the *ātman's* only enemy." In this and the following verse I have translated *ātman* as "mind" as well as in its reflexive sense. This follows the approach of Rāmānuja and Madhva. Śaṅkara, on the other hand, follows a different approach. For Śaṅkara, there is only one reality, *brahman* and sometimes that one reality is also referred by the word *ātman*. When this is done many translators translate this *ātman* as the "Self" (upper case). By contrast the illusory individual soul is sometimes translated as "self" (lower case). Following Śaṅkara one might render this verse as "one should elevate the self by the Self and not degrade the self, for the Self is the only friend of the self as well as the self's only enemy." Compare with BG 13. 24.
6. A translation based on Śaṅkara's interpretation may be rendered as: "The self which has been conquered by the Self becomes the very friend of that self, but for one who has not subdued the self the self will become like an enemy."
7. Here again the word *ātman* is taken as mind. Śaṅkara takes it as self.

ज्ञानविज्ञानतृप्तात्मा कूटस्थो विजितेन्द्रियः ।
युक्त इत्युच्यते योगी समलोष्टाश्मकाञ्चनः ॥ ८

jñāna-vijñāna-tṛptātmā kūṭa-stho vijitendriyaḥ
yukta ity ucyate yogī sama-loṣṭrāśma-kāñcanaḥ

सुहृन्मित्रार्युदासीनमध्यस्थद्वेष्यबन्धुषु ।
साधुष्वपि च पापेषु समबुद्धिर्विशिष्यते ॥ ९

suhṛn-mitrāry-udāsīna-madhyastha-dveṣya-bandhuṣu
sādhuṣv api ca pāpeṣu sama-buddhir viśiṣyate

योगी युञ्जीत सततमात्मानं रहसि स्थितः ।
एकाकी यतचित्तात्मा निराशीरपरिग्रहः ॥ १०

yogī yuñjīta satatam ātmānaṁ rahasi sthitaḥ
ekākī yata-cittātmā nirāśīr aparigrahaḥ

Sameness of Vision

8) The person of discipline who is complete in both knowledge and wisdom,[8] whose senses are subdued and who is situated in transcendence[9] is called a *yogī*. Such a person sees a lump of earth, a stone or a piece of gold as the same.

9) One who sees a close friend, a companion, an enemy, a common acquaintance, an arbiter, the hateful, one's relatives and even all that is good or all that is evil with equal vision, is most advanced.

The Practice of Meditation

10) Without aspirations or possessions, the *yogī* should prepare oneself in a secluded place, and practice controlling body and mind.[10]

---

8. Śaṅkara explains knowledge (*jñāna*) as knowledge gained through study of scripture (*śāstra*). He explains wisdom (*vijñāna*) as realized knowledge gained through practical experience. Rāmānuja interprets *jñāna* as knowledge of the soul in matter and *vijñāna* as knowledge of the soul distinct from matter. Madhva explains *jñāna* as awareness of God and *vijñāna* as direct vision of God. See BG 3.41, 7.2 and 9.1
9. What is here translated as "situated in transcendence" is a rendering of *kūṭa-sthaḥ*, which literally means "situated at the top." The expression is used again in BG 12.3 and 15.16.
10. In the expression "controlling mind and body" (*yata-cittātmā*), Śaṅkara takes *citta* as mind and *ātman* as body. Rāmānuja takes *citta* as reasoning or thinking power and *ātman* as mind. *Ātman* could also be taken as a simple reflexive pronoun. Thus, *yata-cittātmā* could mean, "controlling one's thinking."

शुचौ देशे प्रतिष्ठाप्य स्थिरमासनमात्मनः ।
नात्युच्छ्रितं नातिनीचं चैलाजिनकुशोत्तरम् ॥ ११

śucau deśe pratiṣṭhāpya sthiram āsanam ātmanaḥ
nāty-ucchritaṁ nāti-nīcaṁ cailājina-kuśottaram

तत्रैकाग्रं मनः कृत्वा यतचित्तेन्द्रियक्रियः ।
उपविश्यासने युञ्ज्याद्योगमात्मविशुद्धये ॥ १२

tatraikāgraṁ manaḥ kṛtvā yata-cittendriya-kriyaḥ
upaviśyāsane yuñjyād yogam ātma-viśuddhaye

समं कायशिरोग्रीवं धारयन्नचलं स्थिरः ।
संप्रेक्ष्य नासिकाग्रं स्वं दिशश्चानवलोकयन् ॥ १३

samaṁ kāya-śiro grīvaṁ dhārayann acalaṁ sthiraḥ
samprekṣya nāsikāgraṁ svaṁ diśaś cānavalokayan

प्रशान्तात्मा विगतभीर्ब्रह्मचारिव्रते स्थितः ।
मनः संयम्य मच्चित्तो युक्त आसीत मत्परः ॥ १४

praśāntātmā vigata-bhīr brahmacāri-vrate sthitaḥ
manaḥ saṁyamya mac-citto yukta āsīta mat-paraḥ

युञ्जन्नेवं सदात्मानं योगी नियतमानसः ।
शान्तिं निर्वाणपरमां मत्संस्थामधिगच्छति ॥ १५

yuñjann evaṁ sadātmānaṁ yogī niyata-mānasaḥ
śāntiṁ nirvāṇa-paramāṁ mat-saṁsthām adhigacchati

नात्यश्नतस्तु योगोऽस्ति न चैकान्तमनश्नतः ।
न चातिस्वप्नशीलस्य जाग्रतो नैव चार्जुन ॥ १६

nāty-aśnatas tu yogo 'sti na caikāntam anaśnataḥ
na cāti-svapna-śīlasya jāgrato naiva cārjuna

11-12) Establishing oneself in a sacred place, on a firm seat that is neither too high or too low, covered with a cloth, a deerskin and sacred grass,[11] the *yogī* should fix the mind on a single point and control the thoughts and senses. Sitting on that seat let one practice the discipline of *yoga* for self-purification.

13-14) Holding the body, neck and head in a straight line, remaining motionless and fixed, gazing at the tip of the nose without looking in any other direction, with a peaceful mind and without fear, the *yogī* should become fixed in the vow of celibacy and control the mind with thoughts focused on Me.

15) Ever disciplined in this way, the *yogī*, with controlled mind, attains to the peace that comes from the cessation of material activities.[12] Such peace arises from My nature.

16) O Arjuna, the discipline of *yoga* never arises, for one who eats too much or eats too little, or who sleeps too much or sleeps too little.

---

11. This set of verses is similar to the description of the practice of *yoga* described in the ŚU 2.8-10.

12. The expression "that peace which comes from the cessation of material activities" is a gloss of *śāntiṁ nirvāṇa-paramām*. See fn. under BG 5.24 for a discussion of *nirvāṇa*. Śaṅkara takes *nirvāṇa-paramām* as a *bahuvṛhi* compound meaning "whose culmination is liberation (*mokṣa*)." Madhva glosses it as that peace "belonging to a time posterior to death."

युक्ताहारविहारस्य युक्तचेष्टस्य कर्मसु ।
युक्तस्वप्नावबोधस्य योगो भवति दुःखहा ॥ १७

yuktāhāra-vihārasya yukta-ceṣṭasya karmasu
yukta-svapnāvabodhasya yogo bhavati duḥkha-hā

यदा विनियतं चित्तमात्मन्येवावतिष्ठते ।
निःस्पृहः सर्वकामेभ्यो युक्त इत्युच्यते तदा ॥ १८

yadā viniyataṁ cittam ātmany evāvatiṣṭhate
nispṛhaḥ sarva-kāmebhyo yukta ity ucyate tadā

यथा दीपो निवातस्थो नेङ्गते सोपमा स्मृता ।
योगिनो यतचित्तस्य युञ्जतो योगमात्मनः ॥ १९

yathā dīpo nivāta-stho neṅgate sopamā smṛtā
yogino yata-cittasya yuñjato yogam ātmanaḥ

यत्रोपरमते चित्तं निरुद्धं योगसेवया ।
यत्र चैवात्मनात्मानं पश्यन्नात्मनि तुष्यति ॥ २०

yatroparamate cittaṁ niruddhaṁ yoga-sevayā
yatra caivātmanātmānaṁ paśyann ātmani tuṣyati

सुखमात्यन्तिकं यत्तद्बुद्धिग्राह्यमतीन्द्रियम् ।
वेत्ति यत्र न चैवायं स्थितश्चलति तत्त्वतः ॥ २१

sukham ātyantikaṁ yat tad buddhi-grāhyam atīndriyam
vetti yatra na caivāyaṁ sthitaś calati tattvataḥ

17) The discipline of *yoga,* which removes all suffering, only arises for one who is regulated in food and recreation, whose activities are moderate, and who is disciplined[13] in sleep and wakefulness.

18) One is said to have attained to the discipline of *yoga* when the controlled mind has become fixed on the soul alone and is free of all desires.

19) As a lamp situated in a windless place never wavers, so the *yogī,* who disciplines the mind,[14] never wavers.

The Goal of Meditation

20) When all thoughts come to an end, being blocked by the practice of *yoga,* one finds satisfaction seeing the soul in one's self through the mind.[15]

21) Transcending the reach of the senses, the *yogī* experiences unbounded happiness, grasped through spiritual perception.[16] Being so fixed one never deviates from the truth.

---

13. What is here translated as "regulated," "moderate" and "disciplined" is a rendering of the word "*yukta.*" The literal meaning of *yukta* is "fit" or "proper."
14. "Who disciplines the mind" (*yogam ātmanaḥ*) is literally, "the *yoga* of the *ātman*" and like similar sections of this chapter its meaning depends on how *ātman* is translated.
15. "Seeing the soul in one's self through the mind" is a translation of *ātmanātmānaṁ paśyann ātmani.* Here again there is the repeated use of the word *ātman* with all its potential for various meanings. See fn. under BG 6.5. Madhva takes it as "seeing the Lord in the body with the help of the mind." Śaṅkara takes it as "seeing the Self in the self by the Self."
16. "Grasped through spiritual perception" (*buddhi-grāhyam*) is literally, "grasped by the intellect." Śaṅkara glosses it as "not obtained through the senses." Rāmānuja takes it as an "intellect focused on the soul."

यं लब्ध्वा चापरं लाभं मन्यते नाधिकं ततः ।
यस्मिन्स्थितो न दुःखेन गुरुणापि विचाल्यते ॥ २२

yaṁ labdhvā cāparaṁ lābhaṁ manyate nādhikaṁ tataḥ
yasmin sthito na duḥkhena guruṇāpi vicālyate

तं विद्याद्दुःखसंयोगवियोगं योगसंज्ञितम् ।
स निश्चयेन योक्तव्यो योगोऽनिर्विण्णचेतसा ॥ २३

taṁ vidyād duḥkha-saṁyoga-viyogaṁ yoga-saṁjñitam
sa niścayena yoktavyo yogo 'nirviṇṇa-cetasā

संकल्पप्रभवान्कामांस्त्यक्त्वा सर्वानशेषतः ।
मनसैवेन्द्रियग्रामं विनियम्य समन्ततः ॥ २४

saṅkalpa-prabhavān kāmāṁs tyaktvā sarvān aśeṣataḥ
manasaivendriya-grāmaṁ viniyamya samantataḥ

शनैः शनैरुपरमेद्बुद्ध्या धृतिगृहीतया ।
आत्मसंस्थं मनः कृत्वा न किंचिदपि चिन्तयेत् ॥ २५

śanaiḥ śanair uparamed buddhyā dhṛti-gṛhītayā
ātma-saṁsthaṁ manaḥ kṛtvā na kiñcid api cintayet

यतो यतो निश्चरति मनश्चञ्चलमस्थिरम् ।
ततस्ततो नियम्यैतदात्मन्येव वशं नयेत् ॥ २६

yato yato niścarati manaś cañcalam asthiram
tatas tato niyamyaitad ātmany eva vaśaṁ nayet

प्रशान्तमनसं ह्येनं योगिनं सुखमुत्तमम् ।
उपैति शान्तरजसं ब्रह्मभूतमकल्मषम् ॥ २७

praśānta-manasaṁ hy enaṁ yoginaṁ sukham uttamam
upaiti śānta-rajasaṁ brahma-bhūtam akalmaṣam

22) Upon achieving this, one thinks there is no greater gain. Being firmly situated, one is never swayed from the truth, no matter what the difficulty.

23) Such a position is called the discipline of *yoga.* It is the cessation of all misery and must be practiced with determination and an untiring heart.

24-25) Completely abandoning all desires that spring from the mind,[17] controlling the senses on all sides by the intellect, one should gradually bring the mind to rest through the use of firm intelligence and focus the mind on the soul alone.

26) From wherever the fickle and unsteady mind wavers, it should be brought under the control of intelligence.[18]

27) For supreme happiness comes to that *yogī* whose mind and passions are calmed, who is sinless and who has attained the situation of *brahman.*[19]

---

17. Here *saṅkalpa* has been translated as "mind," but the meaning must also include the ideas of "volition," "mental conception," "will" and "intention." See fn. under BG 6.2.
18. "Brought under the control of intelligence" (*ātmany eva vaśaṁ nayet*): from the context *ātmani* is rendered as "intelligence." Śaṅkara takes it as Self.
19. "The situation of *brahman*" is a translation of "*brahma-bhūtam.*" Literally, it means "becomes *brahman.*" Śaṅkara takes it to mean "liberation while still living" (*jīvan-mukta*). Madhva takes it as "devotion to God."

युञ्जन्नेवं सदात्मानं योगी विगतकल्मषः ।
सुखेन ब्रह्मसंस्पर्शमत्यन्तं सुखमश्नुते ।। २८

yuñjann evaṁ sadātmānaṁ yogī vigata-kalmaṣaḥ
sukhena brahma-saṁsparśam atyantaṁ sukham aśnute

सर्वभूतस्थमात्मानं सर्वभूतानि चात्मनि ।
ईक्षते योगयुक्तात्मा सर्वत्र समदर्शनः ।। २९

sarva-bhūta-stham ātmānaṁ sarva-bhūtāni cātmani
īkṣate yoga-yuktātmā sarvatra sama-darśanaḥ

यो मां पश्यति सर्वत्र सर्वं च मयि पश्यति ।
तस्याहं न प्रणश्यामि स च मे न प्रणश्यति ।। ३०

yo māṁ paśyati sarvatra sarvaṁ ca mayi paśyati
tasyāhaṁ na praṇaśyāmi sa ca me na praṇaśyati

सर्वभूतस्थितं यो मां भजत्येकत्वमास्थितः ।
सर्वथा वर्तमानोऽपि स योगी मयि वर्तते ।। ३१

sarva-bhūta-sthiraṁ yo māṁ bhajaty ekatvam āsthitaḥ
sarvathā vartamāno 'pi sa yogī mayi vartate

आत्म्यौपम्येन सर्वत्र समं पश्यति योऽर्जुन ।
सुखं वा यदि वा दुःखं स योगी परमो मतः ।। ३२

ātmaupamyena sarvatra samaṁ paśyati yo 'rjuna
sukhaṁ vā yadi vā duḥkhaṁ sa yogī paramo mataḥ

28) Always disciplining oneself, the *yogī* whose sins are removed is easily in contact with *brahman* and enjoys unbounded happiness.

29) One who is engaged in the discipline of *yoga* and who possesses the vision of equality, sees the Supreme Soul in all beings and all beings in the Supreme Soul.[20]

30) For one who sees Me everywhere and who sees all things in Me, I am never lost, nor is that one ever lost to Me.

31) The person who is established in equal vision,[21] who worships Me in all beings, is a *yogī* and resides in Me in all circumstances.

32) O Arjuna, whether in happiness or distress, one is regarded as a perfect *yogī* who perceives the uniform nature of the soul under all conditions.

---

20. "One who ... sees the Supreme Soul in all beings and all beings in the Supreme Soul" (*sarva-bhūta-stham ātmānaṁ sarva-bhūtāni cātmani)* is literally, "one who sees the *ātman* in all beings and all beings in the *ātman.*" Madhva says that the word *ātman* used here refers to God. Rāmānuja says it means the individual soul. Thus, according to Rāmānuja to "see the soul existing in all beings and all beings existing in the soul" means seeing the qualitative similarity of all souls separate from matter. Śaṅkara says that *ātman* here refers to *brahman.* Thus, "One sees *brahman* in all beings and all being is *brahman.*"

21. "Equal vision" (*ekatva*) is literally "oneness" or "unity."

अर्जुन उवाच ।
योऽयं योगस्त्वया प्रोक्तः साम्येन मधुसूदन ।
एतस्याहं न पश्यामि चञ्चलत्वात्स्थितिं स्थिराम् ॥ ३३

arjuna uvāca
yo 'yaṁ yogas tvayā proktaḥ sāmyena madhusūdana
etasyāhaṁ na paśyāmi cañcalatvāt sthitiṁ sthirām

चञ्चलं हि मनः कृष्ण प्रमाथि बलवद्दृढम् ।
तस्याहं निग्रहं मन्ये वायोरिव सुदुष्करम् ॥ ३४

cañcalaṁ hi manaḥ kṛṣṇa pramāthi balavad dṛḍham
tasyāhaṁ nigrahaṁ manye vāyor iva suduṣkaram

श्रीभगवानुवाच ।
असंशयं महाबाहो मनो दुर्निग्रहं चलम् ।
अभ्यासेन तु कौन्तेय वैराग्येण च गृह्यते ॥ ३५

śrī-bhagavān uvāca
asaṁśayaṁ mahā-bāho mano durnigrahaṁ calam
abhyāsena tu kaunteya vairāgyeṇa ca gṛhyate

असंयतात्मना योगो दुष्प्राप इति मे मतिः ।
वश्यात्मना तु यतता शक्योऽवाप्तुमुपायतः ॥ ३६

asaṁyatātmanā yogo duṣprāpa iti me matiḥ
vaśyātmanā tu yatatā śakyo 'vāptum upāyataḥ

अर्जुन उवाच ।
अयतिः श्रद्धयोपेतो योगाच्चलितमानसः ।
अप्राप्य योगसंसिद्धिं कां गतिं कृष्ण गच्छति ॥ ३७

arjuna uvāca
ayatiḥ śraddhayopeto yogāc calita-mānasaḥ
aprāpya yoga-saṁsiddhiṁ kāṁ gatiṁ kṛṣṇa gacchati

Arjuna's Inadequacy

33) Arjuna said:
O Madhusūdana, Kṛṣṇa, due to the unsteady nature of the mind, I do not see the practical application[22] of this *yoga* of equal vision that you have described.

34) For the mind is unsteady, churning, and possessed of great strength and intensity. O Kṛṣṇa, to control it is more difficult than controlling the wind.

35) Kṛṣṇa Bhagavān said:
Without a doubt, O great armed son of Kuntī, the mind is unsteady and difficult to control, but with practice and detachment[23] it can be controlled.

36) Without self-control the discipline of *yoga* is indeed hard, but for one who endeavors for self-control through proper means, it is possible. This is my opinion.

Arjuna's Fear

37) Arjuna inquired:
O Kṛṣṇa, what is the fate of the unsuccessful *yogī*, who is endowed with faith, but whose mind has departed from the discipline of *yoga* and so does not obtain perfection?

---

22. What is here translated as "practical application" is literally "permanent foundation" (*sthitiṁ sthiram*).
23. The words for "with practice and detachment" are *abhyāsena* and *vairāgyeṇa*. See BG 12.6.

कच्चिन्नोभयविभ्रष्टश्छिन्नाभ्रमिव नश्यति ।
अप्रतिष्ठो महाबाहो विमूढो ब्रह्मणः पथि ॥ ३८
kaccin nobhaya-vibhraṣṭaś chinnābhram iva naśyati
apratiṣṭho mahā-bāho vimūḍho brahmaṇaḥ pathi

एतन्मे संशयं कृष्ण छेत्तुमर्हस्यशेषतः ।
त्वदन्यः संशयस्यास्य छेत्ता न ह्युपपद्यते ॥ ३९
etan me saṁśayaṁ kṛṣṇa chettum arhasy aśeṣataḥ
tvad-anyaḥ saṁśayasyāsya chettā na hy upapadyate

श्रीभगवानुवाच ।
पार्थ नैवेह नामुत्र विनाशस्तस्य विद्यते ।
न हि कल्याणकृत्कश्चिद्दुर्गतिं तात गच्छति ॥ ४०
śrī-bhagavān uvāca
pārtha naiveha nāmutra vināśas tasya vidyate
na hi kalyāṇa-kṛt kaścid durgatiṁ tāta gacchati

प्राप्य पुण्यकृताँल्लोकानुषित्वा शाश्वतीः समाः ।
शुचीनां श्रीमतां गेहे योगभ्रष्टोऽभिजायते ॥ ४१
prāpya puṇya-kṛtāl lokān uṣitvā śāśvatīḥ samāḥ
śucīnāṁ śrīmatāṁ gehe yoga-bhraṣṭo 'bhijāyate

अथ वा योगिनामेव कुले भवति धीमताम् ।
एतद्धि दुर्लभतरं लोके जन्म यदीदृशम् ॥ ४२
atha vā yoginām eva kule bhavati dhīmatām
etad dhi durlabhataraṁ loke janma yad īdṛśam

38) O great-armed One, is that *yogī*, who is unsuccessful in both this world and the next, who is bewildered on the path of *brahman*, not destroyed like a cloud cut away with no position?

39) O Kṛṣṇa, please dispel my doubt. Other than you, no one can remove this uncertainty.

The Result of Yoga

40) Kṛṣṇa Bhagavān said:
O Pārthā, my friend, one who does good in this world is never overcome by evil, either in this life or the life to come.

41) After achieving the worlds of the pious and dwelling there for countless years, the unsuccessful *yogī* is born in the home of the pure and the fortunate.

42) Then again, the *yogī* may be born in a family of enlightened *yoga* practitioners. Indeed, a birth of this kind is exceedingly rare in this world.

तत्र तं बुद्धिसंयोगं लभते पौर्वदेहिकम् ।
यतते च ततो भूयः संसिद्धौ कुरुनन्दन ॥ ४३

tatra taṁ buddhi-saṁyogaṁ labhate paurva-dehikam
yatate ca tato bhūyaḥ saṁsiddhau kuru-nandana

पूर्वाभ्यासेन तेनैव ह्रियते ह्यवशोऽपि सः ।
जिज्ञासुरपि योगस्य शब्दब्रह्मातिवर्तते ॥ ४४

pūrvābhyāsena tenaiva hriyate hy avaśo 'pi saḥ
jijñāsur api yogasya śabda-brahmātivartate

प्रयत्नाद्यतमानस्तु योगी संशुद्धकिल्बिषः ।
अनेकजन्मसंसिद्धस्ततो याति परां गतिम् ॥ ४५

prayatnād yatamānas tu yogī saṁśuddha-kilbiṣaḥ
aneka-janma-saṁsiddhas tato yāti parāṁ gatim

तपस्विभ्योऽधिको योगी ज्ञानिभ्योऽपि मतोऽधिकः ।
कर्मिभ्यश्चाधिको योगी तस्माद्योगी भवार्जुन ॥ ४६

tapasvibhyo 'dhiko yogī jñānibhyo 'pi mato 'dhikaḥ
karmibhyaś cādhiko yogī tasmād yogī bhavārjuna

योगिनामपि सर्वेषां मद्गतेनान्तरात्मना ।
श्रद्धावान्भजते यो मां स मे युक्ततमो मतः ॥ ४७

yogīnām api sarveṣāṁ mad-gatenāntar-ātmanā
śraddhāvān bhajate yo māṁ sa me yuktatamo mataḥ

43) O joy of the Kurus, in that situation the *yogī* regains contact with the consciousness from the previous life and again strives for perfection.

44) By dint of previous practice one is automatically elevated. Even one who merely desires to understand the discipline of *yoga* stands above the words of the *Vedas.*[24]

45) The *yogī* who is cleansed of sin, who endeavors with great effort, and who has achieved perfection after many births, finally attains the supreme destination.

The Greatness of a Yogī

46) A *yogī* is considered greater than the ascetic, greater than the person of learning and greater than the performer of ritual action. Therefore, by all means become a *yogī.*

47) O Arjuna, the one whose innermost soul[25] has surrendered to Me and who worships Me with great faith, I consider to be the highest of all *yogīs.*[26]

---

24. "Words of the *Vedas*" is literally "the *brahman* that consists of words" (*śabda-brahman*). This is often understood as the ritualistic practices described in the *Vedas.*
25. Both Śaṅkara and Rāmānuja understand "inner most soul" (*antar-ātma*) to be the mind.
26. Compare with BG 12.2.

श्रीभगवानुवाच ।

मय्यासक्तमनाः पार्थ योगं युञ्जन्मदाश्रयः ।
असंशयं समग्रं मां यथा ज्ञास्यसि तच्छृणु ॥ १

śrī-bhagavān uvāca
mayy āsakta-manāḥ pārtha yogaṁ yuñjan mad-āśrayaḥ
asaṁśayaṁ samagraṁ māṁ yathā jñāsyasi tac chṛṇu

ज्ञानं तेऽहं सविज्ञानमिदं वक्ष्याम्यशेषतः ।
यज्ज्ञात्वा नेह भूयोऽन्यज्ज्ञातव्यमवशिष्यते ॥ २

jñānaṁ te 'haṁ sa-vijñānam idaṁ vakṣyāmy aśeṣataḥ
yaj jñātvā neha bhūyo 'nyaj jñātavyam avaśiṣyate

मनुष्याणां सहस्रेषु कश्चिद्यतति सिद्धये ।
यततामपि सिद्धानां कश्चिन्मां वेत्ति तत्त्वतः ॥ ३

manuṣyāṇāṁ sahasreṣu kaścid yatati siddhaye
yatatām api siddhānāṁ kaścin māṁ vetti tattvataḥ

भूमिरापोऽनलो वायुः खं मनो बुद्धिरेव च ।
अहंकार इतीयं मे भिन्ना प्रकृतिरष्टधा ॥ ४

bhūmir āpo 'nalo vāyuḥ khaṁ mano buddhir eva ca
ahaṅkāra itīyaṁ me bhinnā prakṛtir aṣṭadhā

Chapter Seven

Knowledge and Wisdom

1) Kṛṣṇa Bhagavān said:
O son of Pṛthā, listen as I tell you how by practicing *yoga* and taking shelter of Me, with mind attached to Me, you can come to know Me free from doubt.

2) I shall declare to you in detail this knowledge that is both theoretical as well as realized,[1] knowing which nothing more is to be known in this world.

3) Among thousands of human beings one may strive for perfection; of those who have sought perfection, hardly anyone knows Me in truth.

4) Earth, water, fire, air, space, mind, intellect and sense of self[2]—together this is my material nature divided eight-fold.

Chapter Seven is traditionally entitled *jñānā-vijñāna-yoga*, The *Yoga* of Knowledge and Wisdom.

1. "Knowledge that is both theoretical as well as realized" is a translation of *jñāna* and *vijñāna*. See BG 3.41, 6.8 and 9.1.

2. Here *ahaṅkāra* has been translated as "sense of self." *Ahaṅkāra* is often rendered as ego or egotism. This usage has been avoided because the word ego is used in psychoanalytic theory in very specific ways. In addition, the term has the sense of pride or arrogance in common speech. What is meant, however, is the sense of self-identity.

अपरेयमितस्त्वन्यां प्रकृतिं विद्धि मे पराम् ।
जीवभूतां महाबाहो ययेदं धार्यते जगत् ॥ ५

apareyam itas tv anyāṁ prakṛtiṁ viddhi me parām
jīva-bhūtāṁ mahā-bāho yayedaṁ dhāryate jagat

एतद्योनीनि भूतानि सर्वाणीत्युपधारय ।
अहं कृत्स्नस्य जगतः प्रभवः प्रलयस्तथा ॥ ६

etad-yonīni bhūtāni sarvāṇīty upadhāraya
ahaṁ kṛtsnasya jagataḥ prabhavaḥ pralayas tathā

मत्तः परतरं नान्यत्किंचिदस्ति धनंजय ।
मयि सर्वमिदं प्रोतं सूत्रे मणिगणा इव ॥ ७

mattaḥ parataraṁ nānyat kiñcid asti dhanañjaya
mayi sarvam idaṁ protaṁ sūtre maṇi-gaṇā iva

रसोऽहमप्सु कौन्तेय प्रभास्मि शशिसूर्ययोः ।
प्रणवः सर्ववेदेषु शब्दः खे पौरुषं नृषु ॥ ८

raso 'ham apsu kaunteya prabhāsmi śaśi-sūryayoḥ
praṇavaḥ sarva-vedeṣu śabdaḥ khe pauruṣaṁ nṛṣu

पुण्यो गन्धः पृथिव्यां च तेजश्चास्मि विभावसौ ।
जीवनं सर्वभूतेषु तपश्चास्मि तपस्विषु ॥ ९

puṇyo gandhaḥ pṛthivyāṁ ca tejaś cāsmi vibhāvasau
jīvanaṁ sarva-bhūteṣu tapaś cāsmi tapasviṣu

बीजं मां सर्वभूतानां विद्धि पार्थ सनातनम् ।
बुद्धिर्बुद्धिमतामस्मि तेजस्तेजस्विनामहम् ॥ १०

bījaṁ māṁ sarva-bhūtānāṁ viddhi pārtha sanātanam
buddhir buddhi-matām asmi tejas tejasvinām aham

5) O greatly armed Arjuna, besides this lower nature there is another that is higher, which consists of the living beings that sustain this universe.[3]

6) All beings arise from these two natures.[4] Be assured, I am both the origin and dissolution of this entire universe.

7) O conqueror of wealth, there is nothing that is superior to Me. This whole world is bound to Me as pearls are strung on a thread.

8) O son of Kuntī, I am the taste in water, the light of the sun and the moon, the syllable Om heard in the all the *Vedas*; I am sound in space and the vitality of mankind.

9) I am the sweet fragrance of the earth and the warmth in fire. I am the life in all creatures and the penance of all ascetics.

10) O Pārtha, know that I am the eternal seed of all beings, the intellect of those who possess intelligence, and the splendor of all things splendorous.

---

3. Verses four and five describe two natures (*prakṛti*), one lower and one higher. The lower form of nature consists of the eight elements mentioned in verse four. These eight elements are characterized by unconsciousness. The higher form of nature, which consists of the *jīva-bhūta* or the living beings is characterized by consciousness.
4. That is to say, unconscious matter, which comprises the eight elements and the consciousness of the soul.

बलं बलवतां चाहं कामरागविवर्जितम् ।
धर्माविरुद्धो भूतेषु कामोऽस्मि भरतर्षभ ॥ ११

balaṁ balavatāṁ cāhaṁ kāma-rāga-vivarjitam
dharmāviruddho bhūteṣu kāmo 'smi bharatarṣabha

ये चैव सात्त्विका भावा राजसास्तामसाश्च ये ।
मत्त एवेति तान्विद्धि न त्वहं तेषु ते मयि ॥ १२

ye caiva sāttvikā bhāvā rājasās tāmasāś ca ye
matta eveti tān viddhi na tv ahaṁ teṣu te mayi

त्रिभिर्गुणमयैर्भावैरेभिः सर्वमिदं जगत् ।
मोहितं नाभिजानाति मामेभ्यः परमव्ययम् ॥ १३

tribhir guṇa-mayair bhāvair ebhiḥ sarvam idaṁ jagat
mohitaṁ nābhijānāti mām ebhyaḥ param avyayam

दैवी ह्येषा गुणमयी मम माया दुरत्यया ।
मामेव ये प्रपद्यन्ते मायामेतां तरन्ति ते ॥ १४

daivī hy eṣā guṇa-mayī mama māyā duratyayā
mām eva ye prapadyante māyām etāṁ taranti te

न मां दुष्कृतिनो मूढाः प्रपद्यन्ते नराधमाः ।
माययापहृतज्ञाना आसुरं भावमाश्रिताः ॥ १५

na māṁ duṣkṛtino mūḍhāḥ prapadyante narādhamāḥ
māyayāpahṛta-jñānā āsuraṁ bhāvam āśritāḥ

चतुर्विधा भजन्ते मां जनाः सुकृतिनोऽर्जुन ।
आर्तो जिज्ञासुरर्थार्थी ज्ञानी च भरतर्षभ ॥ १६

catur-vidhā bhajante māṁ janāḥ sukṛtino 'rjuna
ārto jijñāsur arthārthī jñānī ca bharatarṣabha

11) O bull of the Bhāratas, I am the strength of the strong, devoid of yearning and passion. I am desire[5] found in all beings that is not contrary to *dharma.*

12) Know that all states of being, whether of *sattva, rajas* or *tamas,*[6] come from Me alone. But I am not in them; they are in Me.

13) Deluded by these states of being consisting of the three *guṇas,* this whole world is unable to recognize Me, who am above these *guṇas* and imperishable.

14) Indeed, My divine energy,[7] composed of the *guṇas,* is difficult to overcome, but those who approach Me can transcend this energy.

15) But the evil, who are ignorant, who are the lowest of mankind, whose learning has been carried away by illusion, or who follow the malevolent nature, can not approach Me.[8]

16) O bull of the Bhāratas, four kinds of righteous persons worship Me: the afflicted, the inquisitive, those who desire personal gain, and the truly learned.

---

5. The word used here for desire is *kāma. Kāma* often denotes sexual desire as well as desire in general.
6. This is the first actual mentioning of the three *guṇas* (qualities of matter): *sattva* (goodness), *rajas* (passion) and *tamas* (darkness). See BG 3.5 and 3.27.
7. Here nature is called divine energy (*daivī māyā*).
8. This verse can also be interpreted as a simple description of evil-doers or to four specific categories of evil-doers.

तेषां ज्ञानी नित्ययुक्त एकभक्तिर्विशिष्यते ।
प्रियो हि ज्ञानिनोऽत्यर्थमहं स च मम प्रियः ॥ १७

teṣāṁ jñānī nitya-yukta eka-bhaktir viśiṣyate
priyo hi jñānino 'tyartham ahaṁ sa ca mama priyaḥ

उदाराः सर्व एवैते ज्ञानी त्वात्मैव मे मतम् ।
आस्थितः स हि युक्तात्मा मामेवानुत्तमां गतिम् ॥ १८

udārāḥ sarva evaite jñānī tv ātmaiva me matam
āsthitaḥ sa hi yuktātmā mām evānuttamāṁ gatim

बहूनां जन्मनामन्ते ज्ञानवान्मां प्रपद्यते ।
वासुदेवः सर्वमिति स महात्मा सुदुर्लभः ॥ १९

bahūnāṁ janmanām ante jñānavān māṁ prapadyate
vāsudevaḥ sarvam iti sa mahātmā su-durlabhaḥ

कामैस्तैस्तैर्हृतज्ञानाः प्रपद्यन्तेऽन्यदेवताः ।
तं तं नियममास्थाय प्रकृत्या नियताः स्वया ॥ २०

kāmais tais tair hṛta-jñānāḥ prapadyante 'nya-devatāḥ
taṁ taṁ niyamam āsthāya prakṛtyā niyatāḥ svayā

यो यो यां यां तनुं भक्तः श्रद्धयार्चितुमिच्छति ।
तस्य तस्याचलां श्रद्धां तामेव विदधाम्यहम् ॥ २१

yo yo yāṁ yāṁ tanuṁ bhaktaḥ śraddhayārcitum icchati
tasya tasyācalāṁ śraddhāṁ tām eva vidadhāmy aham

स तया श्रद्धया युक्तस्तस्या राधनमीहते ।
लभते च ततः कामान्मयैव विहितान्हि तान् ॥ २२

sa tayā śraddhayā yuktas tasyārādhanam īhate
labhate ca tataḥ kāmān mayaiva vihitān hi tān

17) Amongst these great souls, the one who is truly learned, whose devotion is single pointed and who is constantly disciplined, is best. For I am exceedingly dear to the person of learning, and that person is dear to Me.

18) All these are indeed exalted souls, but the one who is truly learned is My very Self. Such a devoted soul has taken shelter of Me as the highest goal. This is my opinion.

19) At the end of many births the person of learning surrenders unto Me thinking, "Vāsudeva is all things."[9] Indeed, such a great soul is rare.

20) Those whose knowledge has been carried away by countless desires surrender unto other gods[10] and follow different religious regulations governed by their particular nature.

21) To whatever divine manifestation they faithfully choose to worship, I alone make their faith strong.

22) Being endowed with such faith they endeavor to worship that particular deity and thereby fulfill their desires. In fact, this is all arranged by Me.

---

9. Literally, *vāsudeva* means the son of Vasudeva, Kṛṣṇa. According to Śaṅkara the word "*vāsudeva*" is used as a symbol for God. According to Rāmānuja and Madhva the word "*vāsudeva*" is specific. It means the son of Vasudeva, Kṛṣṇa, who is God.
10. Other gods (*anya-devataḥ*) according to Śaṅkara means gods other than the Self (*ātman*). According to Rāmānuja it means the Vedic pantheon headed by Indra, etc. In other words, gods other than Kṛṣṇa.

अन्तवत्तु फलं तेषां तद्भवत्यल्पमेधसाम् ।
देवान्देवयजो यान्ति मद्भक्ता यान्ति मामपि ॥ २३

antavat tu phalaṁ teṣāṁ tad bhavaty alpa-medhasām
devān deva-yajo yānti mad-bhaktā yānti mām api

अव्यक्तं व्यक्तिमापन्नं मन्यन्ते मामबुद्धयः ।
परं भावमजानन्तो ममाव्ययमनुत्तमम् ॥ २४

avyaktaṁ vyaktim āpannaṁ manyante mām abuddhayaḥ
paraṁ bhāvam ajānanto mamāvyayam anuttamam

नाहं प्रकाशः सर्वस्य योगमायासमावृतः ।
मूढोऽयं नाभिजानाति लोको मामजमव्ययम् ॥ २५

nāhaṁ prakāśaḥ sarvasya yoga-māyā-samāvṛtaḥ
mūḍho 'yaṁ nābhijānāti loko mām ajam avyayam

वेदाहं समतीतानि वर्तमानानि चार्जुन ।
भविष्याणि च भूतानि मां तु वेद न कश्चन ॥ २६

vedāhaṁ samatītāni vartamānāni cārjuna
bhaviṣyāṇi ca bhūtāni māṁ tu veda na kaścana

इच्छाद्वेषसमुत्थेन द्वंद्वमोहेन भारत ।
सर्वभूतानि संमोहं सर्गे यान्ति परंतप ॥ २७

icchā-dveṣa-samutthena dvandva-mohena bhārata
sarva-bhūtāni sammohaṁ sarge yānti parantapa

येषां त्वन्तगतं पापं जनानां पुण्यकर्मणाम् ।
ते द्वंद्वमोहनिर्मुक्ता भजन्ते मां दृढव्रताः ॥ २८

yeṣāṁ tv anta-gataṁ pāpaṁ janānāṁ puṇya-karmaṇām
te dvandva-moha-nirmuktā bhajante māṁ dṛḍha-vratāḥ

23) But the rewards of their worship are perishable and their intelligence is meager. Those who worship the gods go to the gods, while My devotees come to Me.

24) Those with limited intelligence think of Me as being once unmanifest, now become manifest.[11] They do not know My higher nature, which is imperishable and unsurpassed.

25) Covered by My divine creative power,[12] I am not visible to all. This deluded world knows Me not, who am unborn and imperishable.

26) O Arjuna, I know all beings that have existed in the past; I know all beings existing in the present, and I know all beings who will exist in the future, but no one in fact knows Me.

27) O scorcher of the foe, descendant of Bharata, at the very moment of their birth beings become bewildered by the dualities of illusion that arise from desire and hatred.

28) But for persons whose evil has come to an end and whose deeds have become virtuous, being freed from the duality of illusion, they worship Me with steady resolve.

---

11. This verse refers to those who think that Kṛṣṇa was an ordinary human being who appeared in this world due to his own *karma.*
12. Here the words used for "divine creative power" is *yoga-māyā,* God's divine energy. See fn. Under BG 4.6.

जरामरणमोक्षाय मामाश्रित्य यतन्ति ये ।
ते ब्रह्म तद्विदुः कृत्स्नमध्यात्मं कर्म चाखिलम् ॥ २९

jarā-maraṇa-mokṣāya mām āśritya yatanti ye
te brahma tad viduḥ kṛtsnam adhyātmaṁ karma cākhilam

साधिभूताधिदैवं मां साधियज्ञं च ये विदुः ।
प्रयाणकालेऽपि च मां ते विदुर्युक्तचेतसः ॥ ३०

sādhibhūtādhidaivaṁ māṁ sādhiyajñaṁ ca ye viduḥ
prayāṇa-kāle 'pi ca māṁ te viduḥ yukta-cetasaḥ

29-30) Those who take shelter of Me and who strive for release from old age and death come to know all aspects of *brahman.*[13] They know the *adhyātman*, the entirety of *karma*, the *adhibhūta*, the *adhidaiva*, and the *adhiyajña.* In this way, those whose hearts are devoted, know Me even at the hour of death.

---

13. The idea behind this section of the *Gītā* is similar to BG 4.24, namely, how all things are *brahman.* Here Kṛṣṇa discusses how *brahman* relates to the soul as the *adhyātman*, to action as *karma*, to creation as the *adhibhūta*, to the divinities as the *adhidaiva* and to sacrifice as the *adhiyajña.* The precise meaning of these terms will be discussed in Chapter Eight, verses 1 through 4.

अर्जुन उवाच ।
किं तद्ब्रह्म किमध्यात्मं किं कर्म पुरुषोत्तम ।
अधिभूतं च किं प्रोक्तमधिदैवं किमुच्यते ॥ १

arjuna uvāca
kiṁ tad brahma kim adhyātmaṁ kiṁ karma puruṣottama
adhibhūtaṁ ca kiṁ proktam adhidaivaṁ kim ucyate

अधियज्ञः कथं कोऽत्र देहेऽस्मिन्मधुसूदन ।
प्रयाणकाले च कथं ज्ञेयोऽसि नियतात्मभिः ॥ २

adhiyajñaḥ kathaṁ ko 'tra dehe 'smin madhusūdana
prayāṇa-kāle ca kathaṁ jñeyo 'si niyatātmabhiḥ

श्रीभगवानुवाच ।
अक्षरं ब्रह्म परमं स्वभावोऽध्यात्ममुच्यते ।
भूतभावोद्भवकरो विसर्गः कर्मसंज्ञितः ॥ ३

śrī-bhagavān uvāca
akṣaraṁ brahma paramaṁ svabhāvo 'dhyātmam ucyate
bhūta-bhāvodbhava-karo visargaḥ karma-saṁjñitaḥ

Chapter Eight

The Unchanging Brahman

Definitions

1) Arjuna asked:
O Highest Person, what is *brahman?* What is the *adhyātman*? What is *karma*? What is the *adhibhūta*? And what is the *adhidaiva*? Please explain these things.

2) O Madhusūdana, please explain who the *adhiyajña* is and how he resides in the body. And how can those who are self-controlled know You at the moment of death?

3) Kṛṣṇa Bhagavān said:
The Supreme Unchanging Principle[1] is *brahman.* The soul's individuality[2] is the *adhyātman.* The creative act, which gives rise to the diverse forms of living beings is defined as *karma.*[3]

Chapter Eight is traditionally entitled *akṣara-brahma-yoga,* The *Yoga* of the Unchangeable *Brahman.*

1. *Brahman* is here defined as "the Supreme Unchanging Principle" (*parama akṣara*). This Supreme Unchanging Principle then manifests itself as the various aspects of creation: the soul, action, matter, the divinities and sacrifice. How *brahman* pertains to these aspects of creation is called *adhyātman, karma, adhidaiva, adhibhūta* and *adhiyajña.*

2. "The soul's individuality"(*svabhāva*) is the unique and particular nature that adheres to each individual soul. *Brahman* manifests itself as the individual nature of each soul.

3. "The creative act" (*visarga*) is the outgoing creative force that gives rise to material entities in this world. *Karma* is the grand work of creation. *Brahman* manifests as this generating principle of creation.

अधिभूतं क्षरो भावः पुरुषश्चाधिदैवतम् ।
अधियज्ञोऽहमेवात्र देहे देहभृतां वर ॥ ४

adhibhūtaṁ kṣaro bhāvaḥ puruṣaś cādhidaivatam
adhiyajño 'ham evātra dehe deha-bhṛtāṁ vara

अन्तकाले च मामेव स्मरन्मुक्त्वा कलेवरम् ।
यः प्रयाति स मद्भावं याति नास्त्यत्र संशयः ॥ ५

anta-kāle ca mām eva smaran muktvā kalevaram
yaḥ prayāti sa mad-bhāvaṁ yāti nāsty atra saṁśayaḥ

यं यं वापि स्मरन्भावं त्यजत्यन्ते कलेवरम् ।
तं तमेवैति कौन्तेय सदा तद्भावभावितः ॥ ६

yaṁ yaṁ vāpi smaran bhāvaṁ tyajaty ante kalevaram
taṁ tam evaiti kaunteya sadā tad-bhāva-bhāvitaḥ

तस्मात्सर्वेषु कालेषु मामनुस्मर युध्य च ।
मय्यर्पितमनोबुद्धिर्मामेवैष्यस्यसंशयः ॥ ७

tasmāt sarveṣu kāleṣu mām anusmara yudhya ca
mayy arpita-mano-buddhir mām evaiṣyasy asaṁśayaḥ

अभ्यासयोगयुक्तेन चेतसा नान्यगामिना ।
परमं पुरुषं दिव्यं याति पार्थानुचिन्तयन् ॥ ८

abhyāsa-yoga-yuktena cetasā nānya-gāminā
paramaṁ puruṣaṁ divyaṁ yāti pārthānucintayan

4) O best of embodied souls, the principle of change[4] is the *adhibhūta*. The Universal Person[5] is the *adhidaiva*, and it is I, who am situated within the body as the *adhiyajña*.[6]

The Moment of Death

5) Upon quitting this body, one who exclusively remembers Me at the moment of death attains to My nature.[7] Of this, there is no doubt.

6) O son of Kuntī, whatever state of being one remembers at the end, while leaving the body, that state one surely attains.

7) Therefore, at all times think of Me and fight. With intellect and mind intent on Me, you will come to Me.

8) O Pārtha, with mind firmly fixed in the practice of *yoga*, constantly meditating, one attains the Supreme Divine Person.[8]

---

4. "The principle of change" (*kṣara*) is the defining feature of matter. *Brahman* manifests as this principle of change or perishability. This principle of change is called *adhibhūta*.
5. "The Universal Person" (*puruṣa*) is described in Chapter Eleven. *Brahman* manifests as this Universal Person who is the foundation of the gods.
6. Here Kṛṣṇa describes himself as the recipient of sacrifice, *adhiyajña*.
7. "My nature" (*mad-bhāvam*) is literally, "My state of being." For other uses see BG 4.10, 13.18 and 14.19.
8. Śaṅkara says that "the Supreme Divine Person" (*paramam puruṣam divyam*), means the sun deity. He takes *divya* as "residing in the orb of the sun." Rāmānuja and Madhva say that it means Kṛṣṇa.

कविं पुराणमनुशासितार-
मणोरणीयांसमनुस्मरेद्यः ।
सर्वस्य धातारमचिन्त्यरूप-
मादित्यवर्णं तमसः परस्तात् ॥ ९

kaviṁ purāṇam anuśāsitāram aṇor aṇīyāṁsam anusmared yaḥ
sarvasya dhātāram acintya-rūpam āditya-varṇaṁ tamasaḥ parastāt

प्रयाणकाले मनसाचलेन
भक्त्या युक्तो योगबलेन चैव ।
भ्रुवोर्मध्ये प्राणमावेश्य सम्य-
क्स तं परं पुरुषमुपैति दिव्यम् ॥ १०

prayāṇa-kāle manasācalena bhaktyā yukto yoga-balena caiva
bhruvor madhye prāṇam āveśya samyak sa taṁ paraṁ puruṣam upaiti divyam

यदक्षरं वेदविदो वदन्ति
विशन्ति यद्यतयो वीतरागाः ।
यदिच्छन्तो ब्रह्मचर्यं चरन्ति
तत्ते पदं संग्रहेण प्रवक्ष्ये ॥ ११

yad akṣaraṁ veda-vido vadanti viśanti yad yatayo vīta-rāgāḥ
yad icchanto brahmacaryaṁ caranti tat te padaṁ saṅgraheṇa pravakṣye

सर्वद्वाराणि संयम्य मनो हृदि निरुध्य च ।
मूर्ध्न्याधायात्मनः प्राणमास्थितो योगधारणाम् ॥१२

sarva-dvārāṇi saṁyamya mano hṛdi nirudhya ca
mūrdhny ādhāyātmanaḥ prāṇam āsthito yoga-dhāraṇām

9) One should meditate on that Supreme Divine Person as the ancient seer, as the ruler, as the one smaller than the smallest atom, as the support of all, with inconceivable form, and who has the radiance of the sun beyond all darkness.

10) With a firm mind, disciplined with devotion and the power of *yoga*, fixing the life-air[9] between the eyebrows, one attains that Supreme Divine Person at the time of death.

11) I shall now declare to you that state which the knowers of the *Vedas* call the unchangeable, to which the ascetics who are freed of passion enter, and for which those who practice celibacy live.

12) Closing all the gates of the body[10] and fixing the mind on the heart, the *yogī* establishes the life-breath at the top of the head and becomes situated in the process of *yoga*.

---

9. For a note on "life-air" see BG 4.27 and 4.29 fn.
10. The gates of the body are nine, ten or even eleven in number depending on the list: eyes, nose, ears, mouth, genital, anus and sometimes the navel and fontanel.

ओमित्येकाक्षरं ब्रह्म व्याहरन्मामनुस्मरन् ।
यः प्रयाति त्यजन्देहं स याति परमां गतिम् ॥ १३

oṁ ity ekākṣaraṁ brahma vyāharan mām anusmaran
yaḥ prayāti tyajan dehaṁ sa yāti paramāṁ gatim

अनन्यचेताः सततं यो मां स्मरति नित्यशः ।
तस्याहं सुलभः पार्थ नित्ययुक्तस्य योगिनः ॥ १४

ananya-cetāḥ satataṁ yo māṁ smarati nityaśaḥ
tasyāhaṁ sulabhaḥ pārtha nitya-yuktasya yoginaḥ

मामुपेत्य पुनर्जन्म दुःखालयमशाश्वतम् ।
नाप्नुवन्ति महात्मानः संसिद्धिं परमां गताः ॥ १५

mām upetya punar janma duḥkhālayam aśāśvatam
nāpnuvanti mahātmānaḥ saṁsiddhiṁ paramāṁ gatāḥ

आ ब्रह्मभुवनाल्लोकाः पुनरावर्तिनोऽर्जुन ।
मामुपेत्य तु कौन्तेय पुनर्जन्म न विद्यते ॥ १६

ā-brahma-bhuvanāl lokāḥ punar āvartino 'rjuna
mām upetya tu kaunteya punar janma na vidyate

सहस्रयुगपर्यन्तमहर्यद्ब्रह्मणो विदुः ।
रात्रिं युगसहस्रान्तां तेऽहोरात्रविदो जनाः ॥ १७

sahasra-yuga-paryantam ahar yad brahmaṇo viduḥ
rātriṁ yuga-sahasrāntāṁ te 'ho-rātra-vido janāḥ

13) One who quits the body in this way, while vibrating the syllable Om, the sound of *brahman*, and remembering Me, attains the supreme destination.

14) O Pārtha, I am easily attained by that *yogī* who is ever disciplined and who steadily remembers Me with an unalloyed heart.

15) Those great souls, who have attained the supreme perfection and who have achieved Me, no longer take birth in this place of impermanence and suffering.

16) From the region of the earth to the realm of Brahmā[11] all these worlds are places of repeated birth and death. But having once come to Me, O Arjuna, one need take birth never again.

The Day and Night of Brahmā

17) Those who know day and night understand that a day of Brahmā, by human calculation, is a thousand *yugas* in duration, and that Brahmā's night similarly lasts a thousand *yugas*.[12]

---

11. Brahmā: the four-headed creator deity situated on the highest plane of existence.

12. There are four ages known as *yugas*. (See BG 4.8 fn.) Together a cycle of four *yugas* is known as a *mahā-yuga* or great cycle. A thousand *mahā-yugas* makes a *kalpa*, which is one day of Brahmā. Similarly, one night of Brahmā is one *kalpa* in duration. Brahmā lives for a hundred years. One *mahā-yuga* is said to be 4,320,000 earthly years in duration. Let the reader make the calculations in order to determine the lifetime of Brahmā by human calculation.

अव्यक्ताद्व्यक्तयः सर्वाः प्रभवन्त्यहरागमे ।
रात्र्यागमे प्रलीयन्ते तत्रैवाव्यक्तसंज्ञके ॥ १८

avyaktād vyaktayaḥ sarvāḥ prabhavanty ahar-āgame
rātry-āgame pralīyante tatraivāvyakta-saṁjñake

भूतग्रामः स एवायं भूत्वा भूत्वा प्रलीयते ।
रात्र्यागमेऽवशः पार्थ प्रभवत्यहरागमे ॥ १९

bhūta-grāmaḥ sa evāyaṁ bhūtvā bhūtvā pralīyate
rātry-āgame 'vaśaḥ pārtha prabhavaty ahar-āgame

परस्तस्मात्तु भावोऽन्योऽव्यक्तोऽव्यक्तात्सनातनः ।
यः स सर्वेषु भूतेषु नश्यत्सु न विनश्यति ॥ २०

paras tasmāt tu bhāvo 'nyo 'vyakto 'vyaktāt sanātanaḥ
yaḥ sa sarveṣu bhūteṣu naśyatsu na vinaśyati

अव्यक्तोऽक्षर इत्युक्तस्तमाहुः परमां गतिम् ।
यं प्राप्य न निवर्तन्ते तद्धाम परमं मम ॥ २१

avyakto 'kṣara ity uktas tam āhuḥ paramāṁ gatim
yaṁ prāpya na nivartante tad dhāma paramaṁ mam

पुरुषः स परः पार्थ भक्त्या लभ्यस्त्वनन्यया ।
यस्यान्तःस्थानि भूतानि येन सर्वमिदं ततम् ॥ २२

puruṣaḥ sa paraḥ pārtha bhaktyā labhyas tv ananyayā
yasyāntaḥ-sthāni bhūtāni yena sarvam idaṁ tatam

18) At the beginning of Brahmā's day all things manifest come forth from the great unmanifest.[13] At the coming of Brahmā's night all is again dissolved into that great unmanifest.

19) O son of Pṛthā, repeatedly the same host of beings is brought forth at the coming of Brahmā's day and then again dissolved at the coming of Brahmā's night.

My Supreme Abode

20) Beyond this, however, there is another eternal and imperceptible state of existence that is beyond even the great unmanifest, which, when all beings are destroyed, is itself never destroyed.

21) They call this imperceptible and indestructible realm the most distant destination. This is My supreme abode,[14] and having once gone there, one never returns.

22) O Pārtha, this is the Supreme *Puruṣa*[15] that can only be attained by unalloyed devotion,[16] wherein all beings are situated and by which this entire world is pervaded.

---

13. "From the great unmanifest" (*avyaktāt*) refers to the state of primordial matter called *pradhāna* in Sāṅkhya philosophy. See SK 10-11.
14. What has been translated as "My supreme abode" is derived from *dhāma paramaṁ mama.* Rāmānuja says that *dhāman* refers to the abodes or states of God, which are three in number. The first is Kṛṣṇa's lower nature (BG 7.4) which is the world of dull and unconscious matter; the second is His living nature (BG 7.5), which are the souls of this world interacting with unconscious matter; the third is the realm of the pure souls who are released from unconscious matter. It is this third state that is referred to here. Alternatively he says that *dhāman* may also mean the light of knowledge.
15. The word *puruṣa* literally means man.
16. "By unalloyed devotion" (*bhaktyā ananyayā*) is literally, "by devotion to no other."

यत्र काले त्वनावृत्तिमावृत्तिं चैव योगिनः ।
प्रयाता यान्ति तं कालं वक्ष्यामि भरतर्षभ ॥ २३

yatra kāle tv anāvṛttim āvṛttiṁ caiva yoginaḥ
prayātā yānti taṁ kālaṁ vakṣyāmi bharatarṣabha

अग्निर्ज्योतिरहः शुक्लः षण्मासा उत्तरायणम् ।
तत्र प्रयाता गच्छन्ति ब्रह्म ब्रह्मविदो जनाः ॥ २४

agnir jyotir ahaḥ śuklaḥ ṣaṇ-māsā uttarāyaṇam
tatra prayātā gacchanti brahma brahma-vido janāḥ

धूमो रात्रिस्तथा कृष्णः षण्मासा दक्षिणायनम् ।
तत्र चान्द्रमसं ज्योतिर्योगी प्राप्य निवर्तते ॥ २५

dhūmo rātris tathā kṛṣṇaḥ ṣaṇ-māsā dakṣiṇāyanam
tatra cāndramasaṁ jyotir yogī prāpya nivartate

शुक्लकृष्णे गती ह्येते जगतः शाश्वते मते ।
एकया यात्यनावृत्तिमन्ययावर्तते पुनः ॥ २६

śukla-kṛṣṇe gatī hy ete jagataḥ śāśvate mate
ekayā yāty anāvṛttim anyayāvartate punaḥ

The Destination of the Soul at Death

23) O bull of the Bhāratas, I will now speak of the different times departing *yogīs* leave this world either to return or not to return.

24) Knowers of *brahman* depart this world and attain to *brahman* during the influence of the fire deity, in the light, on an auspicious day, during the bright side of the lunar month,[17] and during the six months while the sun is on the northern course.[18]

25) However, the *yogī* who departs during the influence of smoke, at night, during the dark side of the lunar month, during the six months while the sun is on its southern course attains the moon's light and then returns.[19]

26) These two paths, the path of illumination and the path of darkness, are considered the eternal ways of the world. By one, the *yogī* leaves this world never to return, by the other, the *yogī* again returns.

---

17. The lunar month is divided into two halves. One half is the *śukla-pakṣa* or bright half when the moon increases in luminosity. This occurs from the new moon to the full moon. The other half is the *kṛṣṇa-pakṣa* or dark half when the moon decreases in luminosity. This occurs from the full moon to the new moon. Parallels to this can be found in ChU 5.10.1-2 and 4.15.5, and BU 6.2.15.
18. The sun is said to have two courses. One is the *uttarāyana* or northern course when the sun is increasing in angular height in relation to the horizon. This takes place between December 21st and June 21st. The other is the *dakṣiṇāyāna* or southern course when the sun is decreasing in angular height above the horizon. In the northern hemisphere this translates into longer daylight during *uttarāyana* and shorter daylight during *dakṣiṇāyana.*
19. Compare this verse with ChU 5.10.3-6 and BU 6.2-16.

नैते सृती पार्थ जानन्योगी मुह्यति कश्चन ।
तस्मात्सर्वेषु कालेषु योगयुक्तो भवार्जुन ॥ २७

naite sṛtī pārtha jānan yogī muhyati kaścana
tasmāt sarveṣu kāleṣu yoga-yukto bhavārjuna

वेदेषु यज्ञेषु तपःसु चैव
दानेषु यत्पुण्यफलं प्रदिष्टम् ।
अत्येति तत्सर्वमिदं विदित्वा
योगी परं स्थानमुपैति चाद्यम् ॥ २८

vedeṣu yajñeṣu tapaḥsu caiva dāneṣu yat puṇya-phalaṁ pradiṣṭam
atyeti tat sarvam idaṁ viditvā yogī paraṁ sthānam upaiti cādyam

27) O son of Pṛthā, Arjuna, the *yogī* who understands these two paths is never bewildered. Therefore, in all circumstances become a *yogī*.

28) The *yogī* who knows whatever pious results are derived from the study of the *Vedas*, by the performance of sacrifice, by severe acts of penance or by great acts of charity surpasses them all and goes to that abode of unparalleled glory.

श्रीभगवानुवाच ।
इदं तु ते गुह्यतमं प्रवक्ष्याम्यनसूयवे ।
ज्ञानं विज्ञानसहितं यज्ज्ञात्वा मोक्ष्यसेऽशुभात् ॥ १

śrī-bhagavān uvāca
idaṁ tu te guhyatamaṁ pravakṣyāmy anasūyave
jñānaṁ vijñāna-sahitaṁ yaj jñātvā mokṣyase 'śubhāt

राजविद्या राजगुह्यं पवित्रमिदमुत्तमम् ।
प्रत्यक्षावगमं धर्म्यं सुसुखं कर्तुमव्ययम् ॥ २

rāja-vidyā rāja-guhyaṁ pavitram idam uttamam
pratyakṣāvagamaṁ dharmyaṁ su-sukhaṁ kartum avyayam

अश्रद्दधानाः पुरुषा धर्मस्यास्य परंतप ।
अप्राप्य मां निवर्तन्ते मृत्युसंसारवर्त्मनि ॥ ३

aśraddadhānāḥ puruṣā dharmasyāsya parantapa
aprāpya māṁ nivartante mṛtyu-saṁsāra-vartmani

मया ततमिदं सर्वं जगदव्यक्तमूर्तिना ।
मत्स्थानि सर्वभूतानि न चाहं तेष्ववस्थितः ॥ ४

mayā tatam idaṁ sarvaṁ jagad avyakta-mūrtinā
mat-sthāni sarva-bhūtāni na cāhaṁ teṣv avasthitaḥ

न च मत्स्थानि भूतानि पश्य मे योगमैश्वरम् ।
भूतभृन्न च भूतस्थो ममात्मा भूतभावनः ॥ ५

na ca mat-sthāni bhūtāni paśya me yogam aiśvaram
bhūta-bhṛn na ca bhūta-stho mamātmā bhūta-bhāvanaḥ

Chapter Nine

Imperial Knowledge

The Supreme Wisdom

1) Kṛṣṇa Bhagavān said.
My dear Arjuna, because you are without envy, I shall now declare this most secret wisdom along with what is most practical.[1] Knowing this you shall overcome all that is inauspicious.

2) Such learning is the imperial wisdom and a supreme mystery.[2] It is the most pure knowledge, directly perceived and established in *dharma.* It is everlasting and a joy to perform.

3) O scorcher of the enemy, those who have no faith in these teachings cannot attain Me and so return to this path of repeated birth and death.

4) In My unmanifest form I pervade this entire universe. All beings rest in Me; I do not rest in them.

5) And yet beings do not rest in Me. Behold My mystic wonder! I am both the cause and the support of all beings and yet I am never touched by them.

Chapter Nine is traditionally entitled *rāja-vidyā-rāja-guhya-yoga,* The *Yoga* of Royal Knowledge and Royal Mystery.

1. "Wisdom along with what is most practical" (*jñānaṁ vijñānaṁ sahitam*): See BG 3.41, 6.8 and 7.2 for previous uses.

2. "Such learning is the imperial wisdom and supreme mystery (*rāja-vidyā rāja-guhyaṁ*) may also be read "This learning is the wisdom and mystery of kings."

यथाकाशस्थितो नित्यं वायुः सर्वत्रगो महान् ।
तथा सर्वाणि भूतानि मत्स्थानीत्युपधारय ॥ ६

yathākāśa-sthito nityaṁ vāyuḥ sarvatra-go mahān
tathā sarvāṇi bhūtāni mat-sthānīty upadhāraya

सर्वभूतानि कौन्तेय प्रकृतिं यान्ति मामिकाम् ।
कल्पक्षये पुनस्तानि कल्पादौ विसृजाम्यहम् ॥ ७

sarva-bhūtāni kaunteya prakṛtiṁ yānti māmikām
kalpa-kṣaye punas tāni kalpādau viṣṛjāmy aham

प्रकृतिं स्वामवष्टभ्य विसृजामि पुनः पुनः ।
भूतग्राममिमं कृत्स्नमवशं प्रकृतेर्वशात् ॥ ८

prakṛtiṁ svām avaṣṭabhya visṛjāmi punaḥ punaḥ
bhūta-grāmam imaṁ kṛtsnam avaśaṁ prakṛter vaśāt

न च मां तानि कर्माणि निबध्नन्ति धनंजय ।
उदासीनवदासीनमसक्तं तेषु कर्मसु ॥ ९

na ca māṁ tāni karmāṇi nibadhnanti dhanañjaya
udāsīna-vad āsīnam asaktaṁ teṣu karmasu

मयाध्यक्षेण प्रकृतिः सूयते सचराचरम् ।
हेतुनानेन कौन्तेय जगद्विपरिवर्तते ॥ १०

mayādhyakṣeṇa prakṛtiḥ sūyate sa-carācaram
hetunānena kaunteya jagad viparivartate

अवजानन्ति मां मूढा मानुषीं तनुमाश्रितम् ।
परं भावमजानन्तो मम भूतमहेश्वरम् ॥ ११

avajānanti māṁ mūḍhā mānuṣīṁ tanum āśritam
paraṁ bhāvam ajānanto mama bhūta-maheśvaram

6) As the mighty wind forever blows in the sky, so all beings eternally rest in Me. Try to understand this.

7) At the end of time,[3] all beings enter into My nature; then at the beginning of time, I again send forth all of creation.

8) Through the agency of My material energy,[4] I repeatedly send forth this host of beings, who struggle powerlessly under the control of matter.

9) O conqueror of wealth, I am never bound by these actions, for I am seated as though neutral, unattached to all things.

10) I am the overseer of material nature, which brings forth both moving and the non-moving beings. O son of Kuntī, this entire universe forever moves with material nature as its cause.

Kṛṣṇa's Humanlike Form

11) Because I have assumed this humanlike form, fools scorn Me, not understanding My supreme nature as the Lord of beings.

---

3. What is here translated as "time" is *kalpa.* A *kalpa* is a day of Brahmā. See the note under BG 8.17.
4. Here "material energy" (*prakṛti*) is the same as what is described in BG 7.4: The eight elements: earth, water, fire, air, space, mind, intellect and sense of self.

मोघाशा मोघकर्माणो मोघज्ञाना विचेतसः ।
राक्षसीमासुरीं चैव प्रकृतिं मोहिनीं श्रिताः ॥ १२

moghāśā mogha-karmāṇo mogha-jñānā vicetasaḥ
rākṣasīm āsurīṁ caiva prakṛtiṁ mohinīṁ śritāḥ

महात्मानस्तु मां पार्थ दैवीं प्रकृतिमाश्रिताः ।
भजन्त्यनन्यमनसो ज्ञात्वा भूतादिमव्ययम् ॥ १३

mahātmānas tu māṁ pārtha daivīṁ prakṛtim āśritāḥ
bhajanty ananya-manaso jñātvā bhūtādim avyayam

सततं कीर्तयन्तो मां यतन्तश्च दृढव्रताः ।
नमस्यन्तश्च मां भक्त्या नित्ययुक्ता उपासते ॥ १४

satataṁ kīrtayanto māṁ yatantaś ca dṛḍha-vratāḥ
namasyantaś ca māṁ bhaktyā nitya-yuktā upāsate

ज्ञानयज्ञेन चाप्यन्ये यजन्तो मामुपासते ।
एकत्वेन पृथक्त्वेन बहुधा विश्वतोमुखम् ॥ १५

jñāna-yajñena cāpy anye yajanto mām upāsate
ekatvena pṛthaktvena bahudhā viśvato-mukham

अहं क्रतुरहं यज्ञः स्वधाहमहमौषधम् ।
मन्त्रोऽहमहमेवाज्यमहमग्निरहं हुतम् ॥ १६

ahaṁ kratur ahaṁ yajñaḥ svadhāham aham auṣadham
mantro 'ham aham evājyam aham agnir ahaṁ hutam

पिताहमस्य जगतो माता धाता पितामहः ।
वेद्यं पवित्रमोंकार ऋक्साम यजुरेव च ॥ १७

pitāham asya jagato mātā dhātā pitāmahaḥ
vedyaṁ pavitram oṁkāra ṛk sāma yajur eva ca

12) Those whose hopes are baffled, whose actions are fruitless and whose learning is wasted, who lack all discrimination take shelter of a malevolent and deluding nature.[5]

13) But the great souls, O Pārtha, take shelter of My divine nature and worship Me with undistracted minds. They know Me as the inexhaustible source of all beings.

14) Ever devoted and always praising Me, they strive with firm resolve. They offer homage to Me with great love.

15) And yet there are others who worship Me through the sacrifice of knowledge. Such devoted souls see Me as one and yet diverse, with different forms and faces on all sides.

The Attributes of God

16) It is I who am the ritual, the sacrifice, and the oblation to the ancestors. It is I who am the healing herb, the sacred chant, the sacrificial butter, the fire, and the sacrificial offering.

17) I am the father of this universe, the mother, the support, the grandfather, and the object of all knowledge. I am the purifier, the syllable Om, and the *Ṛg*, *Sāma* and *Yajur Vedas.*

5. Rāmānuja says "the malevolent and deluding nature" means the quality of darkness (*tamo-guṇa*).

गतिर्भर्ता प्रभुः साक्षी निवासः शरणं सुहृत् ।
प्रभवः प्रलयः स्थानं निधानं बीजमव्ययम् ॥ १८

gatir bhartā prabhuḥ sākṣī nivāsaḥ śaraṇaṁ suhṛt
prabhavaḥ pralayaḥ sthānaṁ nidhānaṁ bījam avyayam

तपाम्यहमहं वर्षं निगृह्णाम्युत्सृजामि च ।
अमृतं चैव मृत्युश्च सदसच्चाहमर्जुन ॥ १९

tapāmy aham ahaṁ varṣaṁ nigṛhṇāmy utsṛjāmi ca
amṛtaṁ caiva mṛtyuś ca sad asac cāham arjuna

त्रैविद्या मां सोमपाः पूतपापा
यज्ञैरिष्ट्वा स्वर्गतिं प्रार्थयन्ते ।
ते पुण्यमासाद्य सुरेन्द्रलोक-
मश्नन्ति दिव्यान्दिवि देवभोगान् ॥ २०

trai-vidyā māṁ soma-pāḥ pūta-pāpā yajñair iṣṭvā svar-gatiṁ prārthayante
te puṇyam āsādya surendra-lokam aśnanti divyān divi deva-bhogān

ते तं भुक्त्वा स्वर्गलोकं विशालं
क्षीणे पुण्ये मर्त्यलोकं विशन्ति ।
एवं त्रयीधर्ममनुप्रपन्ना
गतागतं कामकामा लभन्ते ॥ २१

te taṁ bhuktvā svarga-lokaṁ viśālaṁ kṣīṇe puṇye martya-lokaṁ viśanti
evaṁ trayī-dharmam anuprapannā gatāgataṁ kāma-kāmā labhante

18) I am the goal, the maintainer, the Lord, the witness, the abode, the shelter and the friend. I am the origin, the dissolution, the foundation, the reservoir, and the inexhaustible seed.

19) O Arjuna, I create the heat. I hold back and send forth the rain. I am immortality as well as death. I am both what is true and what is untrue.[6]

The Worship of other Deities

20) Those who know the three *Vedas*, who drink the celestial beverage, whose evils are purified worship Me with sacrifice. They desire the path to heaven, and upon reaching the worlds of the pious, they enjoy the celestial delights of heaven in the world of Indra.

21) Having enjoyed the vast realm of heaven, they eventually re-enter the world of mortals when their merit has been exhausted. In this way, those who follow the religion of the three *Vedas* seek to fulfill their desires. They obtain what is merely temporary.[7]

---

6. Rāmānuja explains, "what is true" (*sat*) as that which permanently exists, and "what is untrue" (*asat*) as that which has already existed or which will exist in the future. Madhva explains *sat* and *asat* as cause and effect. S*at* and *asat* may also refer to spirit and matter in the sense of what is permanent and what is temporary. Compare this verse with BG 2.16. and BU 1.3.28.

7. The doctrine of the five mystic fires, taught in the ChU Chp. 5 explains how the soul acquires a new body: "*Pravāhana* traces the course of the soul from the time it ascends to the heavenly world after death in a mortal body. It takes with it the sense organs and the material elements in a subtle state. In the heavenly realm, it gets a suitable body to enjoy the experiences there. When the results of its good *karma* are exhausted, the heavenly body dissolves. The soul then enters a rain cloud, comes down

अनन्याश्चिन्तयन्तो मां ये जनाः पर्युपासते ।
तेषां नित्याभियुक्तानां योगक्षेमं वहाम्यहम् ॥ २२

ananyāś cintayanto māṁ ye janāḥ paryupāsate
teṣāṁ nityābhiyuktānāṁ yoga-kṣemaṁ vahāmy aham

येऽप्यन्यदेवता भक्ता यजन्ते श्रद्धयान्विताः ।
तेऽपि मामेव कौन्तेय यजन्त्यविधिपूर्वकम् ॥ २३

ye 'py anya-devatā-bhaktā yajante śraddhayānvitāḥ
te 'pi mām eva kaunteya yajanty avidhi-pūrvakam

अहं हि सर्वयज्ञानां भोक्ता च प्रभुरेव च ।
न तु मामभिजानन्ति तत्त्वेनातश्च्यवन्ति ते ॥ २४

ahaṁ hi sarva-yajñānāṁ bhoktā ca prabhur eva ca
na tu mām abhijānanti tattvenātaś cyavanti te

यान्ति देवव्रता देवान्पितॄन्यान्ति पितृव्रताः ।
भूतानि यान्ति भूतेज्या यान्ति मद्याजिनोऽपि माम् ॥ २५

yānti deva-vratā devān pitṝn yānti pitṛ-vratāḥ
bhūtāni yānti bhūtejyā yānti mad-yājino 'pi mām

पत्रं पुष्पं फलं तोयं यो मे भक्त्या प्रयच्छति ।
तदहं भक्त्युपहृतमश्नामि प्रयतात्मनः ॥ २६

patraṁ puṣpaṁ phalaṁ toyaṁ yo me bhaktyā prayacchati
tad ahaṁ bhakty-upahṛtam aśnāmi prayatātmanaḥ

22) I bestow the benefits of *yoga* on those who persevere and constantly worship, thinking of Me alone.

23) O son of Kuntī, those devotees who faithfully worship other deities,[8] though with an improper understanding,[9] in fact worship Me alone.

24) For I am the enjoyer and Lord of all sacrifice. But since they fail to recognize Me in the proper way, they eventually fall down.[10]

25) Those who are devoted to the gods go to the gods. Those who are devoted to the forefathers go to the forefathers, and those who worship spirits go to the spirits. Similarly, my devotees come to Me.

Unalloyed Devotion

26) I accept that offering from a devoted soul who offers to Me with love and devotion, a leaf, a flower, a fruit, or even water.

---

to the earth during rains, gets united with food plants, enters a man's body through food, gets united with his semen, enters a woman's womb and there acquires another human body. The cycle then repeats itself."

8. Kṛṣṇa strengthens the faith of those who worship other gods (*anya-devatā-bhaktāḥ*) because Kṛṣṇa is the *adhidaiva* (the basis of all gods) in the form of the *puruṣa* or universal person. See BG 8.4. Rāmānuja describes "other deities" as the Vedic pantheon beginning with Indra.

9. Śaṅkara defines "without proper understanding" (*avidhi-pūrvakam*) as *ajñānam*, without knowledge. Rāmānuja says that it is worship not according to Vedic scripture.

10. Here Kṛṣṇa describes himself as the Lord (*prabhu*) and the enjoyer (*bhoktā*) of all sacrifice. This is what is meant by *adhiyajña*, "the recipient of sacrifice" described in BG 8.4

यत्करोषि यदश्नासि यज्जुहोषि ददासि यत् ।
यत्तपस्यसि कौन्तेय तत्कुरुष्व मदर्पणम् ॥ २७

yat karoṣi yad aśnāsi yaj juhoṣi dadāsi yat
yat tapasyasi kaunteya tat kuruṣva mad-arpaṇam

शुभाशुभफलैरेवं मोक्ष्यसे कर्मबन्धनैः ।
संन्यासयोगयुक्तात्मा विमुक्तो मामुपैष्यसि ॥ २८

śubhāśubha-phalair evaṁ mokṣyase karma-bandhanaiḥ
sannyāsa-yoga-yuktātmā vimukto mām upaiṣyasi

समोऽहं सर्वभूतेषु न मे द्वेष्योऽस्ति न प्रियः ।
ये भजन्ति तु मां भक्त्या मयि ते तेषु चाप्यहम् ॥ २९

samo 'haṁ sarva-bhūteṣu na me dveṣyo 'sti na priyaḥ
ye bhajanti tu māṁ bhaktyā mayi te teṣu cāpy aham

अपि चेत्सुदुराचारो भजते मामनन्यभाक् ।
साधुरेव स मन्तव्यः सम्यग्व्यवसितो हि सः ॥ ३०

api cet su-durācāro bhajate mām ananya-bhāk
sādhur eva sa mantavyaḥ samyag vyavasito hi saḥ

क्षिप्रं भवति धर्मात्मा शश्वच्छान्तिं निगच्छति ।
कौन्तेय प्रतिजानीहि न मे भक्तः प्रणश्यति ॥ ३१

kṣipraṁ bhavati dharmātmā śaśvac-chāntiṁ nigacchati
kaunteya pratijānīhi na me bhaktaḥ praṇaśyati

मां हि पार्थ व्यपाश्रित्य येऽपि स्युः पापयोनयः ।
स्त्रियो वैश्यास्तथा शूद्रास्तेऽपि यान्ति परां गतिम् ॥ ३२

māṁ hi pārtha vyapāśritya ye 'pi syuḥ pāpa-yonayaḥ
striyo vaiśyās tathā śūdrās te 'pi yānti parāṁ gatim

27) O son of Kuntī, whatever deeds you perform, whatever foods you eat, whatever oblations you offer, whatever charity you give, or whatever austerity you perform, do it as an offering for Me.

28) In this way, you will be freed from the bonds of action, whether auspicious or inauspicious. Being so engaged in the discipline of renunciation you will be freed and come to Me.

29) I am equal to all. I hate no one, nor am I partial to anyone. But for those who worship me with devotion, I am in them and they are in Me.

30) Those who exclusively worship Me, even if they perform the most abominable deed, are certainly to be considered righteous, for their resolution is correct.

31) Quickly they become righteous and find eternal peace. O son of Kuntī, know that My devotee never perishes.

32) O Pārtha, for those who take shelter of Me, even though they are of low birth,[11] women, *vaiśyas,* or *śūdras,* also attain the supreme destination.

11. "Those born of low birth" (*pāpa-yonayaḥ*) are literally, "those born of sinful wombs."

किं पुनर्ब्राह्मणाः पुण्या भक्ता राजर्षयस्तथा ।
अनित्यमसुखं लोकमिमं प्राप्य भजस्व माम् ।। ३३

kiṁ punar brāhmaṇāḥ puṇyā bhaktā rājarṣayas tathā
anityam asukhaṁ lokam imaṁ prāpya bhajasva mām

मन्मना भव मद्भक्तो मद्याजी मां नमस्कुरु ।
मामेवैष्यसि युक्त्वैवमात्मानं मत्परायणः ।। ३४

man-manā bhava mad-bhakto mad-yājī māṁ namaskuru
mām evaiṣyasi yuktvaivam ātmānam mat-parāyaṇaḥ

33) So much more are the pious *brāhmaṇas* or the devoted saintly order of princes! Having once come to this temporary world without happiness, just worship Me.

34) Fix your mind upon Me, become My devotee, worship Me, offer homage to Me. In this way, being absorbed in Me, you will come to Me.

श्रीभगवानुवाच ।
भूय एव महाबाहो शृणु मे परमं वचः ।
यत्तेऽहं प्रीयमाणाय वक्ष्यामि हितकाम्यया ॥ १

śrī-bhagavān uvāca
bhūya eva mahā-bāho śṛṇu me paramaṁ vacaḥ
yat te 'haṁ prīyamāṇāya vakṣyāmi hita-kāmyayā

न मे विदुः सुरगणाः प्रभवं न महर्षयः ।
अहमादिर्हि देवानां महर्षीणां च सर्वशः ॥ २

na me viduḥ sura-gaṇāḥ prabhavaṁ na maharṣayaḥ
aham ādir hi devānāṁ maharṣīṇāṁ ca sarvaśaḥ

यो मामजमनादिं च वेत्ति लोकमहेश्वरम् ।
असंमूढः स मर्त्येषु सर्वपापैः प्रमुच्यते ॥ ३

yo mām ajam anādiṁ ca vetti loka-maheśvaram
asammūḍhaḥ sa martyeṣu sarva-pāpaiḥ pramucyate

बुद्धिर्ज्ञानमसंमोहः क्षमा सत्यं दमः शमः ।
सुखं दुःखं भवोऽभावो भयं चाभयमेव च ॥ ४

buddhir jñānam asammohaḥ kṣamā satyaṁ damaḥ śamaḥ
sukhaṁ duḥkhaṁ bhavo 'bhāvo bhayaṁ cābhayam eva ca

अहिंसा समता तुष्टिस्तपो दानं यशोऽयशः ।
भवन्ति भावा भूतानां मत्त एव पृथग्विधाः ॥ ५

ahiṁsā samatā tuṣṭis tapo dānaṁ yaśo 'yaśaḥ
bhavanti bhāvā bhūtānāṁ matta eva pṛthag-vidhāḥ

Chapter Ten

The Divine Manifestations

Kṛṣṇa, the Origin of All

1) Kṛṣṇa Bhagavān said:
O mighty-armed Arjuna, listen again to My supreme words, which I shall speak for your benefit and which will give you great joy.

2) Neither the host of gods nor the great seers know My origin.[1] For in all respects I am the source of both the gods and the great seers.

3) One who knows Me as the unborn,[2] without beginning,[3] as the great Lord of the world, undeluded among mortals is freed from all evils.

4-5) Understand that reasoning, knowledge, freedom from delusion, patience, truth, self-control, peace, happiness, distress, birth, death, fear, as well as fearlessness, nonviolence, equanimity, satisfaction, austerity, charity, fame, and infamy all arise from Me.

Chapter Ten is traditionally entitled *vibhūti-yoga*, The *Yoga* of Manifestation.

1. "My origin" (*prabhava*) may also be taken as "My power" or "My majestic glory."

2. Rāmānuja makes the point that "unborn" (*ajam*) means that God's appearance in this world is categorically different from the ordinary soul who lives in association with matter.

3. Rāmānuja further asserts that "without beginning" (*anādim*) means that God is distinct even from the souls who are liberated from matter.

महर्षयः सप्त पूर्वे चत्वारो मनवस्तथा ।
मद्भावा मानसा जाता येषां लोक इमाः प्रजाः ॥ ६

maharṣayaḥ sapta pūrve catvāro manavas tathā
mad-bhāvā mānasā jātā yeṣāṁ loka imāḥ prajāḥ

एतां विभूतिं योगं च मम यो वेत्ति तत्त्वतः ।
सोऽविकम्पेन योगेन युज्यते नात्र संशयः ॥ ७

etāṁ vibhūtiṁ yogaṁ ca mama yo vetti tattvataḥ
so 'vikampena yogena yujyate nātra saṁśayaḥ

अहं सर्वस्य प्रभवो मत्तः सर्वं प्रवर्तते ।
इति मत्वा भजन्ते मां बुधा भावसमन्विताः ॥ ८

ahaṁ sarvasya prabhavo mattaḥ sarvaṁ pravartate
iti matvā bhajante māṁ budhā bhāva-samanvitāḥ

मच्चित्ता मद्गतप्राणा बोधयन्तः परस्परम् ।
कथयन्तश्च मां नित्यं तुष्यन्ति च रमन्ति च ॥ ९

mac-cittā mad-gata-prāṇā bodhayantaḥ parasparam
kathayantaś ca māṁ nityaṁ tuṣyanti ca ramanti ca

तेषां सततयुक्तानां भजतां प्रीतिपूर्वकम् ।
ददामि बुद्धियोगं तं येन मामुपयान्ति ते ॥ १०

teṣāṁ satata-yuktānāṁ bhajatāṁ prīti-pūrvakam
dadāmi buddhi-yogaṁ taṁ yena mām upayānti te

6) The seven great seers[4] as well as the four ancient progenitors of mankind[5] arise from My being. They spring from My mind, and all beings in this world descend from them.

7) One who truly understands My greatness and mystic power is united with Me through steadfast *yoga.* Of this there is no doubt.

8) For I am the source of all creation. From Me all things come to be. Knowing this, the wise who are saturated with love[6] worship Me.

9) With their thoughts focused on Me and their lives dedicated to Me, they find satisfaction and joy enlightening one another and forever conversing about Me.

10) To those who are ever resolute, who worship Me with love, I give the understanding[7] by which they can come to Me.

---

4. According to Madhva the seven seers are Marīca, Atri, Aṅgiras Pulastya, Pulaha, Kratu and Vasiṣṭha. These seven seers are the sages associated with the seven original family *gotras.* They are also the names of the seven stars in Ursa Major, the big dipper. Śaṅkara and Rāmānuja suggest another list of seven sages starting with Bhṛgu, without mentioning the names.
5. Madhva says the four progenitors of mankind (*manus*) are Svāyambhuva, Rociṣa, Raivata and Uttama.
6. "Full of love" (*bhāva-samanvitāḥ*) is taken by Śaṅkara to be equivalent with *bhāvanā* or a state of meditation on the Supreme. Rāmānuja takes it as "eager desire."
7. "I give the understanding" (*dadāmi buddhi-yogam*) is literally, "I give the discipline of intellect."

तेषामेवानुकम्पार्थमहमज्ञानजं तमः ।
नाशयाम्यात्मभावस्थो ज्ञानदीपेन भास्वता ॥ ११

teṣām evānukampārtham aham ajñāna-jaṁ tamaḥ
nāśayāmy ātma-bhāva-stho jñāna-dīpena bhāsvatā

अर्जुन उवाच ।
परं ब्रह्म परं धाम पवित्रं परमं भवान् ।
पुरुषं शाश्वतं दिव्यमादिदेवमजं विभुम् ॥ १२

arjuna uvāca
paraṁ brahma paraṁ dhāma pavitraṁ paramaṁ bhavān
puruṣaṁ śāśvataṁ divyam ādi-devam ajaṁ vibhum

आहुस्त्वामृषयः सर्वे देवर्षिर्नारदस्तथा ।
असितो देवलो व्यासः स्वयं चैव ब्रवीषि मे ॥ १३

āhus tvām ṛṣayaḥ sarve devarṣir nāradas tathā
asito devalo vyāsaḥ svayaṁ caiva bravīṣi me

सर्वमेतदृतं मन्ये यन्मां वदसि केशव ।
न हि ते भगवन्व्यक्तिं विदुर्देवा न दानवाः ॥ १४

sarvam etad ṛtaṁ manye yan māṁ vadasi keśava
na hi te bhagavan vyaktiṁ vidur devā na dānavāḥ

स्वयमेवात्मनात्मानं वेत्थ त्वं पुरुषोत्तम ।
भूतभावन भूतेश देवदेव जगत्पते ॥ १५

svayam evātmanātmānaṁ vettha tvaṁ puruṣottama
bhūta-bhāvana bhūteśa deva-deva jagat-pate

वक्तुमर्हस्यशेषेण दिव्या ह्यात्मविभूतयः ।
याभिर्विभूतिभिर्लोकानिमांस्त्वं व्याप्य तिष्ठसि ॥ १६

vaktum arhasy aśeṣeṇa divyā hy ātma-vibhūtayaḥ
yābhir vibhūtibhir lokān imāṁs tvaṁ vyāpya tiṣṭhasi

11) I am situated in their innermost being[8] and out of compassion for them, I destroy with the shining lamp of knowledge, the darkness born of ignorance.

Kṛṣṇa is the Highest of All

12) Arjuna said:
You are the Supreme *brahman,* the highest abode,[9] and the most pure One. You are the ultimate person, eternal and divine, the primal God and the unborn Lord.

13) All the sages including the divine Nārada, as well as Asita Devala and Vyāsa[10] declare this of You, and now You directly proclaim this to me.

14) O Keśava, O Bhagavān, I hold to be true all that You tell me, for even the gods and demons fail to understand Your true nature.

15) O highest person, *puruṣottama,* resting place of all beings, God of gods, O Lord of the world, You alone know Yourself.

16) Please declare fully Your divine wonders by which You pervade and abide in all these worlds.

---

8. "Situated in their inner most being" (*ātma-bhāva-sthaḥ*) can also be translated as "situated in My own true state."
9. Both Śaṅkara and Rāmānuja take "highest abode" (*paraṁ dhāma*) as supreme light. *Dhāman* has the sense of both abode and light.
10. Nārada is one of the ten mind-born sons of Brahmā. Asita Devala is one of the composers of the hymns of the *Ṛg Veda.* Sometimes Asita Devala is taken as two separate sages. Vyāsa is the legendary editor of the *Vedas* and compiler of the *Mahābhārata* and *Purāṇas.*

कथं विद्यामहं योगिंस्त्वां सदा परिचिन्तयन् ।
केषु केषु च भावेषु चिन्त्योऽसि भगवन्मया ॥ १७

katham vidyām aham yogiṁs tvāṁ sadā paricintayan
keṣu keṣu ca bhāveṣu cintyo 'si bhagavan mayā

विस्तरेणात्मनो योगं विभूतिं च जनार्दन ।
भूयः कथय तृप्तिर्हि शृण्वतो नास्ति मेऽमृतम् ॥ १८

vistareṇātmano yogaṁ vibhūtiṁ ca janārdana
bhūyaḥ kathaya tṛptir hi śṛṇvato nāsti me 'mṛtam

श्रीभगवानुवाच ।
हन्त ते कथयिष्यामि दिव्या ह्यात्मविभूतयः ।
प्राधान्यतः कुरुश्रेष्ठ नास्त्यन्तो विस्तरस्य मे ॥ १९

śrī-bhagavān uvāca
hanta te kathayiṣyāmi divyā hy ātma-vibhūtayaḥ
prādhānyataḥ kuru-śreṣṭha nāsty anto vistarasya me

अहमात्मा गुडाकेश सर्वभूताशयस्थितः ।
अहमादिश्च मध्यं च भूतानामन्त एव च ॥ २०

aham ātmā guḍākeśa sarva-bhūtāśaya-sthitaḥ
aham ādiś ca madhyaṁ ca bhūtānām anta eva ca

आदित्यानामहं विष्णुर्ज्योतिषां रविरंशुमान् ।
मरीचिर्मरुतामस्मि नक्षत्राणामहं शशी ॥ २१

ādityānām aham viṣṇur jyotiṣāṁ ravir aṁśumān
marīcir marutām asmi nakṣatrāṇām aham śaśī

वेदानां सामवेदोऽस्मि देवानामस्मि वासवः ।
इन्द्रियाणां मनश्चास्मि भूतानामस्मि चेतना ॥ २२

vedānāṁ sāma-vedo 'smi devānām asmi vāsavaḥ
indriyāṇāṁ manaś cāsmi bhūtānām asmi cetanā

17) O mystic One,[11] how am I to understand You? O Blessed Lord, in what forms am I to think of You?

18) O Janārdana, please again describe in detail Your mystic wonder, for I am never satiated hearing such nectar.

Kṛṣṇa is the Quintessence of All Things Great

19) Kṛṣṇa Bhagavān said:
O best of the Kurus, I shall tell you of My divine wonders, but only of those which are most prominent, for there is no limit to My splendor.

20) O sleepless one, I am the soul situated in the heart of all. I am the beginning, the middle and the end of all beings.

21) Of the Ādityas I am Viṣṇu,[12] of luminaries I am the radiant sun, and of Maruts[13] I am Marīci. I am the moon amongst lunar mansions.[14]

22) Of the *Vedas* I am the Sāma Veda, of gods I am Indra, and of the senses I am the mind. I am the consciousness in all beings.

---

11. "O mystic one" (*yogin*): Rāmānuja reads *yogī* instead of *yogin*. Read in this way, *yogī* is nominative and describes Arjuna. *Yogin*, on the other hand, is vocative and is an address to Lord Kṛṣṇa.
12. The sun is given a different name in each month. Thus there are twelve suns known as the twelve Ādityas: Dhātṛ, Aryaman, Mitra, Varuṇa, Indra, Vivasvat, Pūṣan, Aṁśa, Bhaga, Tvaṣṭṛ, Viṣṇu, and Indra. The sun in the month of Kārtika is known as Viṣṇu.
13. The Maruts are the storm gods of which there are forty-nine. Marīci is the head. This Marīci is apparently not one of the seven seers mentioned in verse 10.6.
14. There are twenty-seven lunar mansions or *nakṣatras*. The moon is not one of them, but instead is the lord of the *nakṣatras*.

रुद्राणां शंकरश्चास्मि वित्तेशो यक्षरक्षसाम् ।
वसूनां पावकश्चास्मि मेरुः शिखरिणामहम् ॥ २३

rudrāṇāṁ śaṅkaraś cāsmi vitteśo yakṣa-rakṣasām
vasūnāṁ pāvakaś cāsmi meruḥ śikhariṇām aham

पुरोधसां च मुख्यं मां विद्धि पार्थ बृहस्पतिम् ।
सेनानीनामहं स्कन्दः सरसामस्मि सागरः ॥ २४

purodhasāṁ ca mukhyaṁ māṁ viddhi pārtha bṛhaspatim
senānīnām ahaṁ skandaḥ sarasām asmi sāgaraḥ

महर्षीणां भृगुरहं गिरामस्म्येकमक्षरम् ।
यज्ञानां जपयज्ञोऽस्मि स्थावराणां हिमालयः ॥ २५

maharṣīṇāṁ bhṛgur ahaṁ girām asmy ekam akṣaram
yajñānāṁ japa-yajño 'smi sthāvarāṇāṁ himālayaḥ

अश्वत्थः सर्ववृक्षाणां देवर्षीणां च नारदः ।
गन्धर्वाणां चित्ररथः सिद्धानां कपिलो मुनिः ॥ २६

aśvatthaḥ sarva-vṛkṣāṇāṁ devarṣīṇāṁ ca nāradaḥ
gandharvāṇāṁ citrarathaḥ siddhānāṁ kapilo muniḥ

उच्चैःश्रवसमश्वानां विद्धि माममृतोद्भवम् ।
ऐरावतं गजेन्द्राणां नराणां च नराधिपम् ॥ २७

uccaiḥśravasam aśvānāṁ viddhi mām amṛtodbhavam
airāvataṁ gajendrāṇāṁ narāṇāṁ ca narādhipam

23) Of Rudras I am Śiva,[15] among Yakṣas and Rakṣas I am the lord of wealth, Kubera.[16] Of Vasus[17] I am fire, and of mountain peaks I am Meru.[18]

24) O Pārtha, among priests I am the chief priest, Bṛhaspati.[19] Among generals I am Skanda,[20] and of bodies of water I am the ocean.

25) Of great sages I am Bhṛgu,[21] of utterances I am the single syllable Om. I am the sacrifice of chanting among sacrifices, and I am the Himalayas of mountain ranges.

26) Among trees I am the holy fig, among divine sages I am Nārada. I am Citraratha of Gandharvas,[22] and I am the sage Kapila[23] of perfected beings.

27) Of horses I am Uccaiḥśravas, who arose from nectar. Of royal elephants I am Airāvata,[24] and of men I am the king.

---

15. There are eleven Rudras of which Śiva is the head.
16. The Yakṣas and Rakṣa are various spirits, some malevolent and others benevolent. Kubera, the lord of wealth, is their head.
17. There are eight Vasus: fire, earth, wind, atmosphere, sun, sky, moon, and stars. Fire is their mouth.
18. Meru is the mountain that stands at the center of creation.
19. Bṛhaspati is the priest for Indra and all the gods.
20. Skanda is the son of Śiva. He is also known as Kārttikeya, the god of war. He is often seen with six heads and twelve arms.
21. Bhṛgu is an ancient sage and first of the patriarchs created by the first Manu. His name is associated with an ancient system of astrology.
22. Gandharvas are a class of divine musicians.
23. Kapila is the founder of the Sāṅkhya system of philosophy.
24. Uccaiḥśravas and Airāvata are great beings that were brought forth when the gods and demons churned the ocean of milk in search of the nectar of immortality. They were given to Indra as his horse and elephant respectively.

आयुधानामहं वज्रं धेनूनामस्मि कामधुक् ।
प्रजनश्चास्मि कन्दर्पः सर्पाणामस्मि वासुकिः ॥ २८

āyudhānām ahaṁ vajraṁ dhenūnām asmi kāmadhuk
prajanaś cāsmi kandarpaḥ sarpāṇām asmi vāsukiḥ

अनन्तश्चास्मि नागानां वरुणो यादसामहम् ।
पितॄणामर्यमा चास्मि यमः संयमतामहम् ॥ २९

anantaś cāsmi nāgānāṁ varuṇo yādasām aham
pitṝṇām aryamā cāsmi yamaḥ saṁyamatām aham

प्रह्लादश्चास्मि दैत्यानां कालः कलयतामहम् ।
मृगाणां च मृगेन्द्रोऽहं वैनतेयश्च पक्षिणाम् ॥ ३०

prahlādaś cāsmi daityānāṁ kālaḥ kalayatām aham
mṛgāṇāṁ ca mṛgendro 'haṁ vainateyaś ca pakṣiṇām

पवनः पवतामस्मि रामः शस्त्रभृतामहम् ।
झषाणां मकरश्चास्मि स्रोतसामस्मि जाह्नवी ॥ ३१

pavanaḥ pavatām asmi rāmaḥ śastra-bhṛtām aham
jhaṣāṇāṁ makaraś cāsmi srotasām asmi jāhnavī

28) Of weapons I am the thunderbolt, among cows I am the *kāmadhuk*.[25] I am the principle of procreation, Kandarpa, the god of passion. Among serpents I am Vāsuki.[26]

29) Among celestial serpents[27] I am Ananta, among those who dwell in water I am Varuṇa,[28] of forefathers I am Aryamā, and among regulators I am Yama.[29]

30) Among Daityas I am Prahlāda,[30] of reckoners I am time, of beasts I am the lion, and among birds I am the son of Vinatā, Garuḍa.[31]

31) I am the wind among purifiers. I am Rāma[32] among wielders of weapons. I am the shark[33] among aquatics, and I am the Ganges[34] among rivers.

---

25. The *kāmadhuk* or wish-yielding cow is a celestial cow that was churned from the ocean of milk and given to Indra. It is a cow that gives forth all desires.
26. Vāsuki is the celestial serpent, or *sarpa*, used to churn the ocean of milk. *Sarpas* are single-headed snakes.
27. *Nāgas* are many-headed snakes. Ananta Śeṣa is the divine snake used by Lord Viṣṇu.
28. Beings that live in water are governed by Varuṇa.
29. Aryamā is the chief of the ancestors known as Pitṛs. Yama, the lord of death, is the son of the sun god.
30. The Daityas are the demon sons of Diti. Prahlāda is one of the Daityas and the son of Hiraṇyakaśipu. He became a famous follower of Viṣṇu.
31. Garuḍa is the great carrier of Viṣṇu.
32. Rāma means either the hero of the *Rāmāyaṇa* or Paraśurāma, another incarnation of Viṣṇu famous for the destruction of the *kṣatriya* or warrior class.
33. "*Makara*" is here translated as shark. Sometimes it is translated as a crocodile or even dolphin. In fact, it is a type of huge sea monster, known as the carrier of Varuṇa.
34. Here the Ganges is called Jāhnavī, who is the daughter of Jahnu. Jahnu was a sage who drank up the Ganges. Later it flowed from his ear.

सर्गाणामादिरन्तश्च मध्यं चैवाहमर्जुन ।
अध्यात्मविद्या विद्यानां वादः प्रवदतामहम् ॥ ३२

sargāṇām ādir antaś ca madhyaṁ caivāham arjuna
adhyātma-vidyā vidyānāṁ vādaḥ pravadatām aham

अक्षराणामकारोऽस्मि द्वंद्वः सामासिकस्य च ।
अहमेवाक्षयः कालो धाताहं विश्वतोमुखः ॥ ३३

akṣarāṇām a-kāro 'smi dvandvaḥ sāmāsikasya ca
aham evākṣayaḥ kālo dhātāhaṁ viśvato-mukhaḥ

मृत्युः सर्वहरश्चाहमुद्भवश्च भविष्यताम् ।
कीर्तिः श्रीर्वाक्च नारीणां स्मृतिर्मेधा धृतिः क्षमा ॥ ३४

mṛtyuḥ sarva-haraś cāham udbhavaś ca bhaviṣyatām
kīrtiḥ śrīr vāk ca nārīṇāṁ smṛtir medhā dhṛtiḥ kṣamā

बृहत्साम तथा साम्नां गायत्री छन्दसामहम् ।
मासानां मार्गशीर्षोऽहमृतूनां कुसुमाकरः ॥ ३५

bṛhat-sāma tathā sāmnāṁ gāyatrī chandasām aham
māsānāṁ mārga-śīrṣo 'ham ṛtūnāṁ kusumākaraḥ

द्यूतं छलयतामस्मि तेजस्तेजस्विनामहम् ।
जयोऽस्मि व्यवसायोऽस्मि सत्त्वं सत्त्ववतामहम् ॥ ३६

dyūtaṁ chalayatām asmi tejas tejasvinām aham
jayo 'smi vyavasāyo 'smi sattvaṁ sattvavatām aham

32) O Arjuna, among creations I am the beginning, middle and the end. Of sciences I am the spiritual science of the soul,[35] and of those who speak I am speech.

33) Of syllables I am the letter A, of compounds I am the dual compound.[36] Indeed, I am indestructible time as well as the creator with faces in every direction.

34) I am death that steals away all things, and I am the source of all things to be. Of things feminine I am fame, opulence, fine speech, memory, intellect, firmness and patience.

35) Amongst hymns from the *Sāma-veda* I am the *Bṛhat-sāma,*[37] of meters I am the *gāyatrī,*[38] of months I am Mārgaśīrṣa,[39] and of seasons I am flower-bearing spring.

36) Among cheaters I am gambling, and among all things splendorous I am splendor. I am victory, I am adventure, and I am the vitality in all things vital.

---

35. "Spiritual science of the soul (*adhyātma-vidyā*): for other uses of *adhyātma* see BG 7.30, 8.3 and 11.1.
36. A *dvandva* is a dual compound as "mother-father" for mother and father.
37. The *Bṛhat-sāma* is a hymn to God in the form of Indra.
38. *Gāyatrī* is a meter consisting of twenty-four syllables (three lines of eight syllables). It is perhaps the most important of meters used in the *Vedas.*
39. Mārgaśīrṣa is the month when the moon is full in the *nakṣatra* known as Mṛgaśiras. It corresponds to November-December. This reference, however, refers to a time when the spring equinox actually occurred when the sun was in the zodiac sign of Taurus. This is where part of Mṛgaśiras resides. Due to the precession of the equinoxes, the spring equinox now occurs in Pisces. During the time when the spring equinox was in Mṛgaśīrṣa this *nakṣatra* was considered the first of the 27 *nakṣatras.* Back dating suggests that this verse refers to a tradition that existed around 2500 BC.

वृष्णीनां वासुदेवोऽस्मि पाण्डवानां धनंजयः ।
मुनीनामप्यहं व्यासः कवीनामुशना कविः ॥ ३७

vṛṣṇīnāṁ vāsudevo 'smi pāṇḍavānāṁ dhanañjayaḥ
munīnām apy ahaṁ vyāsaḥ kavīnām uśanā kaviḥ

दण्डो दमयतामस्मि नीतिरस्मि जिगीषताम् ।
मौनं चैवास्मि गुह्यानां ज्ञानं ज्ञानवतामहम् ॥ ३८

daṇḍo damayatām asmi nītir asmi jigīṣatām
maunaṁ caivāsmi guhyānāṁ jñānaṁ jñānavatām aham

यच्चापि सर्वभूतानां बीजं तदहमर्जुन ।
न तदस्ति विना यत्स्यान्मया भूतं चराचरम् ॥ ३९

yac cāpi sarva-bhūtānāṁ bījaṁ tad aham arjuna
na tad asti vinā yat syān mayā bhūtaṁ carācaram

नान्तोऽस्ति मम दिव्यानां विभूतीनां परंतप ।
एष तूद्देशतः प्रोक्तो विभूतेर्विस्तरो मया ॥ ४०

nānto 'sti mama divyānāṁ vibhūtīnāṁ parantapa
eṣa tūddeśataḥ prokto vibhūter vistaro mayā

यद्यद्विभूतिमत्सत्त्वं श्रीमदूर्जितमेव वा ।
तत्तदेवावगच्छ त्वं मम तेजोंऽशसंभवम् ॥ ४१

yad yad vibhūtimat sattvaṁ śrīmad ūrjitam eva vā
tat tad evāvagaccha tvaṁ mama tejo 'ṁśa-sambhavam

अथ वा बहुनैतेन किं ज्ञातेन तवार्जुन ।
विष्टभ्याहमिदं कृत्स्नमेकांशेन स्थितो जगत् ॥ ४२

atha vā bahunaitena kiṁ jñātena tavārjuna
viṣṭabhyāham idaṁ kṛtsnam ekāṁśena sthito jagat

37) Among the descendants of Vṛṣṇi I am Vāsudeva,[40] among the descendants of Pāṇḍu I am Dhanañjaya,[41] of silent sages I am Vyāsa,[42] and of hermits I am the wise Uśanā.[43]

38) I am the rod of chastisement among subdoers, and I am political wisdom among those who desire conquest. Of things secret I am silence, and of the wise I am wisdom.

39) O Arjuna, I am the seed of all beings. Indeed, there are no beings, moving or unmoving, that exist or even could exist without Me.

40) O scorcher of the enemy, there is no limit to My divine wonders. What I have declared to you is but a mere indication of My power.

41) You must understand that whatever is possessed of great wonder, opulence or splendor has sprung from a mere fragment of My greatness.

42) But what need is there, O Arjuna, for so much knowledge? With but a fragment of Myself I pervade and support this entire universe.

---

40. Vṛṣṇi is the family line from which Kṛṣṇa descends. Vāsudeva is Kṛṣṇa.
41. Dhanañjaya is Arjuna.
42. Vyāsa is the traditional compiler of the *Vedas.*
43. Uśanā is a name for Śukrācārya, preceptor for the *asuras* and son of Bhṛgu.

अर्जुन उवाच ।
मदनुग्रहाय परमं गुह्यमध्यात्मसंज्ञितम् ।
यत्त्वयोक्तं वचस्तेन मोहोऽयं विगतो मम ॥ १

arjuna uvāva
mad-anugrahāya paramaṁ guhyam adhyātma-saṁjñitam
yat tvayoktaṁ vacas tena moho 'yaṁ vigato mama

भवाप्ययौ हि भूतानां श्रुतौ विस्तरशो मया ।
त्वत्तः कमलपत्राक्ष माहात्म्यमपि चाव्ययम् ॥ २

bhavāpyayau hi bhūtānāṁ śrutau vistaraśo mayā
tvattaḥ kamala-patrākṣa māhātmyam api cāvyayam

एवमेतद्यथात्थ त्वमात्मानं परमेश्वर ।
द्रष्टुमिच्छामि ते रूपमैश्वरं पुरुषोत्तम ॥ ३

evam etad yathāttha tvam ātmānaṁ parameśvara
draṣṭum icchāmi te rūpam aiśvaraṁ puruṣottama

मन्यसे यदि तच्छक्यं मया द्रष्टुमिति प्रभो ।
योगेश्वर ततो मे त्वं दर्शयात्मानमव्ययम् ॥ ४

manyase yadi tac chakyaṁ mayā draṣṭum iti prabho
yogeśvara tato me tvaṁ darśayātmānam avyayam

श्रीभगवानुवाच ।
पश्य मे पार्थ रूपाणि शतशोऽथ सहस्रशः ।
नानाविधानि दिव्यानि नानावर्णाकृतीनि च ॥ ५

paśya me pārtha rūpāṇi śataśo 'tha sahasraśaḥ
nānā-vidhāni divyāni nānā-varṇākṛtīni ca

Chapter Eleven

Vision of the Universal Form

Arjuna Asks to see Kṛṣṇa's Universal Form

1) Arjuna said:
Out of kindness You have proclaimed the science of the soul,[1] which is the supreme secret. My illusion is now dispelled.

2) O lotus-eyed Kṛṣṇa, I have heard from You in detail about the origin and dissolution of all beings and about Your inexhaustible glories.

3) O Supreme Lord, Highest Person, all that You have declared is true. I now desire to see your mighty form.

4) O Lord, master of all mysticism, if you think that I can witness such a form, kindly show me Your inexhaustible Self.

Arjuna Receives Divine Eyes

5) Kṛṣṇa Bhagavān said:
My dear Arjuna, behold hundreds and thousands of celestial forms, all with unlimited colors and shapes.

Chapter Eleven is traditionally entitled *viśvarūpa-darśana-yoga*, The *Yoga* of the Vision of the Universal Form.

1. "The science of the soul" (*adhyātman*): In this context the prefix *adhi* is used in its sense of "pertaining to." Thus *adhyātman* becomes "the science of the *ātman* (soul)." For other uses see BG 7.30, 8.3 and 10.32.

पश्यादित्यान्वसून्रुद्रानश्विनौ मरुतस्तथा ।
बहून्यदृष्टपूर्वाणि पश्याश्चर्याणि भारत ॥ ६

paśyādityān vasūn rudrān aśvinau marutas tathā
bahūny adṛṣṭa-pūrvāṇi paśyāścaryāṇi bhārata

इहैकस्थं जगत्कृत्स्नं पश्याद्य सचराचरम् ।
मम देहे गुडाकेश यच्चान्यद्द्रष्टुमिच्छसि ॥ ७

ihaika-sthaṁ jagat kṛtsnaṁ paśyādya sa-carācaram
mama dehe guḍākeśa yac cānyad draṣṭum icchasi

न तु मां शक्यसे द्रष्टुमनेनैव स्वचक्षुषा ।
दिव्यं ददामि ते चक्षुः पश्य मे योगमैश्वरम् ॥ ८

na tu māṁ śakyase draṣṭum anenaiva sva-cakṣuṣā
divyaṁ dadāmi te cakṣuḥ paśya me yogam aiśvaram

संजय उवाच ।
एवमुक्त्वा ततो राजन्महायोगेश्वरो हरिः ।
दर्शयामास पार्थाय परमं रूपमैश्वरम् ॥ ९

sañjaya uvāca
evam uktvā tato rājan mahā-yogeśvaro hariḥ
darśayām āsa pārthāya paramaṁ rūpam aiśvaram

अनेकवक्त्रनयनमनेकाद्भुतदर्शनम् ।
अनेकदिव्याभरणं दिव्यानेकोद्यतायुधम् ॥ १०

aneka-vaktra-nayanam anekādbhuta-darśanam
aneka-divyābharaṇaṁ divyānekodyatāyudham

दिव्यमाल्याम्बरधरं दिव्यगन्धानुलेपनम् ।
सर्वाश्चर्यमयं देवमनन्तं विश्वतोमुखम् ॥ ११

divya-mālyāmbara-dharaṁ divya-gandhānulepanam
sarvāścarya-mayaṁ devam anantaṁ viśvato-mukham

6) See the Ādityas, the Vasus, the Rudras, the two Aśvins[2] as well as the Maruts. O descendant of Bharata, witness these marvels, never before seen.

7) In one place you may observe both the moving and the nonmoving worlds. O Arjuna,[3] view whatever you wish to see in My body.

8) But you cannot perceive Me with your present eyes. I therefore give to you divine eyes.[4] Behold my mystic wonders.

The Universal Form

9) Sañjaya said;
O king, the great Lord of mysticism, Kṛṣṇa, then showed to the son of Pṛthā that supreme majestic form.

10) Arjuna saw endless mouths and eyes, unlimited wonderful sights, celestial ornaments, and divine weapons raised on high.

11) With infinite faces staring in all directions, he saw that God adorned with divine garlands, celestial fragrances, garments and ointments—all full of wonder.

---

2. The Aśvins are celestial horsemen, always seen as a pair and known for healing and heralding in the dawn. They are the divine fathers of the two Pāṇḍava, Nakula and Sahadeva.
3. Here Arjuna is actually addressed as Guḍākeśa, conqueror of sleep.
4. "Divine eyes" (*divyaṁ cakṣuḥ*) is literally a divine eye.

दिवि सूर्यसहस्रस्य भवेद्युगपदुत्थिता ।
यदि भाः सदृशी सा स्याद्भासस्तस्य महात्मनः ॥ १२

divi sūrya-sahasrasya bhaved yugapad utthitā
yadi bhāḥ sadṛśī sā syād bhāsas tasya mahātmanaḥ

तत्रैकस्थं जगत्कृत्स्नं प्रविभक्तमनेकधा ।
अपश्यद्देवदेवस्य शरीरे पाण्डवस्तदा ॥ १३

tatraika-sthaṁ jagat kṛtsnaṁ pravibhaktam anekadhā
apaśyad deva-devasya śarīre pāṇḍavas tadā

ततः स विस्मयाविष्टो हृष्टरोमा धनंजयः ।
प्रणम्य शिरसा देवं कृताञ्जलिरभाषत ॥ १४

tataḥ sa vismayāviṣṭo hṛṣṭa-romā dhanañjayaḥ
praṇamya śirasā devaṁ kṛtāñjalir abhāṣata

अर्जुन उवाच ।
पश्यामि देवांस्तव देव देहे
सर्वांस्तथा भूतविशेषसंघान् ।
ब्रह्माणमीशं कमलासनस्थ-
मृषींश्च सर्वानुरगांश्च दिव्यान् ॥ १५

arjuna uvāca
paśyāmi devāṁs tava deva dehe sarvāṁs tathā bhūta-viśeṣa-saṅghān
brahmāṇam īśaṁ kamalāsana-stham ṛṣīṁś ca sarvān uragāṁś ca divyān

अनेकबाहूदरवक्त्रनेत्रं
पश्यामि त्वा सर्वतोऽनन्तरूपम् ।
नान्तं न मध्यं न पुनस्तवादिं
पश्यामि विश्वेश्वर विश्वरूप ॥ १६

aneka-bāhūdara-vaktra-netraṁ paśyāmi tvāṁ sarvato 'nanta-rūpam
nāntaṁ na madhyaṁ na punas tavādiṁ paśyāmi viśveśvara viśva-rūpa

12) If a thousand suns at once rose into the sky, their brilliance still could not outshine the radiance of that exalted Lord.

13) The son of Pāṇḍu then beheld in the body of that God of gods the whole universe standing as one, and yet divided as many.

14) Overwhelmed with amazement, hair standing on end, Arjuna[5] bowed with folded hands and spoke to that great God.

15) Arjuna said:
O Lord, I see in Your body all the gods and the host of beings. I see Brahmā seated on the lotus. I see the sages and all celestial serpents.

16) O Lord of the universe, on all sides and with infinite form I see you with unlimited arms, bellies, mouths and eyes. O Universal Form, I see you without beginning, middle or end.

5. Arjuna is here called Dhanañjaya, conqueror of wealth.

किरीटिनं गदिनं चक्रिणं च
तेजोराशिं सर्वतो दीप्तिमन्तम् ।
पश्यामि त्वां दुर्निरीक्ष्यं समन्ता-
द्दीप्तानलार्कद्युतिमप्रमेयम् ॥ १७

kirīṭinaṁ gadinaṁ cakriṇaṁ ca tejo-rāśiṁ sarvato dīptimantam
paśyāmi tvāṁ durnirīkṣyaṁ samantād dīptānalārka-dyutim aprameyam

त्वमक्षरं परमं वेदितव्यं
त्वमस्य विश्वस्य परं निधानम् ।
त्वमव्ययः शाश्वतधर्मगोप्ता
सनातनस्त्वं पुरुषो मतो मे ॥ १८

tvam akṣaraṁ paramaṁ veditavyaṁ tvam asya viśvasya paraṁ nidhānam
tvam avyayaḥ śāśvata-dharma-goptā sanātanas tvaṁ puruṣo mato me

अनादिमध्यान्तमनन्तवीर्य-
मनन्तबाहुं शशिसूर्यनेत्रम् ।
पश्यामि त्वां दीप्तहुताशवक्त्रं
स्वतेजसा विश्वमिदं तपन्तम् ॥ १९

anādi-madhyāntam ananta-vīryam ananta-bāhuṁ śaśi-sūrya-netram
paśyāmi tvāṁ dīpta-hutāśa-vaktraṁ sva-tejasā viśvam idaṁ tapantam

द्यावापृथिव्योरिदमन्तरं हि
व्याप्तं त्वयैकेन दिशश्च सर्वाः ।
दृष्ट्वाद्भुतं रूपमिदं तवोग्रं
लोकत्रयं प्रव्यथितं महात्मन् ॥ २०

dyāv ā-pṛthivyor idam antaraṁ hi vyāptaṁ tvayaikena diśaś ca sarvāḥ
dṛṣṭvādbhutaṁ rūpam idaṁ tavograṁ loka-trayaṁ pravyathitaṁ mahātman

17) Shimmering with dazzling radiance you are adorned with crown, club, and disc. With blazing fire and the brilliance of immeasurable suns burning on all sides you are difficult to behold.

18) You are imperishable, the highest object of knowledge, and the final resting place of this universe. You are the immortal protector of everlasting *dharma.* I accept You as the most ancient Spirit.[6]

19) I see You without beginning, middle or end, with infinite power and unlimited arms. Your eyes are the sun and moon. I see you with blazing fire issuing forth from Your mouth and scorching this world with Your effulgence.

20) In all directions You pervade the heaven and earth. O Great Soul, the three worlds tremble upon seeing Your wondrous and terrible form.

---

6. "The most ancient Spirit" (*sanātanas tvaṁ puruṣaḥ*) could also be "primeval person," "everlasting man," etc.

अमी हि त्वा सुरसंघा विशन्ति
केचिद्भीताः प्राञ्जलयो गृणन्ति ।
स्वस्तीत्युक्त्वा महर्षिसिद्धसंघाः
स्तुवन्ति त्वां स्तुतिभिः पुष्कलाभिः ॥ २१

amī hi tvāṁ sura-saṅghā viśanti kecid bhītāḥ prāñjalayo gṛṇanti
svastīty uktvā maharṣi-siddha-saṅghāḥ stuvanti tvāṁ stutibhiḥ puṣkalābhiḥ

रुद्रादित्या वसवो ये च साध्या
विश्वेऽश्विनौ मरुतश्चोष्मपाश्च ।
गन्धर्वयक्षासुरसिद्धसंघा
वीक्षन्ते त्वा विस्मिताश्चैव सर्वे ॥ २२

rudrādityā vasavo ye ca sādhyā viśve 'śvinau marutaś coṣmapāś ca
gandharva-yakṣāsura-siddha-saṅghā vīkṣante tvā vismitāś caiva sarve

रूपं महत्ते बहुवक्त्रनेत्रं
महाबाहो बहुबाहूरुपादम् ।
बहूदरं बहुदंष्ट्राकरालं
दृष्ट्वा लोकाः प्रव्यथितास्तथाहम् ॥ २३

rūpaṁ mahat te bahu-vaktra-netraṁ mahā-bāho bahu-bāhūru-pādam
bahūdaraṁ bahu-daṁṣṭrā-karālaṁ dṛṣṭvā lokāḥ pravyathitās tathāham

नभःस्पृशं दीप्तमनेकवर्णं
व्यात्ताननं दीप्तविशालनेत्रम् ।
दृष्ट्वा हि त्वां प्रव्यथितान्तरात्मा
धृतिं न विन्दामि शमं च विष्णो ॥ २४

nabhaḥ-spṛśaṁ dīptam aneka-varṇaṁ vyāttānanaṁ dīpta-viśāla-netram
dṛṣṭvā hi tvāṁ pravyathitāntar-ātmā dhṛtiṁ na vindāmi śamaṁ ca viṣṇo

21) Assemblies of divine beings enter into You. Out of fear they praise You with hands folded. The great sages and perfected beings cry out, "Peace to all," and applaud You with wondrous hymns.

22) The Rudras, the Ādityas, the Vasus, the Sādhyas,[7] the Viśvadevas,[8] the Aśvins, the Maruts, the forefathers,[9] the host of Gandharvas, Yakṣas, demons and perfected ones—all behold You in wonder.

23) O great-armed Kṛṣṇa, the whole world trembles as I do seeing Your monstrous form with unlimited mouths, eyes, arms, thighs and feet, with so many bellies and dreadful fangs.

24) O Viṣṇu, O Lord, my soul trembles seeing You touching the sky, blazing with many colors and mouths open wide with burning eyes. I can find no steadiness or tranquility.

---

7. The Sādhyas are a class of divine beings that dwell between heaven and earth.
8. The Viśvadevas are a class of divine beings said to be ten in number. They are the sons of Viśvā.
9. What is here translated as "the forefathers" is literally "the steam drinkers" *(ūṣma-pas)*. The steam drinkers are a class of ancestors who receive the hot portions of the sacrificial offerings.

दंष्ट्राकरालानि च ते मुखानि
दृष्ट्वैव कालानलसंनिभानि ।
दिशो न जाने न लभे च शर्म
प्रसीद देवेश जगन्निवास ॥ २५

daṁṣṭrā-karālāni ca te mukhāni dṛṣṭvaiva kālānala-sannibhāni
diśo na jāne na labhe ca śarma prasīda deveśa jagan-nivāsa

अमी च त्वां धृतराष्ट्रस्य पुत्राः
सर्वे सहैवावनिपालसंघैः ।
भीष्मो द्रोणः सूतपुत्रस्तथासौ
सहास्मदीयैरपि योधमुख्यैः ॥ २६

amī ca tvāṁ dhṛtarāṣṭrasya putrāḥ sarve sahaivāvani-pāla-saṅghaiḥ
bhīṣmo droṇaḥ sūta-putras tathāsau sahāsmadīyair api yodha-mukhyaiḥ

वक्त्राणि ते त्वरमाणा विशन्ति
दंष्ट्राकरालानि भयानकानि ।
केचिद्विलग्ना दशनान्तरेषु
संदृश्यन्ते चूर्णितैरुत्तमाङ्गैः ॥ २७

vakrāṇi te tvaramāṇā viśanti daṁṣṭrā-karālāni bhayānakāni
kecid vilagnā daśanāntareṣu sandṛśyante cūrṇitair uttamāṅgaiḥ

यथा नदीनां बहवोऽम्बुवेगाः
समुद्रमेवाभिमुखा द्रवन्ति ।
तथा तवामी नरलोकवीरा
विशन्ति वक्त्राण्यभिविज्वलन्ति ॥ २८

yathā nadīnāṁ bahavo 'mbu-vegāḥ samudram evābhimukhā dravanti
tathā tavāmī nara-loka-vīrā viśanti vaktrāṇy abhivijvalanti

25) I have lost my composure and I can find no peace seeing Your dreadful fangs and mouths like the fire of death. O God of gods, shelter of the world, be merciful unto me.

26-27) I see all the these sons of Dhṛtarāṣṭra including Karṇa, the charioteer's son, along with Bhīṣma, Droṇa and the hosts of kings, and our chief warriors, all rushing headlong into Your mouths, which are dreadful with terrifying fangs. Some are seen crushed between Your teeth with heads smashed.

28) As great rivers flow headlong into the sea, so these heroes of mankind enter into Your blazing mouths.

यथा प्रदीप्तं ज्वलनं पतंगा
विशन्ति नाशाय समृद्धवेगाः ।
तथैव नाशाय विशन्ति लोका-
स्तवापि वक्त्राणि समृद्धवेगाः ॥ २९

yathā pradīptaṁ jvalanaṁ pataṅgā viśanti nāśāya samṛddha-vegāḥ
tathaiva nāśāya viśanti lokās tavāpi vaktrāṇi samṛddha-vegāḥ

लेलिह्यसे ग्रसमानः समन्ता-
ल्लोकान्समग्रान्वदनैर्ज्वलद्भिः ।
तेजोभिरापूर्य जगत्समग्रं
भासस्तवोग्राः प्रतपन्ति विष्णो ॥ ३०

lelihyase grasamānaḥ samantāl lokān samagrān vadanair jvaladbhiḥ
tejobhir āpūrya jagat samagraṁ bhāsas tavogrāḥ pratapanti viṣṇo

आख्याहि मे को भवानुग्ररूपो
नमोऽस्तु ते देववर प्रसीद ।
विज्ञातुमिच्छामि भवन्तमाद्यं
न हि प्रजानामि तव प्रवृत्तिम् ॥ ३१

ākhyāhi me ko bhavān ugra-rūpo namo 'stu te deva-vara prasīda
vijñātum icchāmi bhavantam ādyaṁ na hi prajānāmi tava pravṛttim

श्रीभगवानुवाच ।
कालोऽस्मि लोकक्षयकृत्प्रवृद्धो
लोकान्समाहर्तुमिह प्रवृत्तः ।
ऋतेऽपि त्वा न भविष्यन्ति सर्वे
येऽवस्थिताः प्रत्यनीकेषु योधाः ॥ ३२

śrī-bhagavān uvāca
kālo 'smi loka-kṣaya-kṛt pravṛddho lokān samāhartum iha pravṛttaḥ
ṛte 'pi tvā na bhaviṣyanti sarve ye 'vasthitāḥ pratyanīkeṣu yodhāḥ

29) As moths dash full speed into the blazing fire, so all these worlds enter headlong into Your mouths to their final destruction.

30) O Viṣṇu, O Kṛṣṇa, Your flaming mouths voraciously lick at these worlds from all sides. You scorch this entire universe by Your radiance and terrible splendor.

31) O Lord of lords, who are You with such terrible form? I bow before You. Be merciful. You are the primal one. What is Your mission?

Kṛṣṇa Reveals Himself as Time

32) Kṛṣṇa Bhagavān said:
Time I am, destroyer of worlds. I have come to annihilate all beings. Even without you[10] all these warriors, situated on opposite sides, shall be destroyed.

10. "Even without you (*ṛte 'pi tvā*) could also mean "except you."

तस्मात्त्वमुत्तिष्ठ यशो लभस्व
जित्वा शत्रून्भुङ्क्ष्व राज्यं समृद्धम् ।
मयैवैते निहताः पूर्वमेव
निमित्तमात्रं भव सव्यसाचिन् ॥ ३३

tasmāt tvam uttiṣṭha yaśo labhasva jitvā śatrūn bhuṅkṣva rājyaṁ samṛddham
mayaivaite nihatāḥ pūrvam eva nimitta-mātraṁ bhava savyasācin

द्रोणं च भीष्मं च जयद्रथं च
कर्णं तथान्यानपि योधवीरान् ।
मया हतांस्त्वं जहि मा व्यथिष्ठा
युध्यस्व जेतासि रणे सपत्नान् ॥ ३४

droṇaṁ ca bhīṣmaṁ ca jayadrathaṁ ca karṇaṁ tathānyān api yodha-vīrān
mayā hatāṁs tvaṁ jahi mā vyathiṣṭhā yudhyasva jetāsi raṇe sapatnān

संजय उवाच ।
एतच्छ्रुत्वा वचनं केशवस्य
कृताञ्जलिर्वेपमानः किरीटी ।
नमस्कृत्वा भूय एवाह कृष्णं
सगद्गदं भीतभीतः प्रणम्य ॥ ३५

sañjaya uvāca
etac chrutvā vacanaṁ keśavasya kṛtāñjalir vepamānaḥ kirīṭī
namaskṛtvā bhūya evāha kṛṣṇaṁ sa-gadgadaṁ bhīta-bhītaḥ praṇamya

33) Arise and seize your glory. Conquer these enemies and enjoy a flourishing kingdom. I have destroyed them all. O Arjuna,[11] become but My instrument.

34) I have already destroyed Droṇa, Bhīṣma, Jayadratha, Karṇa and the other great warriors. Do not hesitate; slay them. Fight and you will conquer your enemies in battle.

35) Sañjaya said:
Hearing these words of Kṛṣṇa,[12] the crowned Arjuna[13] spoke in a stammering voice with folded hands, trembling and bowing in fear.

---

11. Here Arjuna is called *Savyasācin,* O ambidextrous one.
12. Here Kṛṣṇa is called Keśava.
13. Literally, the crowned one (*kirīṭī*).

अर्जुन उवाच ।
स्थाने हृषीकेश तव प्रकीर्त्या
जगत्प्रहृष्यत्यनुरज्यते च ।
रक्षांसि भीतानि दिशो द्रवन्ति
सर्वे नमस्यन्ति च सिद्धसंघाः ॥ ३६

arjuna uvāca
sthāne hṛṣīkeśa tava prakīrtyā jagat prahṛṣyaty anurajyate ca
rakṣāṁsi bhītāni diśo dravanti sarve namasyanti ca siddha-saṅghāḥ

कस्माच्च ते न नमेरन्महात्मन्
गरीयसे ब्रह्मणोऽप्यादिकर्त्रे ।
अनन्त देवेश जगन्निवास
त्वमक्षरं सदसत्तत्परं यत् ॥ ३७

kasmāc ca te na nameran mahātman garīyase brahmaṇo 'py ādi-kartre
ananta deveśa jagan-nivāsa tvam akṣaraṁ sad-asat tat-paraṁ yat

त्वमादिदेवः पुरुषः पुराण-
स्त्वमस्य विश्वस्य परं निधानम् ।
वेत्तासि वेद्यं च परं च धाम
त्वया ततं विश्वमनन्तरूप ॥ ३८

tvam ādi-devaḥ puruṣaḥ purāṇas tvam asya viśvasya paraṁ nidhānam
vettāsi vedyaṁ ca paraṁ ca dhāma tvayā tataṁ viśvam ananta-rūpa

वायुर्यमोऽग्निर्वरुणः शशाङ्कः
प्रजापतिस्त्वं प्रपितामहश्च ।
नमो नमस्तेऽस्तु सहस्रकृत्वः
पुनश्च भूयोऽपि नमो नमस्ते ॥ ३९

vāyur yamo 'gnir varuṇaḥ śaśāṅkaḥ prajāpatis tvaṁ prapitāmahaś ca
namo namas te 'stu sahasra-kṛtvaḥ punaś ca bhūyo 'pi namo namas te

Arjuna's Praise

36) Arjuna said:
O Hṛṣīkeśa, Kṛṣṇa, the world rightly rejoices and delights in hearing Your fame. The demons flee in all directions and the perfected beings offer You homage.

37) O great Soul, why should they not bow before You? You are greater than even Brahmā.[14] You are the first creator. O unlimited One, Lord of lords, resting place of the world, You are unchangeable.[15] You are beyond what is both permanent and impermanent.[16]

38) You are the primal God, the most ancient person. You are the supreme shelter of this universe. You are the knower, the object of knowledge and the ultimate abode. With unlimited forms, You pervade this entire universe.

39) You are the wind. You are the supreme controller. You are fire, water and the moon. You are the first progenitor and the great grandfather. I bow before You a thousand times.

---

14. The word *brahmaṇaḥ* can be taken as either masculine or neuter. As masculine it refers to the creator god Brahmā. As neuter it refers to the *brahman*, the Supreme. Here it is taken as masculine.
15. Here the word is *akṣara*. See BG 8.3.
16. "Permanent and impermanent" (*sat* and *asat*) see fn. BG 2.16.

नमः पुरस्तादथ पृष्ठतस्ते
नमोऽस्तु ते सर्वत एव सर्व ।
अनन्तवीर्यामितविक्रमस्त्वं
सर्वं समाप्नोषि ततोऽसि सर्वः ॥ ४०

namaḥ purastād atha pṛṣṭhatas te namo 'stu te sarvata eva sarva
ananta-vīryāmita-vikramas tvaṁ sarvaṁ samāpnoṣi tato 'si sarvaḥ

सखेति मत्वा प्रसभं यदुक्तं
हे कृष्ण हे यादव हे सखेति ।
अजानता महिमानं तवेदं
मया प्रमादात्प्रणयेन वापि ॥ ४१

sakheti matvā prasabhaṁ yad uktaṁ he kṛṣṇa he yādava he sakheti
ajānatā mahimānaṁ tavedaṁ mayā pramādāt praṇayena vāpi

यच्चावहासार्थमसत्कृतोऽसि
विहारशय्यासनभोजनेषु ।
एकोऽथ वाप्यच्युत तत्समक्षं
तत्क्षामये त्वामहमप्रमेयम् ॥ ४२

yac cāvahāsārtham asat-kṛto 'si vihāra-śayyāsana-bhojaneṣu
eko 'tha vāpy acyuta tat-samakṣaṁ tat kṣāmaye tvām aham aprameyam

पितासि लोकस्य चराचरस्य
त्वमस्य पूज्यश्च गुरुर्गरीयान् ।
न त्वत्समोऽस्त्यभ्यधिकः कुतोऽन्यो
लोकत्रयेऽप्यप्रतिमप्रभाव ॥ ४३

pitāsi lokasya carācarasya tvam asya pūjyaś ca gurur garīyān
na tvat-samo 'sty abhyadhikaḥ kuto 'nyo loka-traye 'py apratima-prabhāva

40) Respects to You from the front, from behind and from all sides. O one of unlimited power and of unmeasured strength, You complete all things, therefore You are all things.

41-42) Whatever I have said without knowing Your greatness, thinking of You as my companion and saying out of love or madness, “O Kṛṣṇa, O Yādava, O Friend,” I ask Your forgiveness. Whatever I have done improperly, out of jest, while playing, resting, sitting, or eating, either alone, or in the presence of others, O Acyuta, immeasurable One, I beg Your forgiveness.

43) You are the father of this world and of all beings moving and nonmoving. You are its worshipable and most venerable teacher. No one is equal to You in all these three worlds. O immeasurable Lord, how can anyone be greater?

तस्मात्प्रणम्य प्रणिधाय कायं
प्रसादये त्वामहमीशमीड्यम् ।
पितेव पुत्रस्य सखेव सख्युः
प्रियः प्रियायार्हसि देव सोढुम् ॥ ४४

tasmāt praṇamya praṇidhāya kāyaṁ prasādaye tvām aham īśam īḍyam
piteva putrasya sakheva sakhyuḥ priyaḥ priyāyārhasi deva soḍhum

अदृष्टपूर्वं हृषितोऽस्मि दृष्ट्वा
भयेन च प्रव्यथितं मनो मे ।
तदेव मे दर्शय देव रूपं
प्रसीद देवेश जगन्निवास ॥ ४५

adṛṣṭa-pūrvaṁ hṛṣito 'smi dṛṣṭvā bhayena ca pravyathitaṁ mano me
tad eva me darśaya deva rūpaṁ prasīda deveśa jagan-nivāsa

किरीटिनं गदिनं चक्रहस्त-
मिच्छामि त्वां द्रष्टुमहं तथैव ।
तेनैव रूपेण चतुर्भुजेन
सहस्रबाहो भव विश्वमूर्ते ॥ ४६

kirīṭinaṁ gadinaṁ cakra-hastam icchāmi tvāṁ draṣṭum ahaṁ tathaiva
tenaiva rūpeṇa catur-bhujena sahasra-bāho bhava viśva-mūrte

श्रीभगवानुवाच ।
मया प्रसन्नेन तवार्जुनेदं
रूपं परं दर्शितमात्मयोगात् ।
तेजोमयं विश्वमनन्तमाद्यं
यन्मे त्वदन्येन न दृष्टपूर्वम् ॥ ४७

śrī-bhagavān uvāca
mayā prasannena tavārjunedaṁ rūpaṁ paraṁ darśitam ātma-yogāt
tejo-mayaṁ viśvam anantam ādyaṁ yan me tvad anyena na dṛṣṭa-pūrvam

44) Most worshipable Lord, I bow before You. I beg mercy. Please forgive me, as a father forgives a son, as a friend forgives a companion, or as a lover forgives a beloved.

45) I am thrilled seeing this form that has never been seen before, but in fear my heart trembles. O Lord, show me Your humanlike form as before. O Lord of lords, resting-place of the world, be merciful.

46) O thousand-armed form of the universe, I desire to see You as before, adorned with crown, club and with disc in hand. Please assume that four-armed form.

47) Kṛṣṇa Bhagavān said:
O Arjuna, through My power of *yoga*, I have happily shown you this supreme form. It is splendorous. It is universal and it is primal.

न वेदयज्ञाध्ययनैर्न दानै-
र्न च क्रियाभिर्न तपोभिरुग्रैः ।
एवंरूपः शक्य अहं नृलोके
द्रष्टुं त्वदन्येन कुरुप्रवीर ।। ४८

na veda-yajñādhyayanair na dānair na ca kriyābhir na tapobhir ugraiḥ
evaṁ-rūpaḥ śakya ahaṁ nṛ-loke draṣṭuṁ tvad anyena kuru-pravīra

मा ते व्यथा मा च विमूढभावो
दृष्ट्वा रूपं घोरमीदृङ्ममेदम् ।
व्यपेतभीः प्रीतमनाः पुनस्त्वं
तदेव मे रूपमिदं प्रपश्य ।। ४९

mā te vyathā mā ca vimūḍha-bhāvo dṛṣṭvā rūpaṁ ghoram īdṛṅ mamedam
vyapeta-bhīḥ prīta-manāḥ punas tvaṁ tad eva me rūpam idaṁ prapaśya

संजय उवाच ।
इत्यर्जुनं वासुदेवस्तथोक्त्वा
स्वकं रूपं दर्शयामास भूयः ।
आश्वासयामास च भीतमेनं
भूत्वा पुनः सौम्यवपुर्महात्मा ।। ५०

sañjaya uvāca
ity arjunaṁ vāsudevas tathoktvā svakaṁ rūpaṁ darśayām āsa bhūyaḥ
āśvāsayām āsa ca bhītam enaṁ bhūtvā punaḥ saumya-vapur mahātmā

अर्जुन उवाच ।
दृष्ट्वेदं मानुषं रूपं तव सौम्यं जनार्दन ।
इदानीमस्मि संवृत्तः सचेताः प्रकृतिं गतः ।। ५१

arjuna uvāca
dṛṣṭvedaṁ mānuṣaṁ rūpaṁ tava saumyaṁ janārdana
idānīm asmi saṁvṛttaḥ sa-cetāḥ prakṛtiṁ gataḥ

48) Not by the *Vedas,* nor by sacrifice or study, nor by charity or ritual acts, nor by severe austerities am I to be seen in such a form in this world. O hero of the Kurus, other than you, no one has seen this form.

49) Do not be in anxiety. Do not feel bewildered seeing this terrible form. Let your fear be gone and let your heart be gladdened. Behold My previous form.

Kṛṣṇa Resumes His Humanlike Form

50) Sañjaya said:
Speaking to Arjuna, the son of Vasudeva, the exalted Kṛṣṇa, once again assumed his natural form. This pleasing appearance of Kṛṣṇa consoled Arjuna.

51) Arjuna said:
Seeing Your pleasing humanlike form, O Kṛṣṇa, I have now regained my composure and have been restored to my normal state.

श्रीभगवानुवाच ।
सुदुर्दर्शमिदं रूपं दृष्टवानसि यन्मम ।
देवा अप्यस्य रूपस्य नित्यं दर्शनकाङ्क्षिणः ॥ ५२

śrī-bhagavān uvāca
su-durdarśam idaṁ rūpaṁ dṛṣṭavān asi yan mama
devā apy asya rūpasya nityaṁ darśana-kāṅkṣiṇaḥ

नाहं वेदैर्न तपसा न दानेन न चेज्यया ।
शक्य एवंविधो द्रष्टुं दृष्टवानसि मां यथा ॥ ५३

nāhaṁ vedair na tapasā na dānena na cejyayā
śakya evaṁ-vidho draṣṭuṁ dṛṣṭavān asi māṁ yathā

भक्त्या त्वनन्यया शक्य अहमेवंविधोऽर्जुन ।
ज्ञातुं द्रष्टुं च तत्त्वेन प्रवेष्टुं च परंतप ॥ ५४

bhaktyā tv ananyayā śakya aham evaṁ-vidho 'rjuna
jñātuṁ draṣṭuṁ ca tattvena praveṣṭuṁ ca parantapa

मत्कर्मकृन्मत्परमो मद्भक्तः सङ्गवर्जितः ।
निर्वैरः सर्वभूतेषु यः स मामेति पाण्डव ॥ ५५

mat-karma-kṛn mat-paramo mad-bhaktaḥ saṅga-varjitaḥ
nirvairaḥ sarva-bhūteṣu yaḥ sa mām eti pāṇḍava

52) Kṛṣṇa Bhagavān said:
This form that you have seen[17] is indeed difficult to behold. Even the gods constantly desire to see this form.

53) Not by Vedic study, not by austerities, not by charity, nor even by ritual worship can I be seen as you have seen Me.

54) O scorcher of the enemy, Arjuna, it is nevertheless possible to know Me as I am, for I can be approached by unalloyed devotion.

55) O son of Pāṇḍu, that person alone comes to Me who performs all work on My behalf, who is intent upon Me, who is My devotee, free of attachment, and who is without malice.

---

17. Śaṅkara, Rāmānuja and Madhva all concur that "This form that you have seen" (*idaṁ rūpaṁ dṛṣṭavān asi*) is the *viśva-rūpam*, the universal form.

अर्जुन उवाच ।
एवं सततयुक्ता ये भक्तास्त्वां पर्युपासते ।
ये चाप्यक्षरमव्यक्तं तेषां के योगवित्तमाः ॥ १

arjuna uvāca
evaṁ satata-yuktā ye bhaktās tvāṁ paryupāsate
ye cāpy akṣaram avyaktaṁ teṣāṁ ke yoga-vittamāḥ

श्रीभगवानुवाच ।
मय्यावेश्य मनो ये मां नित्ययुक्ता उपासते ।
श्रद्धया परयोपेतास्ते मे युक्ततमा मताः ॥ २

śrī-bhagavān uvāca
mayy āveśya mano ye māṁ nitya-yuktā upāsate
śraddhayā parayopetās te me yuktatamā matāḥ

Chapter Twelve

Bhakti Yoga

The Best Way to Worship

1) Arjuna inquired,
I wish to know who has the best knowledge of *yoga*: those who are constantly devoted and who worship You in this way, or those who seek You as the unchangeable, the unmanifest?[1]

2) Kṛṣṇa Bhagavān said,
I consider those who approach Me with firm faith, ever devoted, fixing their mind on Me, to be the best of *yogīs*.[2]

Chapter Twelve is traditionally entitled *bhakti-yoga*, the *Yoga* of Devotion.

1. The traditional commentators each have a different interpretation of Arjuna's question. The controversy arises over the meaning of the words "in this way" (*evam*), "unchangeable" (*akṣaram*) and "unmanifest" (*avyaktam*). Śaṅkara says that "*evam*" refers to the universal form (*viśva-rūpa*) described in the previous chapter. He says that the words "unchangeable" (*akṣaram*) and "unmanifest" (*avyaktam*) refer to *brahman*. Therefore, Arjuna's question is between those who approach God in the form of the universal form and those who approach God as *nirguṇa brahman*, the Absolute without attributes. Rāmānuja, on the other hand, says that the word "*evam*" refers to those who approach God as described in the last verse of Chapter Eleven (BG 11.55), in other words, the personal form of God. He says that the words "unchangeable" (*akṣaram*) and "unmanifested" (*avyaktam*) refer to the unchangeable and unmanifest individual soul and not to *brahman*. The question is, therefore, between those who worship a personal form of God or those who attempt to understand the nature of the individual soul. Madhva, with an even different interpretation, states that the question concerns those who approach God in a personal way, in the form of Kṛṣṇa as described in the latter part of the previous chapter, and those who approach God in an impersonal way as the unmanifest in matter.

2. Compare this verse to BG 6.47.

ये त्वक्षरमनिर्देश्यमव्यक्तं पर्युपासते ।
सर्वत्रगमचिन्त्यं च कूटस्थमचलं ध्रुवम् ॥ ३

ye tv akṣaram anirdeśyam avyaktaṁ paryupāsate
sarvatra-gam acintyaṁ ca kūṭa-stham acalaṁ dhruvam

संनियम्येन्द्रियग्रामं सर्वत्र समबुद्धयः ।
ते प्राप्नुवन्ति मामेव सर्वभूतहिते रताः ॥ ४

sanniyamyendriya-grāmaṁ sarvatra sama-buddhayaḥ
te prāpnuvanti mām eva sarva-bhūta-hite ratāḥ

क्लेशोऽधिकतरस्तेषामव्यक्तासक्तचेतसाम् ।
अव्यक्ता हि गतिर्दुःखं देहवद्भिरवाप्यते ॥ ५

kleśo 'dhikataras teṣām avyaktāsakta-cetasām
avyaktā hi gatir duḥkhaṁ dehavadbhir avāpyate

ये तु सर्वाणि कर्माणि मयि संन्यस्य मत्पराः ।
अनन्येनैव योगेन मां ध्यायन्त उपासते ॥ ६

ye tu sarvāṇi karmāṇi mayi sannyasya mat-parāḥ
ananyenaiva yogena māṁ dhyāyanta upāsate

तेषामहं समुद्धर्ता मृत्युसंसारसागरात् ।
भवामि नचिरात्पार्थ मय्यावेशितचेतसाम् ॥ ७

teṣām ahaṁ samuddhartā mṛtyu-saṁsāra-sāgarāt
bhavāmi na cirāt pārtha mayy āveśita-cetasām

मय्येव मन आधत्स्व मयि बुद्धिं निवेशय ।
निवसिष्यसि मय्येव अत ऊर्ध्वं न संशयः ॥ ८

mayy eva mana ādhatsva mayi buddhiṁ niveśaya
nivasiṣyasi mayy eva ata ūrdhvaṁ na saṁśayaḥ

3-4) But they too reach Me, who control the senses and are intent on the welfare of all, who approach the Absolute as the Supreme unchangeable, as the indefinable, as the unmanifest, as the all-pervading One, beyond thought, the highest,[3] immovable and forever fixed—the impersonal form of the Absolute.

5) Trouble is greater, however, for those whose hearts are fixed on the unmanifest. Indeed, the path of the unmanifest is difficult for those who are embodied.

Those Who Worship the Personal God

6-7) O Arjuna, for those who have dedicated their actions to Me, who meditate on Me with undivided attention, and whose minds dwell on Me—for them I become a swift deliverer from the ocean of repeated birth and death.

8) Fix your mind on Me alone. Direct your intelligence towards Me. Thereafter,[4] you will dwell in Me. Of this there is no doubt.

---

3. "The highest" (*kūṭa-stha*) is literally "situated at the top." Compare to BG 6.8 and 15.16.

4. "Thereafter" (*ata ūrdhvam*) means after death.

अथ चित्तं समाधातुं न शक्नोषि मयि स्थिरम् ।
अभ्यासयोगेन ततो मामिच्छाप्तुं धनंजय ॥ ९

atha cittaṁ samādhātuṁ na śaknoṣi mayi sthiram
abhyāsa-yogena tato mām icchāptuṁ dhanañjaya

अभ्यासेऽप्यसमर्थोऽसि मत्कर्मपरमो भव ।
मदर्थमपि कर्माणि कुर्वन्सिद्धिमवाप्स्यसि ॥ १०

abhyāse 'py asamartho 'si mat-karma-paramo bhava
mad-artham api karmāṇi kurvan siddhim avāpsyasi

अथैतदप्यशक्तोऽसि कर्तुं मद्योगमाश्रितः ।
सर्वकर्मफलत्यागं ततः कुरु यतात्मवान् ॥ ११

athaitad apy aśakto 'si kartuṁ mad-yogam āśritaḥ
sarva-karma-phala-tyāgaṁ tataḥ kuru yatātmavān

श्रेयो हि ज्ञानमभ्यासाज्ज्ञानाद्ध्यानं विशिष्यते ।
ध्यानात्कर्मफलत्यागस्त्यागाच्छान्तिरनन्तरम् ॥ १२

śreyo hi jñānam abhyāsāj jñānād dhyānaṁ viśiṣyate
dhyānāt karma-phala-tyāgas tyāgāc chāntir anantaram

9) O Dhanañjaya, if you are unable to fix your mind steadily on Me, then seek to attain Me by the practice of *yoga*.[5]

10) If, however, you are unable to practice *yoga*, then dedicate your actions to Me.[6] By acting for My sake you will attain perfection.

11) If you are even unable to do this, then try to renounce the results of actions and thereby become self-controlled.[7]

12) For knowledge is better than practice, better than knowledge is meditation, better still is the renunciation of the fruits of action, for renunciation leads directly to peace.[8]

---

5. Here the term used for "the practice of *yoga*" is *abhyāsa-yoga*. Literally, *abhyāsa-yoga* is "the *yoga* of repetition." Śaṅkara defines this as the concentration of the mind on a single object, such as the universal form, while withdrawing it from all other things. Rāmānuja explains it as the constant remembrance of God. Compare with verse with BG 6.35.

6. Rāmānuja describes "dedicate your actions to Me" (*mat-karma-parama*) to include such activities as the building of temples, the gathering of flowers for decorating images of God, uttering the names of God, circumambulating temples, etc. This is *bhakti-yoga*.

7. Rāmānuja suggests that if one cannot follow the path of *bhakti* described in the previous verse, then one can take up the path of the unmanifest mentioned earlier in this chapter. For Rāmānuja the path of the unmanifest is meditation not on God, but on the indestructible individual soul. This will eventually lead to meditation on the form of God.

8. This verse presents a problem because it appears to contradict what has preceded in verses nine to eleven. Here "knowledge," according to Rāmānuja, means knowledge of the indestructible soul. Such knowledge is better than the practice of *yoga* in the sense that *yoga* practice (*abhyāsa-yoga*) may not be possible for the person who has little or no love for God. Therefore, from the perspective of such a person self-knowledge or introspection is the best course of action. In a similar way, "meditation," means meditation on the indestructible soul, which, if knowledge of the soul is not possible, is the best course of action. Finally, if meditation on the indestructible soul is even not possible then "renunciation of the fruits of action" is best because at least that will give peace.

अद्वेष्टा सर्वभूतानां मैत्रः करुण एव च ।
निर्ममो निरहंकारः समदुःखसुखः क्षमी ॥ १३

adveṣṭā sarva-bhūtānāṁ maitraḥ karuṇa eva ca
nirmamo nirahaṅkāraḥ sama-duḥkha-sukhaḥ kṣamī

संतुष्टः सततं योगी यतात्मा दृढनिश्चयः ।
मय्यर्पितमनोबुद्धिर्यो मद्भक्तः स मे प्रियः ॥ १४

santuṣṭaḥ satataṁ yogī yatātmā dṛḍha-niścayaḥ
mayy arpita-mano-buddhir yo mad-bhaktaḥ sa me priyaḥ

यस्मान्नोद्विजते लोको लोकान्नोद्विजते च यः ।
हर्षामर्षभयोद्वेगैर्मुक्तो यः स च मे प्रियः ॥ १५

yasmān nodvijate loko lokān nodvijate ca yaḥ
harṣāmarṣa-bhayodvegair mukto yaḥ sa ca me priyaḥ

अनपेक्षः शुचिर्दक्ष उदासीनो गतव्यथः ।
सर्वारम्भपरित्यागी यो मद्भक्तः स मे प्रियः ॥ १६

anapekṣaḥ śucir dakṣa udāsīno gata-vyathaḥ
sarvārambha-parityāgī yo mad-bhaktaḥ sa me priyaḥ

यो न हृष्यति न द्वेष्टि न शोचति न काङ्क्षति ।
शुभाशुभपरित्यागी भक्तिमान्यः स मे प्रियः ॥ १७

yo na hṛṣyati na dveṣṭi na śocati na kāṅkṣati
śubhāśubha-parityāgī bhaktimān yaḥ sa me priyaḥ

Whom God Loves

13-14) The *yogī* who is without hostility, who is friendly and compassionate to all creatures, who lives without a sense of ownership or ego, who is equal in pain and pleasure, who is patient, ever satisfied and self-controlled, whose resolve is firm, and whose intellect and mind are dedicated to Me—such a person is My devotee and is dear to Me.

15) One who neither creates fear in the world nor shrinks from the world, who is free from worldly happiness, jealousy, anxiety and agitation is also dear to Me.

16) The *yogī* who is devoted to Me, who is impartial, pure, expert, free of worry and who has renounced all things is dear to Me.

17) One who neither delights or hates, who neither laments or desires, who is full of devotion and who renounces what is both favorable and unfavorable is dear to Me.

समः शत्रौ च मित्रे च तथा मानावमानयोः ।
शीतोष्णसुखदुःखेषु समः सङ्गविवर्जितः ॥ १८

samaḥ śatrau ca mitre ca tathā mānāvamānayoḥ
śītoṣṇa-sukha-duḥkheṣu samaḥ saṅga-vivarjitaḥ

तुल्यनिन्दास्तुतिर्मौनी संतुष्टो येन केनचित् ।
अनिकेतः स्थिरमतिर्भक्तिमान्मे प्रियो नरः ॥ १९

tulya-nindā-stutir maunī santuṣṭo yena kenacit
aniketaḥ sthira-matir bhaktimān me priyo naraḥ

ये तु धर्म्यामृतमिदं यथोक्तं पर्युपासते ।
श्रद्दधाना मत्परमा भक्तास्तेऽतीव मे प्रियाः ॥ २०

ye tu dharmyāmṛtam idaṁ yathoktaṁ paryupāsate
śraddadhānā mat-paramā bhaktās te 'tīva me priyāḥ

18-19) One who is equal to friend and enemy alike, who is equal in honor and dishonor, heat and cold, happiness and distress, who is free of attachment, to whom criticism and praise are the same, ever silent and satisfied with what comes of its own accord, who is without attachment to home, and whose thoughts are fixed—such a devoted person is dear to Me.

20) Indeed, those who take shelter of this immortal wisdom[9] of which I have spoken, who are full of faith and intent on Me are exceedingly dear to Me.[10]

---

9. "This immortal wisdom" is derived from the expression *dharmyāmṛtam idam. Dharmya* is literally "what concerns *dharma.*" The word *amṛta* can mean both immortality and nectar. Therefore, the expression may also be rendered as "this immortal law" or "this nectar of duty."

10. Śaṅkara says that verses 13 to 20 describe the situation that leads to immortality for those who meditate on *nirguṇa brahman,* the unmanifest. Madhva says that this set of verses describe the followers of *bhakti-yoga.* Rāmānuja says verses 13 to 19 describe the position of a *karma-yogī* and that verse 20 describes the position of a *bhakti-yogī.*

श्रीभगवानुवाच ।
इदं शरीरं कौन्तेय क्षेत्रमित्यभिधीयते ।
एतद्यो वेत्ति तं प्राहुः क्षेत्रज्ञ इति तद्विदः ॥ १

śrī-bhagavān uvāca
idaṁ śarīraṁ kaunteya kṣetraṁ ity abhidhīyate
etad yo vetti taṁ prāhuḥ kṣetra-jña iti tad-vidaḥ

क्षेत्रज्ञं चापि मां विद्धि सर्वक्षेत्रेषु भारत ।
क्षेत्रक्षेत्रज्ञयोर्ज्ञानं यत्तज्ज्ञानं मतं मम ॥ २

kṣetra-jñaṁ cāpi māṁ viddhi sarva-kṣetreṣu bhārata
kṣetra-kṣetra-jñayor jñānaṁ yat taj jñānaṁ mataṁ mama

तत्क्षेत्रं यच्च यादृक्च यद्विकारि यतश्च यत् ।
स च यो यत्प्रभावश्च तत्समासेन मे शृणु ॥ ३

tat kṣetraṁ yac ca yādṛk ca yad-vikāri yataś ca yat
sa ca yo yat-prabhāvaś ca tat samāsena me śṛṇu

Chapter Thirteen

The Field of Action and Its Knower

The Field and the Knower of the Field

1) Kṛṣṇa Bhagavān said:
O son of Kuntī, those in knowledge say that this body is called a field and that one who knows the body is called a knower of the field.[1]

2) Understand that I am the knower of the field in all bodies[2] and that awareness of both the field and the knower of the field constitutes knowledge. O descendant of Bharata, this is My opinion.

3) Now listen as I briefly describe the field, its nature, its transformations, its source, who the knower of the field is, and what his powers are.

Chapter Thirteen is traditionally entitled *kṣetra-kṣetrajña-vibhāga-yoga*, The *Yoga* of the Distinction between the Field and the Knower of the Field.

1. In this chapter two terms are introduced: "the field" (*kṣetra*) and "the knower of the field" (*kṣetra-jña*). The body is considered a "field" in the sense that it is a field of activity. The "knower of the field" is the one who is conscious of the activites of the body, namely, the individual soul. The term "knower of the field" is first used in the *Upaniṣads* (ŚU 6.16 and MaiU 2.5) to describe the soul.

2. Here the expression "knower of the field" (*kṣetra-jña)* is applied to God.

ऋषिभिर्बहुधा गीतं छन्दोभिर्विविधैः पृथक् ।
ब्रह्मसूत्रपदैश्चैव हेतुमद्भिर्विनिश्चितैः ॥ ४

ṛṣibhir bahudhā gītaṁ chandobhir vividhaiḥ pṛthak
brahma-sūtra-padaiś caiva hetumadbhir viniścitaiḥ

महाभूतान्यहंकारो बुद्धिरव्यक्तमेव च ।
इन्द्रियाणि दशैकं च पञ्च चेन्द्रियगोचराः ॥ ५

mahā-bhūtāny ahaṅkāro buddhir avyaktam eva ca
indriyāṇi daśaikaṁ ca pañca cendriya-gocarāḥ

इच्छा द्वेषः सुखं दुःखं संघातश्चेतना धृतिः ।
एतत्क्षेत्रं समासेन सविकारमुदाहृतम् ॥ ६

icchā dveṣaḥ sukhaṁ duḥkhaṁ saṅghātaś cetanā dhṛtiḥ
etat kṣetraṁ samāsena savikāram udāhṛtam

4) Sages have spoken of this matter in Vedic hymns, in special statements that describe *brahman*[3] and through the use of analytical reasoning.

5-6) The primary elements,[4] the sense of self, intellect, the unmanifest,[5] the eleven senses,[6] and the five sense objects, desire, hatred, happiness, distress, the aggregate,[7] consciousness and will—these, along with their changes, constitute the field.

---

3. "Concise statements describing *brahman*" (*brahma-sūtra-padaiḥ*) may refer to the actual *Vedānta-sūtras* or simply to aphorisms about the Supreme. Rāmānuja considers this a direct reference to the *Vedānta-sūtra*. Madhva does not. Śaṅkara considers it a reference to the *Upaniṣads*.
4. The primary elements are five: earth, water, fire, air and space. See BG 7.4 for a complete list.
5. The unmanifest refers to primordial matter as outlined in Sāṅkhya philosophy.
6. The eleven senses include the five commonly understood senses, plus the mind and the five organs of action: hands, feet, voice, anus and genital.
7. "The aggregate" (*saṅghātaḥ*) is literally "the combination." Śaṅkara takes this to mean the combination or interaction of the bodily senses. Rāmānuja takes it to mean the combination necessary for the support of consciousness.

अमानित्वमदम्भित्वमहिंसा क्षान्तिरार्जवम् ।
आचार्योपासनं शौचं स्थैर्यमात्मविनिग्रहः ॥ ७

amānitvam adambhitvam ahiṁsā kṣāntir ārjavam
ācāryopāsanaṁ śaucaṁ sthairyam ātma-vinigrahaḥ

इन्द्रियार्थेषु वैराग्यमनहंकार एव च ।
जन्ममृत्युजराव्याधिदुःखदोषानुदर्शनम् ॥ ८

indriyārtheṣu vairāgyam anahaṅkāra eva ca
janma-mṛtyu-jarā-vyādhi-duḥkha-doṣānudarśanam

असक्तिरनभिष्वङ्गः पुत्रदारगृहादिषु ।
नित्यं च समचित्तत्वमिष्टानिष्टोपपत्तिषु ॥ ९

asaktir anabhiṣvaṅgaḥ putra-dāra-gṛhādiṣu
nityaṁ ca sama-cittatvam iṣṭāniṣṭopapattiṣu

मयि चानन्ययोगेन भक्तिरव्यभिचारिणी ।
विविक्तदेशसेवित्वमरतिर्जनसंसदि ॥ १०

mayi cānanya-yogena bhaktir avyabhicāriṇī
vivikta-deśa-sevitvam aratir jana-saṁsadi

अध्यात्मज्ञाननित्यत्वं तत्त्वज्ञानार्थदर्शनम् ।
एतज्ज्ञानमिति प्रोक्तमज्ञानं यदतोऽन्यथा ॥ ११

adhyātma-jñāna-nityatvaṁ tattva-jñānārtha-darśanam
etaj jñānam iti proktam ajñānaṁ yad ato 'nyathā

ज्ञेयं यत्तत्प्रवक्ष्यामि यज्ज्ञात्वामृतमश्नुते ।
अनादिमत्परं ब्रह्म न सत्तन्नासदुच्यते ॥ १२

jñeyaṁ yat tat pravakṣyāmi yaj jñātvāmṛtam aśnute
anādi mat-paraṁ brahma na sat tan nāsad ucyate

Knowledge

7-11) Modesty, sincerity, nonviolence, patience, straightforwardness, service to teacher, purity, firmness, self-control, detachment from the sense objects, non-egotism, awareness of the troubles caused by birth, death, old age and disease, detachment from sensual passions, absence of worldly attachment for sons, wives, home and the like, steady mindedness in what happens—whether desired or undesired—devotion to Me through constant striving, inhabiting secluded places, aversion to crowds, constancy in seeking knowledge of the soul and God, insight into the objects of knowledge and truth—all this has been declared to be based on knowledge. All other things are based on ignorance.

The Object of Real Knowledge

12) I shall now speak of the object of all knowledge, knowing which one attains immortality. It is *brahman*, without beginning, and it is dependent on Me.[8] It is said to be neither *sat* nor *asat*.[9]

---

8. "It is *brahman*, without beginning, and it is dependent on Me" (*anādi mat-paraṁ brahma*) can also be read as: ***anādi-mat*** *paraṁ brahma*. According to the first reading *mat* is taken as the pronoun "Me." According to the second reading *mat* is taken as a secondary suffix meaning "possessing," in which case the line means "the supreme *brahman* is possessed of no beginning." Both interpretations are grammatically correct. Based on BG 14.27 Rāmānuja follows the former reading, while Śaṅkara follows the latter reading.

9. For an explanation of *sat* and *asat* see fn. BG 2.16. Here Rāmānuja takes *sat* and *asat* to be cause and effect. In other words, *brahman* is beyond the cause and the effects of this world.

सर्वतःपाणिपादं तत्सर्वतोऽक्षिशिरोमुखम् ।
सर्वतःश्रुतिमल्लोके सर्वमावृत्य तिष्ठति ॥ १३

sarvataḥ pāṇi-pādaṁ tat sarvato 'kṣi-śiro-mukham
sarvataḥ śrutimal loke sarvam āvṛtya tiṣṭhati

सर्वेन्द्रियगुणाभासं सर्वेन्द्रियविवर्जितम् ।
असक्तं सर्वभृच्चैव निर्गुणं गुणभोक्तृ च ॥ १४

sarvendriya-guṇābhāsaṁ sarvendriya-vivarjitam
asaktaṁ sarva-bhṛc caiva nirguṇaṁ guṇa-bhoktṛ ca

बहिरन्तश्च भूतानामचरं चरमेव च ।
सूक्ष्मत्वात्तदविज्ञेयं दूरस्थं चान्तिके च तत् ॥ १५

bahir antaś ca bhūtānām acaraṁ caram eva ca
sūkṣmatvāt tad avijñeyaṁ dūra-sthaṁ cāntike ca tat

अविभक्तं च भूतेषु विभक्तमिव च स्थितम् ।
भूतभर्तृ च तज्ज्ञेयं ग्रसिष्णु प्रभविष्णु च ॥ १६

avibhaktaṁ ca bhūteṣu vibhaktam iva ca sthitam
bhūta-bhartṛ ca taj jñeyaṁ grasiṣṇu prabhaviṣṇu ca

ज्योतिषामपि तज्ज्योतिस्तमसः परमुच्यते ।
ज्ञानं ज्ञेयं ज्ञानगम्यं हृदि सर्वस्य विष्ठितम् ॥ १७

jyotiṣām api taj jyotis tamasaḥ param ucyate
jñānaṁ jñeyaṁ jñāna-gamyaṁ hṛdi sarvasya viṣṭhitam

इति क्षेत्रं तथा ज्ञानं ज्ञेयं चोक्तं समासतः ।
मद्भक्त एतद्विज्ञाय मद्भावायोपपद्यते ॥ १८

iti kṣetraṁ tathā jñānaṁ jñeyaṁ coktaṁ samāsataḥ
mad-bhakta etad vijñāya mad-bhāvāyopapadyate

13) On all sides are its hands and feet. Everywhere are its eyes, head and face. It has ears everywhere. Enveloping all, it pervades this entire universe.[10]

14) Devoid of senses, it illuminates the function of the senses.[11] Unattached, it maintains all. Devoid of qualities, it enjoys qualities.

15) It exists both within all things as well as outside of all things. It is moving as well as unmoving; and due to its subtle nature, it is unknowable. It is both distant and yet very near.[12]

16) Undivided, it pervades all things and yet it appears divided. It is known as the source and the destruction as well as the maintainer of all things.

17) Of lights, it is declared to be the light that is beyond darkness. It is knowledge, the object of knowlege and that which is attained through knowledge. It is situated in the heart of all.[13]

18) Thus the field, knowledge, and the object of knowledge have been described in brief. Understanding this, My devotee attains to My state of being.[14]

---

10. This verse is taken right out of the ŚU 3.16. It is based on the theme of the *Puruṣa-sūkta* (RV 10.81.3).
11. Compare this to ŚU 3.17.
12. Compare this to ĪU 5.
13. Compare to the following verses: BU 4.4. 16, MuU 2.2.6, BG 8.9, ŚU 3.8, ŚU 3.13, and ŚU 4.20.
14. "My state of being" (*mad-bhāvam*): see BG 4.10, 8.5 and 14.19.

प्रकृतिं पुरुषं चैव विद्ध्यनादी उभावपि ।
विकारांश्च गुणांश्चैव विद्धि प्रकृतिसंभवान् ॥ १९
prakṛtiṁ puruṣaṁ caiva viddhy anādī ubhāv api
vikārāṁś ca guṇāṁś caiva viddhi prakṛti-sambhavān

कार्यकारणकर्तृत्वे हेतुः प्रकृतिरुच्यते ।
पुरुषः सुखदुःखानां भोक्तृत्वे हेतुरुच्यते ॥ २०
kārya-kāraṇa-kartṛtve hetuḥ prakṛtir ucyate
puruṣaḥ sukha-duḥkhānāṁ bhoktṛtve hetur ucyate

पुरुषः प्रकृतिस्थो हि भुङ्क्ते प्रकृतिजान्गुणान् ।
कारणं गुणसङ्गोऽस्य सदसद्योनिजन्मसु ॥ २१
puruṣaḥ prakṛti-stho hi bhuṅkte prakṛti-jān guṇān
kāraṇaṁ guṇa-saṅgo 'sya sad-asad-yoni-janmasu

उपद्रष्टानुमन्ता च भर्ता भोक्ता महेश्वरः ।
परमात्मेति चाप्युक्तो देहेऽस्मिन्पुरुषः परः ॥ २२
upadraṣṭānumantā ca bhartā bhoktā maheśvaraḥ
paramātmeti cāpy ukto dehe 'smin puruṣaḥ paraḥ

य एवं वेत्ति पुरुषं प्रकृतिं च गुणैः सह ।
सर्वथा वर्तमानोऽपि न स भूयोऽभिजायते ॥ २३
ya evaṁ vetti puruṣaṁ prakṛtiṁ ca guṇaiḥ saha
sarvathā vartamāno 'pi na sa bhūyo 'bhijāyate

Prakṛti *and* Puruṣa

19) You should know that both matter and spirit,[15] *prakṛti* and *puruṣa,* are without beginning. You should also know that the (three) *guṇas* as well as their transformations arise from *prakṛti.*

20) *Prakṛti* is said to be the source of all phases of action: the thing to be done, the means of doing it,[16] and the person who does it. *Puruṣa* is said to be the source of the experience of happiness and suffering.

21) *Puruṣa,* situated within *prakṛti,* experiences the (three) *guṇas* which arise from *prakṛti.* Contact with these *guṇas* causes birth in both good and evil species of life.

22) The highest *puruṣa* in this body has been declared to be the overseer, the permitter, the support and the enjoyer: the great Lord, who is the Supreme Soul.[17]

23) The person who thus understands both *prakṛti* and *puruṣa* along with the (three) *guṇas* does not take birth again, regardless of one's present state of existence.

---

15. "Matter and spirit" (*prakṛti and puruṣa*) means, "the field and the knower of the field."
16. Both Śaṅkara and Rāmānuja read "the thing to be done" (*kārya*) as the body and "the means of doing it" (*kāraṇa*) as the senses. Regarding the idea that the soul performs no action, compare this verse to BG 3.28 and 13.29.
17. According to Madhva the "highest *puruṣa* in the body" (*dehe 'smin puruṣaḥ paraḥ),* the "great Lord" (*maheśvara*) and the "Supreme Soul" (*paramātmā*) all refer to God. Rāmānuja, however, says these terms refer to the individual spirit soul and not to God.

ध्यानेनात्मनि पश्यन्ति केचिदात्मानमात्मना ।
अन्ये सांख्येन योगेन कर्मयोगेन चापरे ॥ २४

dhyānenātmani paśyanti kecid ātmānam ātmanā
anye sāṅkhyena yogena karma-yogena cāpare

अन्ये त्वेवमजानन्तः श्रुत्वान्येभ्य उपासते ।
तेऽपि चातितरन्त्येव मृत्युं श्रुतिपरायणाः ॥ २५

anye tv evam ajānantaḥ śrutvānyebhya upāsate
te 'pi cātitaranty eva mṛtyuṁ śruti-parāyaṇāḥ

यावत्संजायते किंचित्सत्त्वं स्थावरजङ्गमम् ।
क्षेत्रक्षेत्रज्ञसंयोगात्तद्विद्धि भरतर्षभ ॥ २६

yāvat sañjāyate kiñcit sattvaṁ sthāvara-jaṅgamam
kṣetra-kṣetra-jña-saṁyogāt tad viddhi bharatarṣabha

समं सर्वेषु भूतेषु तिष्ठन्तं परमेश्वरम् ।
विनश्यत्स्वविनश्यन्तं यः पश्यति स पश्यति ॥ २७

samaṁ sarveṣu bhūteṣu tiṣṭhantaṁ parameśvaram
vinaśyatsv avinaśyantaṁ yaḥ paśyati sa paśyati

समं पश्यन्हि सर्वत्र समवस्थितमीश्वरम् ।
न हिनस्त्यात्मनात्मानं ततो याति परां गतिम् ॥ २८

samaṁ paśyan hi sarvatra samavasthitam īśvaram
na hinasty ātmanātmānaṁ tato yāti parāṁ gatim

24) Some see that Supreme Soul in themselves by the mind through meditation,[18] others perceive it through *sāṅkhya-yoga*[19] and still others through *karma-yoga.*

25) Then again there are some who are without knowledge, but because they hear from those with knowledge, come to revere this truth. They too cross beyond death.

26) O best of the Bhāratas, understand that all sentient beings, whether moving or unmoving, are but a combination of the field and the knower of the field.

God Resides in All Creatures

27) The Supreme Lord,[20] abiding equally in all beings, is not destroyed when they are destroyed. One who perceives this, truly sees.

28) Seeing that same Lord situated everywhere, one ceases to harm oneself by the mind.[21] One then goes to the supreme destination.

---

18. "Some see that Supreme Soul in themselves by the mind through meditation" (*dhyānenātmani paśyanti kecid ātmānam ātmanā*) is literally "some see the *ātman* in the *ātman* by the *ātman* through meditation." Here *ātman* is taken to refer to the Supreme Soul, one's self (reflexive) and the mind. For an explanation of this use of *ātman* see BG 6.5 fn.
19. For an explanation of *sāṅkhya* see fn. BG 2.39. Here *sāṅkhya* may refer to the formal system of Sāṅkhya philosophy.
20. Here as elsewhere in this chapter Rāmānuja interprets "the Supreme Lord" (*parameśvaram*) as the supreme lord of the body, i.e. the individual soul and not to God as the over-soul.
21. Oneself by the mind" (*ātmanātmānam*) is literally "the *ātman* by the *ātman*." See BG. 13.24.

प्रकृत्यैव च कर्माणि क्रियमाणानि सर्वशः ।
यः पश्यति तथात्मानमकर्तारं स पश्यति ॥ २९

prakṛtyaiva ca karmāṇi kriyamāṇāni sarvaśaḥ
yaḥ paśyati tathātmānam akartāraṁ sa paśyati

यदा भूतपृथग्भावमेकस्थमनुपश्यति ।
तत एव च विस्तारं ब्रह्म संपद्यते तदा ॥ ३०

yadā bhūta-pṛthag-bhāvam eka-stham anupaśyati
tata eva ca vistāraṁ brahma sampadyate tadā

अनादित्वान्निर्गुणत्वात्परमात्मायमव्ययः ।
शरीरस्थोऽपि कौन्तेय न करोति न लिप्यते ॥ ३१

anāditvān nirguṇatvāt paramātmāyam avyayaḥ
śarīra-stho 'pi kaunteya na karoti na lipyate

यथा सर्वगतं सौक्ष्म्यादाकाशं नोपलिप्यते ।
सर्वत्रावस्थितो देहे तथात्मा नोपलिप्यते ॥ ३२

yathā sarva-gataṁ saukṣmyād ākāśaṁ nopalipyate
sarvatrāvasthito dehe tathātmā nopalipyate

यथा प्रकाशयत्येकः कृत्स्नं लोकमिमं रविः ।
क्षेत्रं क्षेत्री तथा कृत्स्नं प्रकाशयति भारत ॥ ३३

yathā prakāśayaty ekaḥ kṛtsnaṁ lokam imaṁ raviḥ
kṣetraṁ kṣetrī tathā kṛtsnaṁ prakāśayati bhārata

क्षेत्रक्षेत्रज्ञयोरेवमन्तरं ज्ञानचक्षुषा ।
भूतप्रकृतिमोक्षं च ये विदुर्यान्ति ते परम् ॥ ३४

kṣetra-kṣetrajñayor evam antaraṁ jñāna-cakṣuṣā
bhūta-prakṛti-mokṣaṁ ca ye vidur yānti te param

29) One who truly sees perceives that all actions are performed entirely by matter and that the soul performs no actions.[22]

30) When one sees that all diverse states of being are based on one source,[23] from which they expand, one attains *brahman.*

31) O son of Kuntī, this imperishable supreme soul,[24] who is without beginning and devoid of the *guṇas,* neither acts nor is tainted by action even though situated in the body.

32) As the all-pervading sky, due to its subtle nature, is never stained, similarly the soul, situated in all bodies, ever remains unstained.

33) O descendant of Bharata, as the single sun illumines this whole world, so the owner of the field illumines this entire body.

34) Those whose eyes are filled with knowledge see the difference between the field and the knower of the field as well as the release of beings from matter. In this way, they attain the Supreme.

---

22. Regarding the idea that the soul performs no action, compare this verse to BG 3.28 and 13.20.

23. That "one source" (*eka-stha*) is literally "standing in one." Rāmānuja says it is material nature (*prakṛti*). Śaṅkara says it is the Self (*ātman*).

24. "This imperishable supreme soul" (*paramātmāyam avyayaḥ*) is here taken to be the individual soul who is the lord of the body. In many places in this chapter there is debate over the meaning of the word. Rāmānuja says that this chapter only discusses the individual soul and matter, *puruṣa* and *prakṛti.* Therefore, all references to *paramātmā* as in BG 13.22 or this verse refer to the individual soul. Madhva, on the other hand, does not agree. For him there are three principles discussed in this chapter: God (*paramātmā*), soul (*ātmā*), and matter (*prakṛti*). This is born out in verse two where Kṛṣṇa identifies himself as the knower in all bodies. This is *paramātmā,* the over-soul.

श्रीभगवानुवाच ।
परं भूयः प्रवक्ष्यामि ज्ञानानां ज्ञानमुत्तमम् ।
यज्ज्ञात्वा मुनयः सर्वे परां सिद्धिमितो गताः ॥ १

śrī-bhagavān uvāca
paraṁ bhūyaḥ pravakṣyāmi jñānānāṁ jñānam uttamam
yaj jñātvā munayaḥ sarve parāṁ siddhim ito gatāḥ

इदं ज्ञानमुपाश्रित्य मम साधर्म्यमागताः ।
सर्गेऽपि नोपजायन्ते प्रलये न व्यथन्ति च ॥ २

idaṁ jñānam upāśritya mama sādharmyam āgatāḥ
sarge 'pi nopajāyante pralaye na vyathanti ca

मम योनिर्महद्ब्रह्म तस्मिन्गर्भं दधाम्यहम् ।
संभवः सर्वभूतानां ततो भवति भारत ॥ ३

mama yonir mahad-brahma tasmin garbhaṁ dadhāmy aham
sambhavaḥ sarva-bhūtānāṁ tato bhavati bhārata

सर्वयोनिषु कौन्तेय मूर्तयः संभवन्ति याः ।
तासां ब्रह्म महद्योनिरहं बीजप्रदः पिता ॥ ४

sarva-yoniṣu kaunteya mūrtayaḥ sambhavanti yāḥ
tāsāṁ brahma mahad yonir ahaṁ bīja-pradaḥ pitā

Chapter Fourteen

The Three Guṇas

1) Kṛṣṇa Bhagavān said:
Again I shall declare this supreme knowledge, which is the best of all learning. Knowing this, sages have achieved the highest perfection.

2) Through this knowledge they attained a nature similar to Mine.[1] Consequently, they are not born at the time of creation, nor are they disturbed at the time of dissolution.

Material Nature is My Womb

3) O descendant of Bharata, material nature[2] is the womb into which I place the seed of life.[3] All beings arise from this source.

4) O son of Kuntī, whatever forms appear in the various species of life, material nature is the womb and I am the seed-giving father.

Chapter Fourteen is traditionally entitled *guṇa-traya-vibhaga-yoga*, The *Yoga* of Distinction between the Three *Guṇas*.

1. Śaṅkara says "a nature similar to Me" (*mama sādharmyam*) means "a similar identity as Me." Rāmānuja says it means "similar qualities as Me."
2. What is here translated as "material nature" is literally "the great *brahman*" (*mahad-brahma*). Śaṅkara, Rāmānuja and Madhva all interpret this as *prakṛti*, material nature.
3. "The seed of life" (*garbha*) is literally "the embyro."

सत्त्वं रजस्तम इति गुणाः प्रकृतिसंभवाः ।
निबध्नन्ति महाबाहो देहे देहिनमव्ययम् ॥ ५

sattvaṁ rajas tama iti guṇāḥ prakṛti-sambhavāḥ
nibadhnanti mahā-bāho dehe dehinam avyayam

तत्र सत्त्वं निर्मलत्वात्प्रकाशकमनामयम् ।
सुखसङ्गेन बध्नाति ज्ञानसङ्गेन चानघ ॥ ६

tatra sattvaṁ nirmalatvāt prakāśakam anāmayam
sukha-saṅgena badhnāti jñāna-saṅgena cānagha

रजो रागात्मकं विद्धि तृष्णासङ्गसमुद्भवम् ।
तन्निबध्नाति कौन्तेय कर्मसङ्गेन देहिनम् ॥ ७

rajo rāgātmakaṁ viddhi tṛṣṇā-saṅga-samudbhavam
tan nibadhnāti kaunteya karma-saṅgena dehinam

तमस्त्वज्ञानजं विद्धि मोहनं सर्वदेहिनाम् ।
प्रमादालस्यनिद्राभिस्तन्निबध्नाति भारत ॥ ८

tamas tv ajñāna-jaṁ viddhi mohanaṁ sarva-dehinām
pramādālasya-nidrābhis tan nibadhnāti bhārata

The Guṇas *of Nature*

5) O great-armed Arjuna, *sattva, rajas* and *tamas*[4] are the *guṇas* born of material nature. They bind the imperishable embodied soul to a physical form.

6) O faultless one, the material quality of *sattva*, which is pure, illuminating and free of disease, binds one through attachment to happiness and knowledge.[5]

7) Understand that *rajas* is founded on desire[6] and that it springs from thirst and attachment. O son of Kuntī, through attachment to action it binds the embodied soul.

8) Know that *tamas* arises from ignorance and causes the bewilderment of all embodied souls. O descendant of Bharata, it binds one through madness, idleness and sleep.

---

4. *Sattva* (goodness), *rajas* (passion) and *tamas* (darkness) are conceived in Sāṅkhya and Vedānta philosophy as the three *guṇas* of matter (*prakṛti*). *Sattva* makes for a steady and balanced condition of matter. *Rajas* stimulates energetic and constructive activity. *Tamas* is responsible for inertia and disintegration. The Sanskrit word *guṇa* has many meanings including quality, mode, constituent element, etc. Consequently, the *guṇas* have been translated into English as the "modes of nature," the "qualities of matter," the "constituents of matter," etc. The idea of mode is perhaps the best translation as it suggests a disposition or an orientation to reality. *Sattva, rajas* and *tamas* are not acts, but ways of acting—dispositions which cause us to act in certain ways. One attains genuine "freedom" when one has managed to transcend the three *guṇas*. According to Śaṅkara *sattva, rajas* and *tamas* are called *guṇas* not because they are qualities of matter, but because the *Sāṅkhyas* chose that particular word as a technical term.
5. Śaṅkara explains that *sattva*, by leading to knowledge and happiness, makes one happy, which then gives rise to attachment. This in turn leads to rebirth. He further points out that the kind of knowledge mentioned in this verse is the pursuit of happiness and not knowledge in relation to the soul.
6. According to Rāmānuja the "desire" (*tṛṣṇa*) meant here is sexual desire. Others take it as desire in general.

सत्त्वं सुखे सञ्जयति रजः कर्मणि भारत ।
ज्ञानमावृत्य तु तमः प्रमादे सञ्जयत्युत ॥ ९

sattvaṁ sukhe sañjayati rajaḥ karmaṇi bhārata
jñānam āvṛtya tu tamaḥ pramāde sañjayaty uta

रजस्तमश्चाभिभूय सत्त्वं भवति भारत ।
रजः सत्त्वं तमश्चैव तमः सत्त्वं रजस्तथा ॥ १०

rajas tamaś cābhibhūya sattvaṁ bhavati bhārata
rajaḥ sattvaṁ tamaś caiva tamaḥ sattvaṁ rajas tathā

सर्वद्वारेषु देहेऽस्मिन्प्रकाश उपजायते ।
ज्ञानं यदा तदा विद्याद्विवृद्धं सत्त्वमित्युत ॥ ११

sarva-dvāreṣu dehe 'smin prakāśa upajāyate
jñānaṁ yadā tadā vidyād vivṛddhaṁ sattvam ity uta

लोभः प्रवृत्तिरारम्भः कर्मणामशमः स्पृहा ।
रजस्येतानि जायन्ते विवृद्धे भरतर्षभ ॥ १२

lobhaḥ pravṛttir ārambhaḥ karmaṇām aśamaḥ spṛhā
rajasy etāni jāyante vivṛddhe bharatarṣabha

अप्रकाशोऽप्रवृत्तिश्च प्रमादो मोह एव च ।
तमस्येतानि जायन्ते विवृद्धे कुरुनन्दन ॥ १३

aprakāśo 'pravṛttiś ca pramādo moha eva ca
tamasy etāni jāyante vivṛddhe kuru-nandana

यदा सत्त्वे प्रवृद्धे तु प्रलयं याति देहभृत् ।
तदोत्तमविदां लोकानमलान्प्रतिपद्यते ॥ १४

yadā sattve pravṛddhe tu pralayaṁ yāti deha-bhṛt
tadottama-vidāṁ lokān amalān pratipadyate

9) O Arjuna, *sattva* causes attachment to happiness, *rajas* to activity, and *tamas,* which obscures knowledge, causes attachment to madness.

10) Sometimes *sattva* dominates, overpowering *rajas* and *tamas.* Likewise, *rajas* overpowers *sattva* and *tamas,* or *tamas* overpowers *sattva* and *rajas.*

11) When knowledge arises, illumining all the gates of this body,[7] know that *sattva* has become strong.

12) O bull of the Bhāratas, when *rajas* has become strong, greed, worldly engagement, great undertakings, turmoil, and desire arise.

13) O joy of the Kurus, when *tamas* intensifies gloom, inactivity, madness and delusion arise.

14) If the embodied soul meets death while *sattva* dominates, one reaches the spotless worlds of those who know the highest.[8]

---

7. "All the gates of this body" (*sarva-dvāreṣu dehe 'smin*) means two eyes, two ears, two nostrils, the mouth, the genital and the anus. Śaṅkara and Rāmānuja say it means the senses.
8. Rāmānuja says that if one dies when *sattva* predominates one is reborn into a family that has knowledge of the soul and one automatically becomes qualified to perform further works to know the soul.

रजसि प्रलयं गत्वा कर्मसङ्गिषु जायते ।
तथा प्रलीनस्तमसि मूढयोनिषु जायते ॥ १५

rajasi pralayaṁ gatvā karma-saṅgiṣu jāyate
tathā pralīnas tamasi mūḍha-yoniṣu jāyate

कर्मणः सुकृतस्याहुः सात्त्विकं निर्मलं फलम् ।
रजसस्तु फलं दुःखमज्ञानं तमसः फलम् ॥ १६

karmaṇaḥ sukṛtasyāhuḥ sāttvikaṁ nirmalaṁ phalam
rajasas tu phalaṁ duḥkham ajñānaṁ tamasaḥ phalam

सत्त्वात्संजायते ज्ञानं रजसो लोभ एव च ।
प्रमादमोहौ तमसो भवतोऽज्ञानमेव च ॥ १७

sattvāt sañjāyate jñānaṁ rajaso lobha eva ca
pramāda-mohau tamaso bhavato 'jñānam eva ca

ऊर्ध्वं गच्छन्ति सत्त्वस्था मध्ये तिष्ठन्ति राजसाः ।
जघन्यगुणवृत्तस्था अधो गच्छन्ति तामसाः ॥ १८

ūrdhvaṁ gacchanti sattva-sthā madhye tiṣṭhanti rājasāḥ
jaghanya-guṇa-vṛtti-sthā adho gacchanti tāmasāḥ

नान्यं गुणेभ्यः कर्तारं यदा द्रष्टानुपश्यति ।
गुणेभ्यश्च परं वेत्ति मद्भावं सोऽधिगच्छति ॥ १९

nānyaṁ guṇebhyaḥ kartāraṁ yadā draṣṭānupaśyati
guṇebhyaś ca paraṁ vetti mad-bhāvaṁ so 'dhigacchati

गुणानेतानतीत्य त्रीन्देही देहसमुद्भवान् ।
जन्ममृत्युजरादुःखैर्विमुक्तोऽमृतमश्नुते ॥ २०

guṇān etān atītya trīn dehī deha-samudbhavān
janma-mṛtyu-jarā-duḥkhair vimukto 'mṛtam aśnute

15) If one meets death while *rajas* dominates, the embodied soul takes birth among those who are attached to activity. If one dies in *tamas,* the embodied soul takes birth in the wombs of the ignorant.[9]

16) The learned say that an action undertaken according to *sattva* produces a result that is pure and good, while an action undertaken in *rajas* leads to suffering. They also say that an action undertaken in *tamas* leads to ignorance.

17) Knowledge arises from *sattva.* Intense longing develops from *rajas,* while madness, delusion and ignorance arise from *tamas.*

18) Those situated in *sattva* rise upwards. Those situated in *rajas* remain midway, while those situated in *tamas* descend downwards.[10]

19) When the embodied soul understands that there is no agent other than these three *guṇas* and he is able to perceive what lies beyond these *guṇas,* such a soul finally attains to My nature.[11]

20) Transcending the three *guṇas,* which originate in the body,[12] the embodied soul becomes free from the sufferings of birth, death and old age and attains immortality.

---

9. "In the wombs of the ignorant" (*mūḍha-yoniṣu*) is described by Śaṅkara as domestic animals. Rāmānuja describes it as dogs and pigs.
10. Śaṅkara defines upwards, middle and downwards as birth as a god, a human being, or an animal. Rāmānuja describes upwards as release from rebirth and downwards (in increasing order of lowness) as birth as an animal, a worm, an insect, or as immovable things such as shrubs and creepers, and finally to the state of stones, wood and straw, etc.
11. "My nature (*mad-bhāvam*) is literally "My state of being." See BG 4.10, 8.5, and 13.18.
12. The expression "which originate in the body," (*deha-samudbhavān*), could also mean "from which the body arises."

अर्जुन उवाच ।
कैर्लिङ्गैस्त्रीन्गुणानेतानतीतो भवति प्रभो ।
किमाचारः कथं चैतांस्त्रीन्गुणानतिवर्तते ॥ २१

arjuna uvāca
kair liṅgais trīn guṇān etān atīto bhavati prabho
kim ācāraḥ kathaṁ caitāṁs trīn guṇān ativartate

श्रीभगवानुवाच ।
प्रकाशं च प्रवृत्तिं च मोहमेव च पाण्डव ।
न द्वेष्टि संप्रवृत्तानि न निवृत्तानि काङ्क्षति ॥ २२

śrī-bhagavān uvāca
prakāśaṁ ca pravṛttiṁ ca moham eva ca pāṇḍava
na dveṣṭi sampravṛttāni na nivṛttāni kāṅkṣati

उदासीनवदासीनो गुणैर्यो न विचाल्यते ।
गुणा वर्तन्त इत्येव योऽवतिष्ठति नेङ्गते ॥ २३

udāsīna-vad āsīno guṇair yo na vicālyate
guṇā vartanta ity eva yo 'vatiṣṭhati neṅgate

समदुःखसुखः स्वस्थः समलोष्टाश्मकाञ्चनः ।
तुल्यप्रियाप्रियो धीरस्तुल्यनिन्दात्मसंस्तुतिः ॥ २४

sama-duḥkha-sukhaḥ sva-sthaḥ sama-loṣṭāśma-kāñcanaḥ
tulya-priyāpriyo dhīras tulya-nindātma-saṁstutiḥ

मानावमानयोस्तुल्यस्तुल्यो मित्रारिपक्षयोः ।
सर्वारम्भपरित्यागी गुणातीतः स उच्यते ॥ २५

mānāvamānayos tulyas tulyo mitrāri-pakṣayoḥ
sarvārambha-parityāgī guṇātītaḥ sa ucyate

21) Arjuna inquired,
My Lord, by what characteristics is one known who has transcended these three *guṇas*? What is that person's conduct? And how does one transcend these *guṇas*?

One Who has Transcended the Three Guṇas

22-23) Kṛṣṇa Bhagavān said,
O son of Pāṇḍu, the person who neither rejects illumination, worldly engagements or even delusion when they occur, nor desires them when they cease, who is indifferent and undisturbed by the *guṇas*, and who thinks, "This is just the *guṇas* interacting" is said to have attained transcendence.

24-25) One who remains fixed and unshaken, who is equal in distress and happiness, self situated, and for whom a lump of earth, a stone or gold are equal, to whom the beloved or unbeloved are the same, who is fixed and equal in blame or praise, who is equal in honor or dishonor and to both friends and enemies alike, and who renounces the results of all undertakings—such a person is said to have transcended the three *guṇas.*

मां च योऽव्यभिचारेण भक्तियोगेन सेवते ।
स गुणान्समतीत्यैतान्ब्रह्मभूयाय कल्पते ।। २६

māṁ ca yo 'vyabhicāreṇa bhakti-yogena sevate
sa guṇān samatītyaitān brahma-bhūyāya kalpate

ब्रह्मणो हि प्रतिष्ठाहममृतस्याव्ययस्य च ।
शाश्वतस्य च धर्मस्य सुखस्यैकान्तिकस्य च ।। २७

brahmaṇo hi pratiṣṭhāham amṛtasyāvyayasya ca
śāśvatasya ca dharmasya sukhasyaikāntikasya ca

26) That person, who serves Me with unfailing devotion, transcending these *guṇas,* is fit for the condition of *brahman.*[13]

27) For I am the foundation of *brahman,*[14] which is immortal and imperishable, and which is the basis of eternal *dharma* and perfect happiness.

---

13. "Fit for the condition of *brahman*" (*brahma-bhūyāya kalpate*) is taken by Śaṅkara as "fit for becoming *brahman.*" Rāmānuja and Madhva take it as "fit for the state of *brahman.*"

14. Here the word *brahman* is interpreted differently by the commentators. Śaṅkara takes it as the Self, Rāmānuja as the individual soul and Madhva as *māyā,* material nature.

श्रीभगवानुवाच ।
ऊर्ध्वमूलमधःशाखमश्वत्थं प्राहुरव्ययम् ।
छन्दांसि यस्य पर्णानि यस्तं वेद स वेदवित् ॥ १

śrī-bhagavān uvāca
ūrdhva-mūlam adhaḥ-śākham aśvatthaṁ prāhur avyayam
chandāṁsi yasya parṇāni yas taṁ veda sa veda-vit

अधश्चोर्ध्वं प्रसृतास्तस्य शाखा
गुणप्रवृद्धा विषयप्रवालाः ।
अधश्च मूलान्यनुसंततानि
कर्मानुबन्धीनि मनुष्यलोके ॥ २

adhaś cordhvaṁ prasṛtās tasya śākhā guṇa-pravṛddhā viṣaya-pravālāḥ
adhaś ca mūlāny anusantatāni karmānubandhīni manuṣya-loke

न रूपमस्येह तथोपलभ्यते
नान्तो न चादिर्न च संप्रतिष्ठा ।
अश्वत्थमेनं सुविरूढमूल-
मसङ्गशस्त्रेण दृढेन छित्त्वा ॥ ३

na rūpam asyeha tathopalabhyate nānto na cādir na ca sampratiṣṭhā
aśvattham enaṁ su-virūḍha-mūlam asaṅga-śastreṇa dṛḍhena chittvā

Chapter Fifteen

The Yoga of the Supreme Puruṣa

The Imperishable Fig Tree

1) Kṛṣṇa Bhagavān said
There is an imperishable *aśvattha* tree[1] with its roots upwards and its branches downwards. Its leaves are the Vedic hymns. One who understands this tree is a knower of the Veda.

2) The branches of this tree extend both downwards and upwards and they are nourished by the three *guṇas*. Its shoots are the sense objects, and the roots that spread downward into this world are the cause of action.

3) The true form of this tree, from its beginning to its end, cannot be perceived in this world. This sacred *aśvattha*, with its firmly grown root, should be cut down with the powerful weapon of detachment.

Chapter Fifteen is traditionally entitled *puruṣottama-yoga*, the *Yoga* of the Highest Person.

1. The "*aśvattha* tree" (*aśvattha*) is the famous pipal, the sacred fig (*ficus religiosa*) that is revered throughout Hinduism. It is also known as the bo tree of enlightenment that is famous as the tree under which Siddhārtha Gautama attained enlightenment to become the Buddha. The *aśvattha* is not to be confused with the banyan tree (*ficus benghalensis/indica*), which is a member of the same botanical family. Like the banyan tree the roots of the *aśvattha* can grow from its branches. A similar analogy of the cosmic pipal tree is found in the KU (6.1) and the TA 1.2.5. The earliest reference to a cosmic tree appears in RV 1.24.7.

ततः पदं तत्परिमार्गितव्यं
यस्मिन्गता न निवर्तन्ति भूयः ।
तमेव चाद्यं पुरुषं प्रपद्ये
यतः प्रवृत्तिः प्रसृता पुराणी ॥ ४

tataḥ padaṁ tat parimārgitavyaṁ yasmin gatā na nivartanti bhūyaḥ
tam eva cādyaṁ puruṣaṁ prapadye yataḥ pravṛttiḥ prasṛtā purāṇī

निर्मानमोहा जितसङ्गदोषा
अध्यात्मनित्या विनिवृत्तकामाः ।
द्वंद्वैर्विमुक्ताः सुखदुःखसंज्ञै-
र्गच्छन्त्यमूढाः पदमव्ययं तत् ॥ ५

nirmāna-mohā jita-saṅga-doṣā
adhyātma-nityā vinivṛtta-kāmāḥ
dvandvair vimuktāḥ sukha-duḥkha-saṁjñair
gacchanty amūḍhāḥ padam avyayaṁ tat

न तद्भासयते सूर्यो न शशाङ्को न पावकः ।
यद्गत्वा न निवर्तन्ते तद्धाम परमं मम ॥ ६

na tad bhāsayate sūryo na śaśāṅko na pāvakaḥ
yad gatvā na nivartante tad dhāma paramaṁ mama

ममैवांशो जीवलोके जीवभूतः सनातनः ।
मनःषष्ठानीन्द्रियाणि प्रकृतिस्थानि कर्षति ॥ ७

mamaivāṁśo jīva-loke jīva-bhūtaḥ sanātanaḥ
manaḥ-ṣaṣṭhānīndriyāṇi prakṛti-sthāni karṣati

शरीरं यदवाप्नोति यच्चाप्युत्क्रामतीश्वरः ।
गृहीत्वैतानि संयाति वायुर्गन्धानिवाशयात् ॥ ८

śarīraṁ yad avāpnoti yac cāpy utkrāmatīśvaraḥ
gṛhītvaitāni saṁyāti vāyur gandhān ivāśayāt

4) That place[2] must be sought from which having once gone one never returns. "I therefore surrender unto that original person from whom this ancient creation has issued forth."[3]

5) Those who are without pride or illusion, who have overcome the evils of attachment, ever fixed in the soul, whose desires have been stopped, and who are freed from the dualities of happiness and distress—undeluded, they go to that imperishable place.[4]

6) The sun does not illumine My supreme abode,[5] nor does the moon or fire. Having once gone there, one never returns.

The Transmigrating Soul

7) An eternal fragment of Myself becomes the living being in this world. It draws to itself the six senses including the mind, which arise from matter.[6]

8) When that lord[7] secures a body and then gives it up, it takes these senses and moves on, like the wind carries fragrance from its source.

---

2. Here the word *pada,* meaning "place" is used, but it may also mean a "condition" or "state of being."
3. The quotations show that Kṛṣṇa is taking the role of a devotee.
4. "Imperishable place" (*padam avyayam*), see fn. BG 15.4.
5. "Supreme abode" (*dhāma paramam*): Here the word *dhāman* like *padam* may be taken as an actual place or a state of being. In this instance Rāmānuja takes *dhāman* as "light" which is another legitimate meaning.
6. "Arise from matter" (*prakṛti-sthāni*) is literally "standing in matter."
7. Madhva takes "lord" (*īśvara*) in this verse to be the Supreme Lord. Śaṅkara and Rāmānuja take it to mean the individual soul as lord of the body.

श्रोत्रं चक्षुः स्पर्शनं च रसनं घ्राणमेव च ।
अधिष्ठाय मनश्चायं विषयानुपसेवते ॥ ९

śrotraṁ cakṣuḥ sparśanaṁ ca rasanaṁ ghrāṇam eva ca
adhiṣṭhāya manaś cāyaṁ viṣayān upasevate

उत्क्रामन्तं स्थितं वापि भुञ्जानं वा गुणान्वितम् ।
विमूढा नानुपश्यन्ति पश्यन्ति ज्ञानचक्षुषः ॥ १०

utkrāmantaṁ sthitaṁ vāpi bhuñjānaṁ vā guṇānvitam
vimūḍhā nānupaśyanti paśyanti jñāna-cakṣuṣaḥ

यतन्तो योगिनश्चैनं पश्यन्त्यात्मन्यवस्थितम् ।
यतन्तोऽप्यकृतात्मानो नैनं पश्यन्त्यचेतसः ॥ ११

yatanto yoginaś cainaṁ paśyanty ātmany avasthitam
yatanto 'py akṛtātmāno nainaṁ paśyanty acetasaḥ

यदादित्यगतं तेजो जगद्भासयतेऽखिलम् ।
यच्चन्द्रमसि यच्चाग्नौ तत्तेजो विद्धि मामकम् ॥ १२

yad āditya-gataṁ tejo jagad bhāsayate 'khilam
yac candramasi yac cāgnau tat tejo viddhi māmakam

गामाविश्य च भूतानि धारयाम्यहमोजसा ।
पुष्णामि चौषधीः सर्वाः सोमो भूत्वा रसात्मकः ॥ १३

gām āviśya ca bhūtāni dhārayāmy aham ojasā
puṣṇāmi cauṣadhīḥ sarvāḥ somo bhūtvā rasātmakaḥ

अहं वैश्वानरो भूत्वा प्राणिनां देहमाश्रितः ।
प्राणापानसमायुक्तः पचाम्यन्नं चतुर्विधम् ॥ १४

ahaṁ vaiśvānaro bhūtvā prāṇināṁ deham āśritaḥ
prāṇāpāna-samāyuktaḥ pacāmy annaṁ catur-vidham

9) Assuming a particular set of senses that include the ear, the eye, the skin, the tongue, and the nose, as well as mind, this lord enjoys the objects of the senses.

10) The ignorant are unable to perceive how this lord departs from the body, or how it remains within the body to enjoy in combination with the *guṇas*. Only those with the eye of knowledge truly see.

11) The striving *yogīs* can see the soul situated within the body. But the foolish, who are without maturity, are unable to perceive it, no matter how they try.

God in All Things

12) The brilliance of the sun, which illumines this entire world, comes from Me. Similarly, the splendor of the moon and the fire also come from Me.

13) I enter the earth and sustain all beings by My strength. I become the moon,[8] full of the vitality that nourishes all vegetation.

14) I am the fire of digestion[9] situated in the body of all beings. In union with the incoming and outgoing breaths[10] I digest the four kinds of food.[11]

---

8. The word used here for "moon" is *soma*. Some take *soma* here to mean the mythic *soma* drink of the gods. The *soma* plant produced a juice that was drunk by priests and other members during Vedic sacrifice.
9. "The fire of digestion" (*vaiśvānara*): See BU V.9.1. The term literally means "that which is common to all men." It usually refers to Agni and is particularly used for the fire of digestion.
10. The breaths (*prāṇas*) of the body are five-fold. The *prāṇa* maintains life, while the *apāna*, the *vyāna*, the *samāna* and the *udāna* airs promote excretion, circulation, digestions and respiration respectively.
11. The four kinds of food are those that are chewed such as bread or sweet cake; that which is swallowed such as milk and juice; that which is sucked such as sugarcane and mango; and that which is licked such as sauce and honey.

सर्वस्य चाहं हृदि संनिविष्टो
मत्तः स्मृतिर्ज्ञानमपोहनं च ।
वेदैश्च सर्वैरहमेव वेद्यो
वेदान्तकृद्वेदविदेव चाहम् ॥ १५

sarvasya cāhaṁ hṛdi sanniviṣṭo mattaḥ smṛtir jñānam apohanaṁ ca
vedaiś ca sarvair aham eva vedyo vedānta-kṛd veda-vid eva cāham

द्वाविमौ पुरुषौ लोके क्षरश्चाक्षर एव च ।
क्षरः सर्वाणि भूतानि कूटस्थोऽक्षर उच्यते ॥ १६

dvāv imau puruṣau loke kṣaraś cākṣara eva ca
kṣaraḥ sarvāṇi bhūtāni kūṭa-stho 'kṣara ucyate

15) I am situated in the hearts of all. From Me come memory, knowledge and forgetfulness.[12] I am to be known by all the *Vedas*. I am the maker of the Veda's conclusions[13] and I alone know the *Vedas*.

Two Puruṣa*s and the Highest* Puruṣa

16) In this world[14] there are two *puruṣas*:[15] the changeable and the unchangeable. The changeable are the living beings, who inhabit this world. The unchangeable are said to be those who occupy the highest place.[16]

---

12. "Forgetfulness" (*apohanam*) is literally removal. However, it also refers to the reasoning faculty. So it could be translated as "reasoning." Śaṅkara takes it as loss of memory and comments that the virtuous, on account of their pious deeds, are blessed with memory and knowledge. The wicked, through their evil deeds, suffer from the loss of these. Rāmānuja agrees, but also points out that *apohanam* may also mean reasoning, derived from *ūha*. Thus *apohana* is the reasoning that removes doubt.
13. "The Veda's conclusions" (*vedānta*): Śaṅkara says *vedānta* means the *Upaniṣads*. Rāmānuja takes it to mean Vedic conclusions in general. Madhva takes it to refer directly to the *Vedānta-sūtras*.
14. "In this world" (*loke*) is glossed as "in the *Vedas*" by Rāmānuja.
15. "Two *puruṣas* (*imau puruṣau*) is literally "two persons." The word *puruṣa* was used in BG 13.19 in conjunction with *prakṛti*, material nature. There *puruṣa* referred to the soul who experiences the sensations that arise through contact with *prakṛti*. Rāmānuja understands the "two *puruṣas*" as two classes of souls. One, the class of souls in association with matter and therefore subject to death, and the other, a class of souls not in association with matter and therefore liberated. Śaṅkara, on the other hand, understands the two *puruṣas* as two categories of existence. One consists of all beings in the world who are described as changeable (*kṣara*), and the other is the illusory power of God (*māyā-śakti*), which he says is eternal and therefore described as unchangeable (*akṣara*). Madhva understands the two *puruṣas* to be all the embodied souls that are said to be the changeable *puruṣa* (*kṣara puruṣa*), and material energy that is said to be the unchangeable *puruṣa* (*akṣara puruṣa*).
16. "Highest place" (*kūṭa-stha*) is literally "standing at the top." See BG 6.8 and 12.3 for other uses of this term.

उत्तमः पुरुषस्त्वन्यः परमात्मेत्युदाहृतः ।
यो लोकत्रयमाविश्य बिभर्त्यव्यय ईश्वरः ॥ १७

uttamaḥ puruṣas tv anyaḥ paramātmety udāhṛtaḥ
yo loka-trayam āviśya bibharty avyaya īśvaraḥ

यस्मात्क्षरमतीतोऽहमक्षरादपि चोत्तमः ।
अतोऽस्मि लोके वेदे च प्रथितः पुरुषोत्तमः ॥ १८

yasmāt kṣaram atīto 'ham akṣarād api cottamaḥ
ato 'smi loke vede ca prathitaḥ puruṣottamaḥ

यो मामेवमसंमूढो जानाति पुरुषोत्तमम् ।
स सर्वविद्भजति मां सर्वभावेन भारत ॥ १९

yo mām evam asammūḍho jānāti puruṣottamam
sa sarva-vid bhajati māṁ sarva-bhāvena bhārata

इति गुह्यतमं शास्त्रमिदमुक्तं मयानघ ।
एतद्बुद्ध्वा बुद्धिमान्स्यात्कृतकृत्यश्च भारत ॥ २०

iti guhyatamaṁ śāstram idam uktaṁ mayānagha
etad buddhvā buddhimān syāt kṛta-kṛtyaś ca bhārata

17) But there is another, the Supreme *Puruṣa*, who is called the Highest Soul, the unchanging controller who enters into the three worlds[17] and maintains them.

18) Since I transcend both the changeable and the unchangeable, I am therefore celebrated as that Supreme *Puruṣa* in both the world[18] and in the *Vedas*.

19) In this way, O descendant of Bharata, one who knows Me as the Supreme *Puruṣa* is free of delusion and is a knower of all things. Such a person worships Me with his whole being.

20) O sinless Arjuna, I have thus revealed this most confidential science, knowing which one becomes enlightened and has accomplished all there is to do.[19]

---

17. The "three worlds" are *bhūloka*, *bhuvarloka*, and *svarloka*.
18. Śaṅkara takes "in the world" (*loke*) to mean "in the three worlds." Rāmānuja takes it as "in the *smṛti*" as opposed to the *śruti* which are the *Vedas*. Madhva's followers take it as "books written by holy men in the world." This amounts to the same thing as *smṛti*.
19. Śaṅkara considers the whole teaching of the *Bhagavad Gītā* and even the *Vedas* to be summed up in this fifteenth chapter.

श्रीभगवानुवाच ।
अभयं सत्त्वसंशुद्धिर्ज्ञानयोगव्यवस्थितिः ।
दानं दमश्च यज्ञश्च स्वाध्यायस्तप आर्जवम् ॥ १

śrī-bhagavān uvāca
abhayaṁ sattva-saṁśuddhir jñāna-yoga-vyavasthitiḥ
dānaṁ damaś ca yajñaś ca svādhyāyas tapa ārjavam

अहिंसा सत्यमक्रोधस्त्यागः शान्तिरपैशुनम् ।
दया भूतेष्वलोलुप्त्वं मार्दवं ह्रीरचापलम् ॥ २

ahiṁsā satyam akrodhas tyāgaḥ śāntir apaiśunam
dayā bhūteṣv aloluptvaṁ mārdavaṁ hrīr acāpalam

तेजः क्षमा धृतिः शौचमद्रोहो नातिमानिता ।
भवन्ति संपदं दैवीमभिजातस्य भारत ॥ ३

tejaḥ kṣamā dhṛtiḥ śaucam adroho nāti-mānitā
bhavanti sampadaṁ daivīm abhijātasya bhārata

दम्भो दर्पोऽतिमानश्च क्रोधः पारुष्यमेव च ।
अज्ञानं चाभिजातस्य पार्थ संपदमासुरीम् ॥ ४

dambho darpo 'timānaś ca krodhaḥ pāruṣyam eva ca
ajñānaṁ cābhijātasya pārtha sampadam āsurīm

दैवी संपद्विमोक्षाय निबन्धायासुरी मता ।
मा शुचः संपदं दैवीमभिजातोऽसि पाण्डव ॥ ५

daivī sampad vimokṣāya nibandhāyāsurī matā
mā śucaḥ sampadaṁ daivīm abhijāto 'si pāṇḍava

Chapter Sixteen

The Divine and Malevolent Natures

Divine and Malevolent Qualities

1-3) Kṛṣṇa Bhagavān said:
O descendant of Bharata, fearlessness, purification of one's existence,[1] steadiness in the discipline of knowledge, charity, self-restraint, religious sacrifice, sacred study,[2] austerity, straightforwardness, nonviolence, truth, freedom from anger, renunciation, peace, freedom from faultfinding, compassion towards other beings, absence of greed, gentleness, modesty, steadiness, vigor, patience, fortitude, purity, absence of malice, and freedom from pride—these are the blessings of one born with a divine nature.

4) O Pārtha, deceit, arrogance, pride, anger, harshness, as well as ignorance are the attributes of one born of the malevolent nature.

5) The divine blessings lead to liberation; the malevolent attributes leads to further bondage. Grieve not, O son of Pāṇḍu, for you are born with the blessings of the divine nature.

Chapter Sixteen is traditionally entitled *daivāsura-saṁpad-vibhāga-yoga,* The *Yoga* of the Distinction between the Divine and the Malevolent Natures.

1. "Purification of one's existence" (*sattva-saṁśuddhi*) is literally "purification of being." Śaṅkara and Rāmānuja take it as purity of mind.

2. "Sacred study (*svādhyāya*) can also be taken as self-study, i.e., introspection.

द्वौ भूतसर्गौ लोकेऽस्मिन्दैव आसुर एव च ।
दैवो विस्तरशः प्रोक्त आसुरं पार्थ मे शृणु ॥ ६

dvau bhūta-sargau loke 'smin daiva āsura eva ca
daivo vistaraśaḥ prokta āsuraṁ pārtha me śṛṇu

प्रवृत्तिं च निवृत्तिं च जना न विदुरासुराः ।
न शौचं नापि चाचारो न सत्यं तेषु विद्यते ॥ ७

pravṛttiṁ ca nivṛttiṁ ca janā na vidur āsurāḥ
na śaucaṁ nāpi cācāro na satyaṁ teṣu vidyate

असत्यमप्रतिष्ठं ते जगदाहुरनीश्वरम् ।
अपरस्परसंभूतं किमन्यत्कामहैतुकम् ॥ ८

asatyam apratiṣṭhaṁ te jagad āhur anīśvaram
aparaspara-sambhūtaṁ kim anyat kāma-haitukam

एतां दृष्टिमवष्टभ्य नष्टात्मानोऽल्पबुद्धयः ।
प्रभवन्त्युग्रकर्माणः क्षयाय जगतोऽहिताः ॥ ९

etāṁ dṛṣṭim avaṣṭabhya naṣṭātmāno 'lpa-buddhayaḥ
prabhavanty ugra-karmāṇaḥ kṣayāya jagato 'hitāḥ

काममाश्रित्य दुष्पूरं दम्भमानमदान्विताः ।
मोहाद्गृहीत्वासद्ग्राहान्प्रवर्तन्तेऽशुचिव्रताः ॥ १०

kāmam āśritya duṣpūraṁ dambha-māna-madānvitāḥ
mohād gṛhītvāsad-grāhān pravartante 'śuci-vratāḥ

चिन्तामपरिमेयां च प्रलयान्तामुपाश्रिताः ।
कामोपभोगपरमा एतावदिति निश्चिताः ॥ ११

cintām aparimeyāṁ ca pralayāntām upāśritāḥ
kāmopabhoga-paramā etāvad iti niścitāḥ

6) O son of Pṛthā, in this world there are two kinds of created beings: one divine, the other malevolent. The divine nature has been explained at length. Now hear from Me of the malevolent nature.

The Malevolent Heart

7) Persons of the malevolent nature do not know how to act or how not to act. Neither purity, proper conduct nor even truth itself is found in them.

8) They say the world is unreal, without a foundation; that it is without a God, and that it has arisen out of chance.[3] They say desire[4] alone has caused the world.

9) Holding to this view, these lost souls are without intelligence. They arise as enemies of the world and perform terrible deeds that lead to destruction.

10) They are filled with insatiable desire, hypocrisy, arrogance and pride. Based on delusion their undertakings are impure.

11) They are overflowing with anxieties that never cease. Gratification of desire is the supreme object of life. They are convinced that there is no higher goal.

---

3. "Arisen out of chance" (*aparaspara-saṁbhūtam*) is literally "brought about without mutual relation." Śaṅkara and Rāmānuja take it as "brought about by mutual union of male and female."
4. The Sanskrit word *kāma* is literally "desire," but here it specifically indicates sexual desire.

आशापाशशतैर्बद्धाः कामक्रोधपरायणाः ।
ईहन्ते कामभोगार्थमन्यायेनार्थसंचयान् ॥ १२

āśā-pāśa-śatair baddhāḥ kāma-krodha-parāyaṇāḥ
īhante kāma-bhogārtham anyāyenārtha-sañcayān

इदमद्य मया लब्धमिदं प्राप्स्ये मनोरथम् ।
इदमस्तीदमपि मे भविष्यति पुनर्धनम् ॥ १३

idam adya mayā labdham imaṁ prāpsye manoratham
idam astīdam api me bhaviṣyati punar dhanam

असौ मया हतः शत्रुर्हनिष्ये चापरानपि ।
ईश्वरोऽहमहं भोगी सिद्धोऽहं बलवान्सुखी ॥ १४

asau mayā hataḥ śatrur haniṣye cāparān api
īśvaro 'ham ahaṁ bhogī siddho 'haṁ balavān sukhī

आढ्योऽभिजनवानस्मि कोऽन्योऽस्ति सदृशो मया ।
यक्ष्ये दास्यामि मोदिष्य इत्यज्ञानविमोहिताः ॥ १५

āḍhyo 'bhijanavān asmi ko 'nyo 'sti sadṛśo mayā
yakṣye dāsyāmi modiṣya ity ajñāna-vimohitāḥ

अनेकचित्तविभ्रान्ता मोहजालसमावृताः ।
प्रसक्ताः कामभोगेषु पतन्ति नरकेऽशुचौ ॥ १६

aneka-citta-vibhrāntā moha-jāla-samāvṛtāḥ
prasaktāḥ kāma-bhogeṣu patanti narake 'śucau

12) Bound by an endless chain of expectations, subject to desire and anger, they hoard wealth in order to fulfill their desires by any means possible.

13) "Today I have acquired so much wealth. I shall obtain even more in the future. This much is mine and tomorrow more wealth will be mine."

14) "I have destroyed this enemy and I will destroy the others also. I am the lord. I am the enjoyer. I am successful, strong and happy."

15) "I am wealthy and of noble birth. Who is my equal? I shall perform sacrifice, give charity and rejoice." In this way, they are deluded by ignorance.

16) Bewildered by endless desires, surrounded by a network of illusion, attached to the fulfillment of desires, they descend to the most abominable hell.[5]

---

5. 'They descend to the most abominable hell" (*patanti narake 'śucau)* is literally "they fall to an unclean hell."

आत्मसंभाविताः स्तब्धा धनमानमदान्विताः ।
यजन्ते नामयज्ञैस्ते दम्भेनाविधिपूर्वकम् ॥ १७

ātma-sambhāvitāḥ stabdhā dhana-māna-madānvitāḥ
yajante nāma-yajñais te dambhenāvidhi-pūrvakam

अहंकारं बलं दर्पं कामं क्रोधं च संश्रिताः ।
मामात्मपरदेहेषु प्रद्विषन्तोऽभ्यसूयकाः ॥ १८

ahaṅkāraṁ balaṁ darpaṁ kāmaṁ krodhaṁ ca saṁśritāḥ
mām ātma-para-deheṣu pradviṣanto 'bhyasūyakāḥ

तानहं द्विषतः क्रूरान्संसारेषु नराधमान् ।
क्षिपाम्यजस्रमशुभानासुरीष्वेव योनिषु ॥ १९

tān ahaṁ dviṣataḥ krūrān saṁsāreṣu narādhamān
kṣipāmy ajasram aśubhān āsurīṣv eva yoniṣu

आसुरीं योनिमापन्ना मूढा जन्मनि जन्मनि ।
मामप्राप्यैव कौन्तेय ततो यान्त्यधमां गतिम् ॥ २०

āsurīṁ yonim āpannā mūḍhā janmani janmani
mām aprāpyaiva kaunteya tato yānty adhamāṁ gatim

त्रिविधं नरकस्येदं द्वारं नाशनमात्मनः ।
कामः क्रोधस्तथा लोभस्तस्मादेतत्त्रयं त्यजेत् ॥ २१

tri-vidhaṁ narakasyedaṁ dvāraṁ nāśanam ātmanaḥ
kāmaḥ krodhas tathā lobhas tasmād etat trayaṁ tyajet

17) Self-possessed, stubborn, full of pride and the conceit of wealth, they perform religious rites in name only without sincerity or regard for scriptural injunctions.

18) Out of egotism, violence, pride, desire and anger they are envious and hateful of Me, who dwells both within their body and the bodies of others.

19) I send back those who are hateful, cruel and inauspicious, who are the lowest of mankind, to repeated birth in malevolent wombs.[6]

20) O son of Kuntī, deluded birth after birth in such malevolent species of life, they are unable to attain Me and thereby sink to the lowest conditions of life.

The Triple Gates of Hell

21) Desire, anger and greed are the three gateways to hell that lead to the destruction of the soul. They must, therefore, be given up.

---

6. Śaṅkara suggests "malevolent wombs" (*āsurīṣv eva yoniṣu*) means in the wombs of cruel species such as lions and tigers, etc. Rāmānuja suggests that it means situations that are unfavorable for communion with God.

एतैर्विमुक्तः कौन्तेय तमोद्वारैस्त्रिभिर्नरः ।
आचरत्यात्मनः श्रेयस्ततो याति परां गतिम् ॥ २२

etair vimuktaḥ kaunteya tamo-dvārais tribhir naraḥ
ācaraty ātmanaḥ śreyas tato yāti parāṁ gatim

यः शास्त्रविधिमुत्सृज्य वर्तते कामकारतः ।
न स सिद्धिमवाप्नोति न सुखं न परां गतिम् ॥ २३

yaḥ śāstra-vidhim utsṛjya vartate kāma-kārataḥ
na sa siddhim avāpnoti na sukhaṁ na parāṁ gatim

तस्माच्छास्त्रं प्रमाणं ते कार्याकार्यव्यवस्थितौ ।
ज्ञात्वा शास्त्रविधानोक्तं कर्म कर्तुमिहार्हसि ॥ २४

tasmāc chāstraṁ pramāṇaṁ te kāryākārya-vyavasthitau
jñātvā śāstra-vidhānoktaṁ karma kartum ihārhasi

22) O son of Kuntī, a person who is released from these three gateways to darkness, performs what is best for the soul and thereby achieves the supreme goal.

23) One who lives according to one's own desire, rejecting the authority of *śāstra,*[7] achieves neither perfection, happiness, nor the supreme goal.

24) Therefore, let *śāstra* be your authority in determining what should be done and what should not be done. Knowing what has been stated in *śāstra,* you are obliged to act accordingly in this world.

---

7. *Śāstra* means scripture. Rāmānuja specifies scripture as the *Vedas* including *Dharma-śāstra, Itihāsa* and the *Purāṇas.*

अर्जुन उवाच ।

ये शास्त्रविधिमुत्सृज्य यजन्ते श्रद्धयान्विताः ।
तेषां निष्ठा तु का कृष्ण सत्त्वमाहो रजस्तमः ॥ १

arjuna uvāca
ye śāstra-vidhim utsṛjya yajante śraddhayānvitāḥ
teṣāṁ niṣṭhā tu kā kṛṣṇa sattvam āho rajas tamaḥ

श्रीभगवानुवाच ।

त्रिविधा भवति श्रद्धा देहिनां सा स्वभावजा ।
सात्त्विकी राजसी चैव तामसी चेति तां शृणु ॥ २

śrī-bhagavān uvāca
tri-vidhā bhavati śraddhā dehināṁ sā svabhāva-jā
sāttvikī rājasī caiva tāmasī ceti tāṁ ś ṛṇu

सत्त्वानुरूपा सर्वस्य श्रद्धा भवति भारत ।
श्रद्धामयोऽयं पुरुषो यो यच्छ्रद्धः स एव सः ॥ ३

sattvānurūpā sarvasya śraddhā bhavati bhārata
śraddhā-mayo 'yaṁ puruṣo yo yac-chraddhaḥ sa eva saḥ

Chapter Seventeen

Three Kinds of Faith

A Person Who Worships without the Authority of Śāstra

1) Arjuna inquired:
O Kṛṣṇa, what is the position of a person who worships with faith,[1] but who has abandoned the injunctions of *śāstra*? Does that person worship in *sattva, rajas* or *tamas*?[2]

2) Kṛṣṇa Bhagavān said:
Faith takes three forms for those who are embodied. It arises from the particular constitution[3] of the individual and is characterized by *sattva, rajas* or *tamas.* Now hear about this.

3) O descendant of Bharata, a person's faith corresponds to the state of their existence. Indeed, faith is the very essence of a person.[4]

Chapter Seventeen is traditionally entitled *śraddhā-traya-vibhāga-yoga,* The *Yoga* of the Threefold Division of Faith.

1. Here faith is a rendering of the word *śraddhā,* which is a compound of two words: *śrat* (heart) and *dhā* (to put or place). Thus *śraddhā* is literally "to set one's heart on."
2. For a discussion of the three qualities of nature (*sattva, rajas* and *tamas),* see Chapter Fourteen.
3. "Particular constitution" (*svabhāva*) is defined by Śaṅkara as the impression of good and other kinds of action performed in past births that become manifest at the time of death. Rāmānuja defines *svabhāva* as the natural disposition peculiar to one's nature. It is individual taste (*ruci*) that arises due to the unconscious subtle impressions from past lives.
4. "Faith is the very essence of a person" (*yo yac chraddhaḥ sa eva saḥ*) is literally, "As a man's faith is, so is he."

यजन्ते सात्त्विका देवान्यक्षरक्षांसि राजसाः ।
प्रेतान्भूतगणांश्चान्ये यजन्ते तामसा जनाः ॥ ४

yajante sāttvikā devān yakṣa-rakṣāṁsi rājasāḥ
pretān bhūta-gaṇāṁś cānye yajante tāmasā janāḥ

अशास्त्रविहितं घोरं तप्यन्ते ये तपो जनाः ।
दम्भाहंकारसंयुक्ताः कामरागबलान्विताः ॥ ५

aśāstra-vihitaṁ ghoraṁ tapyante ye tapo janāḥ
dambhāhaṅkāra-saṁyuktāḥ kāma-rāga-balānvitāḥ

कर्शयन्तः शरीरस्थं भूतग्राममचेतसः ।
मां चैवान्तःशरीरस्थं तान्विद्ध्यासुरनिश्चयान् ॥ ६

karṣayantaḥ śarīra-sthaṁ bhūta-grāmam acetasaḥ
māṁ caivāntaḥ śarīra-sthaṁ tān viddhy āsura-niścayān

आहारस्त्वपि सर्वस्य त्रिविधो भवति प्रियः ।
यज्ञस्तपस्तथा दानं तेषां भेदमिमं शृणु ॥ ७

āhāras tv api sarvasya tri-vidho bhavati priyaḥ
yajñas tapas tathā dānaṁ teṣāṁ bhedam imaṁ śṛṇu

आयुःसत्त्वबलारोग्यसुखप्रीतिविवर्धनाः ।
रस्याः स्निग्धाः स्थिरा हृद्या आहाराः सात्त्विकप्रियाः ८

āyuḥ-sattva-balārogya-sukha-prīti-vivardhanāḥ
rasyāḥ snigdhāḥ sthirā hṛdyā āhārāḥ sāttvika-priyāḥ

कट्वम्ललवणात्युष्णतीक्ष्णरूक्षविदाहिनः ।
आहारा राजसस्येष्टा दुःखशोकामयप्रदाः ॥ ९

kaṭv-amla-lavaṇāty-uṣṇa-tīkṣṇa-rūkṣa-vidāhinaḥ
āhārā rājasasyeṣṭā duḥkha-śokāmaya-pradāḥ

4) Those who are characterized by *sattva* worship God and the gods. Those who are characterized by *rajas* worship spirits and demons, and others, who are characterized by *tamas*, worship departed souls and ghosts.[5]

Those Who Torment the Flesh

5-6) Those who perform terrible austerities not sanctioned in scripture, who are controlled by deceit and egotism, who are filled with desire, passion and violence, torment the elements of the body as well as the Supreme Soul within. Such fools have a malevolent purpose.

7) Even the kind of food, the type of sacrifice, the kind of austerity and the type of charity that a person enjoys is of three kinds. Now listen to the differences as I explain them.

Food and the Three Guṇas

8) Foods that are characterized as *sattva* increase the duration of life, vitality, strength, health, happiness and satisfaction. Such foods are savory, agreeable, substantial and hearty.

9) Foods that are characterized as *rajas* are pungent, sour, salty, hot, sharp, astringent and burning. Such foods cause distress, misery and disease.

---

5. Compare this verse with BG 7. 20-23 and BG 9. 20-5.

यातयामं गतरसं पूति पर्युषितं च यत् ।
उच्छिष्टमपि चामेध्यं भोजनं तामसप्रियम् ॥ १०

yāta-yāmaṁ gata-rasaṁ pūti paryuṣitaṁ ca yat
ucchiṣṭam api cāmedhyaṁ bhojanaṁ tāmasa-priyam

अफलाकाङ्क्षिभिर्यज्ञो विधिदृष्टो य इज्यते ।
यष्टव्यमेवेति मनः समाधाय स सात्त्विकः ॥ ११

aphalākāṅkṣibhir yajño vidhi-dṛṣṭo ya ijyate
yaṣṭavyam eveti manaḥ samādhāya sa sāttvikaḥ

अभिसंधाय तु फलं दम्भार्थमपि चैव यत् ।
इज्यते भरतंश्रेष्ठ तं यज्ञं विद्धि राजसम् ॥ १२

abhisandhāya tu phalaṁ dambhārtham api caiva yat
ijyate bharata-śreṣṭha taṁ yajñaṁ viddhi rājasam

विधिहीनमसृष्टान्नं मन्त्रहीनमदक्षिणम् ।
श्रद्धाविरहितं यज्ञं तामसं परिचक्षते ॥ १३

vidhi-hīnam asṛṣṭānnaṁ mantra-hīnam adakṣiṇam
śraddhā-virahitaṁ yajñaṁ tāmasaṁ paricakṣate

देवद्विजगुरुप्राज्ञपूजनं शौचमार्जवम् ।
ब्रह्मचर्यमहिंसा च शारीरं तप उच्यते ॥ १४

deva-dvija-guru-prājña-pūjanaṁ śaucam ārjavam
brahmacaryam ahiṁsā ca śārīraṁ tapa ucyate

अनुद्वेगकरं वाक्यं सत्यं प्रियहितं च यत् ।
स्वाध्यायाभ्यसनं चैव वाङ्मयं तप उच्यते ॥ १५

anudvega-karaṁ vākyaṁ satyaṁ priya-hitaṁ ca yat
svādhyāyābhyasanaṁ caiva vāṅ-mayaṁ tapa ucyate

10) Foods that are characterized as *tamas* are spoiled, tasteless, putrid, stale,[6] leftover, and filthy.

Sacrifice and the Three Guṇas

11) That sacrifice which is performed without desire for a result and according to scriptural injunctions while thinking, "Sacrifice is duty," is of the nature of *sattva.*

12) But that sacrifice, O best of the Bhāratas, which is performed for a result and out of pride, is of the nature of *rajas.*

13) Sacrifice not sanctioned by scriptural injunction, which is without distribution of sacred food, wherein no Vedic hymns are recited or sacrificial fees[7] paid, and which is bereft of faith, is declared to be of the nature of *tamas.*

Austerity and the Three Guṇas

14) Austerity pertaining to the body involves the worship of God and the gods, the twice-born,[8] teachers, and the learned. Such austerity is characterized by cleanliness, straightforwardness, chastity and nonviolence.

15) Austerity pertaining to speech consists of words that cause no anxiety. Such speech is truthful, pleasing, beneficial, and includes the recitation and study of sacred texts.

---

6. Here the word "stale" (*yāta-yāma*) is taken by Śaṅkara as "cooked too slowly." Rāmānuja takes it as "that has stood around too long." Literally, it means, "gone for three hours."
7. "No sacrificial fees" (*adakṣiṇam*) is derived from *dakṣiṇā. Dakṣiṇā* is a gift offered to a priest after the performance of a religious ceremony.
8. "Twice-born" (*dvija*) refers to *brāhmaṇas.*

मनःप्रसादः सौम्यत्वं मौनमात्मविनिग्रहः ।
भावसंशुद्धिरित्येतत्तपो मानसमुच्यते ॥ १६

manaḥ-prasādaḥ saumyatvaṁ maunam ātma-vinigrahaḥ
bhāva-saṁśuddhir ity etat tapo mānasam ucyate

श्रद्धया परया तप्तं तपस्तत्त्रिविधं नरैः ।
अफलाकाङ्क्षिभिर्युक्तैः सात्त्विकं परिचक्षते ॥ १७

śraddhayā parayā taptaṁ tapas tat tri-vidhaṁ naraiḥ
aphalākāṅkṣibhir yuktaiḥ sāttvikaṁ paricakṣate

सत्कारमानपूजार्थं तपो दम्भेन चैव यत् ।
क्रियते तदिह प्रोक्तं राजसं चलमध्रुवम् ॥ १८

satkāra-māna-pūjārthaṁ tapo dambhena caiva yat
kriyate tad iha proktaṁ rājasaṁ calam adhruvam

मूढग्राहेणात्मनो यत्पीडया क्रियते तपः ।
परस्योत्सादनार्थं वा तत्तामसमुदाहृतम् ॥ १९

mūḍha-grāheṇātmano yat pīḍayā kriyate tapaḥ
parasyotsādanārthaṁ vā tat tāmasam udāhṛtam

दातव्यमिति यद्दानं दीयतेऽनुपकारिणे ।
देशे काले च पात्रे च तद्दानं सात्त्विकं स्मृतम् ॥ २०

dātavyam iti yad dānaṁ dīyate 'nupakāriṇe
deśe kāle ca pātre ca tad dānaṁ sāttvikaṁ smṛtam

यत्तु प्रत्युपकारार्थं फलमुद्दिश्य वा पुनः ।
दीयते च परिक्लिष्टं तद्दानं राजसं स्मृतम् ॥ २१

yat tu pratyupakārārthaṁ phalam uddiśya vā punaḥ
dīyate ca parikliṣṭaṁ tad dānaṁ rājasaṁ smṛtam

16) Austerity pertaining to the mind produces mental tranquility, gentleness, silence, self-restraint and the purification of one's existence.[9]

17) When persons of the highest faith practice austerity without a motivation and with discipline they are characterized by *sattva.*

18) Austerity undertaken for respect, honor and reverence, and which is arrogant is characterized by *rajas.* Such endeavors are transitory and impermanent.

19) Austerity performed out of foolishness, which harms another or one's self is characterized by *tamas.*

Charity and the Three Guṇas

20) Charity, which is given out of duty, without expectation of return, and which is given in a suitable location, at a proper time and to a worthy person is charity characterized by *sattva.*

21) But charity, which is given for the sake of obtaining a return or which causes harm is characterized by *rajas.*

9. "Purification of one's existence" (*bhāva-saṁśuddhiḥ*): Compare with BG 16.1, *sattva-saṁśuddhi.*

अदेशकाले यद्दानमपात्रेभ्यश्च दीयते ।
असत्कृतमवज्ञातं तत्तामसमुदाहृतम् ॥ २२

adeśa-kāle yad dānam apātrebhyaś ca dīyate
asat-kṛtam avajñātaṁ tat tāmasam udāhṛtam

ॐ तत्सदिति निर्देशो ब्रह्मणस्त्रिविधः स्मृतः ।
ब्राह्मणास्तेन वेदाश्च यज्ञाश्च विहिताः पुरा ॥ २३

oṁ tat sad iti nirdeśo brahmaṇas tri-vidhaḥ smṛtaḥ
brāhmaṇās tena vedāś ca yajñāś ca vihitāḥ purā

तस्मादोमित्युदाहृत्य यज्ञदानतपःक्रियाः ।
प्रवर्तन्ते विधानोक्ताः सततं ब्रह्मवादिनाम् ॥ २४

tasmād oṁ ity udāhṛtya yajña-dāna-tapaḥ-kriyāḥ
pravartante vidhānoktāḥ satataṁ brahma-vādinām

तदित्यनभिसंधाय फलं यज्ञतपःक्रियाः ।
दानक्रियाश्च विविधाः क्रियन्ते मोक्षकाङ्क्षिभिः ॥ २५

tad ity anabhisandhāya phalaṁ yajña-tapaḥ-kriyāḥ
dāna-kriyāś ca vividhāḥ kriyante mokṣa-kāṅkṣibhiḥ

सद्भावे साधुभावे च सदित्येतत्प्रयुज्यते ।
प्रशस्ते कर्मणि तथा सच्छब्दः पार्थ युज्यते ॥ २६

sad-bhāve sādhu-bhāve ca sad ity etat prayujyate
praśaste karmaṇi tathā sac-chabdhaḥ pārtha yujyate

यज्ञे तपसि दाने च स्थितिः सदिति चोच्यते ।
कर्म चैव तदर्थीयं सदित्येवाभिधीयते ॥ २७

yajñe tapasi dāne ca sthitiḥ sad iti cocyate
karma caiva tad-arthīyaṁ sad ity evābhidhīyate

अश्रद्धया हुतं दत्तं तपस्तप्तं कृतं च यत् ।
असदित्युच्यते पार्थ न च तत्प्रेत्य नो इह ॥ २८

aśraddhayā hutaṁ dattaṁ tapas taptaṁ kṛtaṁ ca yat
asad ity ucyate pārtha na ca tat pretya no iha

22) Charity, which is given at an unsuitable location and time, and to an unworthy person, without respect and with disregard is charity characterized by *tamas.*

The Utterance: Oṁ Tat Sat

23) In former times, the utterance: *oṁ tat sat,*[10] composed of three syllables, designated *brahman.* The priestly class, the *Vedas,* and sacrifices arose from this.

24) Those who follow the sacred injunctions and who recite the *Vedas* utter the syllable *om* before acts of sacrifice, charity and austerity.

25) Those who desire liberation without seeking a gainful result utter the syllable *tat* before they perform acts of sacrifice, austerity and charity.

26) O son of Pṛthā, the word *sat* is used in its sense of what is "permanent" and what is "good."[11] Similarly, *sat* is used to indicate any pious action.

27) Faithful determination while performing sacrifice, austerity and charity is also called *sat.* Even an action serving that purpose is called *sat.*

28) O son of Pṛthā, any oblation that is offered, any gift that is given, any austerity that is performed or any action that is undertaken, if it is done without faith[12] is called *asat.* It has no value in this world or in the next.

---

10. This ancient formula, "*oṁ tat sat*" literally means "Yes, it exists." See BG 8.13.
11. See BG 2.16.
12. "Without faith" (*aśraddhayā*) is literally, "without one's heart being in it." See fn under BG 17.1

अर्जुन उवाच ।
संन्यासस्य महाबाहो तत्त्वमिच्छामि वेदितुम् ।
त्यागस्य च हृषीकेश पृथक्केशिनिषूदन ॥ १

arjuna uvāca
sannyāsasya mahā-bāho tattvam icchāmi veditum
tyāgasya ca hṛṣīkeśa pṛthak keśi-niṣūdana

श्रीभगवानुवाच ।
काम्यानां कर्मणां न्यासं संन्यासं कवयो विदुः ।
सर्वकर्मफलत्यागं प्राहुस्त्यागं विचक्षणाः ॥ २

śrī-bhagavān uvāca
kāmyānāṁ karmaṇāṁ nyāsaṁ sannyāsaṁ kavayo viduḥ
sarva-karma-phala-tyāgaṁ prāhus tyāgaṁ vicakṣaṇāḥ

त्याज्यं दोषवदित्येके कर्म प्राहुर्मनीषिणः ।
यज्ञदानतपःकर्म न त्याज्यमिति चापरे ॥ ३

tyājyaṁ doṣa-vad ity eke karma prāhur manīṣiṇaḥ
yajña-dāna-tapaḥ-karma na tyājyam iti cāpare

निश्चयं शृणु मे तत्र त्यागे भरतसत्तम ।
त्यागो हि पुरुषव्याघ्र त्रिविधः संप्रकीर्तितः ॥ ४

niścayaṁ śṛṇu me tatra tyāge bharata-sattama
tyāgo hi puruṣa-vyāghra tri-vidhaḥ samprakīrtitaḥ

Chapter Eighteen

The Perfection of Renunciation

Sannyāsa *and* Tyāga

1) Arjuna said,
O great-armed Kṛṣṇa, slayer of Keśī, I wish to know the difference between *sannyāsa* and *tyāga*.[1]

2) Kṛṣṇa Bhagavān said:
Sages with clear vision understand *sannyāsa* to be the giving up of actions intended for the satisfaction of desires, and *tyāga* to be the giving up of the results of all activities.[2]

3) Some declare that after renunciation prescribed actions should be given up as an evil, yet another group says that acts of sacrifice, charity and austerity should never be given up.

4) O best of the Bhāratas, tiger among men, hear my decision on this matter. *Tyāga* is declared to be of three kinds.[3]

Chapter Eighteen is traditionally entitled *mokṣa-sannyāsa-yoga,* The *Yoga* of Release by Renunciation.

1. Some commentators translate *sannyāsa* as renunciation and *tyāga* as abandonment. Rāmānuja says that Arjuna is asking if what is meant by these two words are two different things or actually the same thing.

2. Here *sannyāsa* is defined as the cessation of those actions that are intended to fulfill a particular desire. By contrast, *tyāga* involves the performance of those same actions, but in a manner that is not intended to achieve any personal gain.

3. This verse seems out of place and would be better placed after verse six.

यज्ञदानतपःकर्म न त्याज्यं कार्यमेव तत् ।
यज्ञो दानं तपश्चैव पावनानि मनीषिणाम् ॥ ५

yajña-dāna-tapaḥ-karma na tyājyaṁ kāryam eva tat
yajño dānaṁ tapaś caiva pāvanāni manīṣiṇām

एतान्यपि तु कर्माणि सङ्गं त्यक्त्वा फलानि च ।
कर्तव्यानीति मे पार्थ निश्चितं मतमुत्तमम् ॥ ६

etāny api tu karmāṇi saṅgaṁ tyaktvā phalāni ca
kartavyānīti me pārtha niścitaṁ matam uttamam

नियतस्य तु संन्यासः कर्मणो नोपपद्यते ।
मोहात्तस्य परित्यागस्तामसः परिकीर्तितः ॥ ७

niyatasya tu sannyāsaḥ karmaṇo nopapadyate
mohāt tasya parityāgas tāmasaḥ parikīrtitaḥ

दुःखमित्येव यत्कर्म कायक्लेशभयात्त्यजेत् ।
स कृत्वा राजसं त्यागं नैव त्यागफलं लभेत् ॥ ८

duḥkham ity eva yat karma kāya-kleśa-bhayāt tyajet
sa kṛtvā rājasaṁ tyāgaṁ naiva tyāga-phalaṁ labhet

कार्यमित्येव यत्कर्म नियतं क्रियतेऽर्जुन ।
सङ्गं त्यक्त्वा फलं चैव स त्यागः सात्त्विको मतः ॥ ९

kāryam ity eva yat karma niyataṁ kriyate 'rjuna
saṅgaṁ tyaktvā phalaṁ caiva sa tyāgaḥ sāttviko mataḥ

न द्वेष्ट्यकुशलं कर्म कुशले नानुषज्जते ।
त्यागी सत्त्वसमाविष्टो मेधावी छिन्नसंशयः ॥ १०

na dveṣṭy akuśalaṁ karma kuśale nānuṣajjate
tyāgī sattva-samāviṣṭo medhāvī chinna-saṁśayaḥ

5) Acts of sacrifice, charity and austerity are never to be given up, but must always be performed. For sacrifice, charity and austerity are purifying even for the wise.[4]

6) Such prescribed actions, however, must only be performed after setting aside attachment and desire for the result. O Pārtha, this is My highest and settled opinion.

7) To give up a prescribed action is improper. An act of *tyāga* performed out of illusion is said to be characterized by *tamas.*

8) A person who gives up a prescribed action as distressful or out of fear for bodily discomfort performs an act of *tyāga* that is characterized by *rajas.* Indeed, such a person never obtains the true results of *tyāga.*

9) O Arjuna, *tyāga* is understood to be characterized by *sattva* when it is performed without attachment for the result, simply because it must be done.

10) One who is endowed with *sattva* qualities, who is wise and whose doubts are destroyed, is neither repelled nor attracted to any action, whether auspicious or inauspicious.

4. Śaṅkara says that acts of sacrifice, charity and austerity should be performed only until the desire to know *brahman* arises and that they should be given up thereafter. Rāmānuja says these acts should be performed until death. Madhva agrees that such works are necessary even for ascetics: their sacrifice is the sacrifice of wisdom, their charity is the charity of giving knowledge and their austerity is the austerity of purity and abstinence.

न हि देहभृता शक्यं त्यक्तुं कर्माण्यशेषतः ।
यस्तु कर्मफलत्यागी स त्यागीत्यभिधीयते ॥ ११

na hi deha-bhṛtā śakyaṁ tyaktuṁ karmāṇy aśeṣataḥ
yas tu karma-phala-tyāgī sa tyāgīty abhidhīyate

अनिष्टमिष्टं मिश्रं च त्रिविधं कर्मणः फलम् ।
भवत्यत्यागिनां प्रेत्य न तु संन्यासिनां क्वचित् ॥ १२

aniṣṭam iṣṭaṁ miśraṁ ca tri-vidhaṁ karmaṇaḥ phalam
bhavaty atyāgināṁ pretya na tu sannyāsināṁ kvacit

पञ्चैतानि महाबाहो कारणानि निबोध मे ।
सांख्ये कृतान्ते प्रोक्तानि सिद्धये सर्वकर्मणाम् ॥ १३

pañcaitāni mahā-baho kāraṇāni nibodha me
sāṅkhye kṛtānte proktāni siddhaye sarva-karmaṇām

अधिष्ठानं तथा कर्ता करणं च पृथग्विधम् ।
विविधाश्च पृथक्चेष्टा दैवं चैवात्र पञ्चमम् ॥ १४

adhiṣṭhānaṁ tathā kartā karaṇaṁ ca pṛthag-vidham
vividhāś ca pṛthak ceṣṭā daivaṁ caivātra pañcamam

11) An embodied soul is never able to completely give up action in this world. Instead, one who gives up the results of action is properly situated in *tyāga*.

12) For those who have failed to give up the results of their actions, the three fruits of action—desired, mixed or undesired[5]—accrue after death. This is never the case for those who have renounced the results of their actions.

The Five Components of Action

13-14) O mighty-armed Arjuna, listen as I explain, according to logical reasoning,[6] the five components that affect the accomplishment of an action. They include the location, the performer, the various instruments, the activity, and providence.[7]

---

5. Rāmānuja says that "undesired" fruits means hell, etc. "Desired" fruits means heaven, etc. and "mixed" fruits means such things as sons, cows and food, etc. Śaṅkara says "undesired" means hell or an animal birth. "Desired" means birth as a god and "mixed" means a human birth.
6. Madhva says that "logical reasoning" (*sāṅkhye*) refers to the system of Sāṅkhya philosophy. Rāmānuja takes the word to mean reasoned conclusions and not to the specific system of philosophy. Śaṅkara says it means the teachings of the *Upaniṣads.*
7. The commentators vary somewhat on this verse. According to Śaṅkara "the location" (*adhiṣṭhānam*) is the body, "the performer" (*kartā*) is the individual self, "the various instruments" (*karaṇam*) are the ten senses and the mind, "the activity" (*ceṣṭās*) is the activities of the vital airs, and "providence" (*daiva)* is the sun god and other divinities who help the senses, etc. According to Rāmānuja *adhiṣṭhānam* is the body, the individual soul is the *kartā,* the *karaṇa* are the organs of the body including the mind, *ceṣṭās* are the vital airs of the body and *daiva* is Viṣṇu as the *paramātma* or supersoul. Madhva say that the *adhiṣṭhānam* is the basis of action, the *kartā* is Viṣṇu, that *ceṣṭā* refers to the action, and that *daiva* is the unseen.

शरीरवाङ्मनोभिर्यत्कर्म प्रारभते नरः ।
न्याय्यं वा विपरीतं वा पञ्चैते तस्य हेतवः ॥ १५

śarīra-vāṅ-manobhir yat karma prārabhate naraḥ
nyāyyaṁ vā viparītaṁ vā pañcaite tasya hetavaḥ

तत्रैवं सति कर्तारमात्मानं केवलं तु यः ।
पश्यत्यकृतबुद्धित्वान्न स पश्यति दुर्मतिः ॥ १६

tatraivaṁ sati kartāram ātmānaṁ kevalaṁ tu yaḥ
paśyaty akṛta-buddhitvān na sa paśyati durmatiḥ

यस्य नाहंकृतो भावो बुद्धिर्यस्य न लिप्यते ।
हत्वापि स इमाँल्लोकान्न हन्ति न निबध्यते ॥ १७

yasya nāhaṅkṛto bhāvo buddhir yasya na lipyate
hatvāpi sa imāl lokān na hanti na nibadhyate

ज्ञानं ज्ञेयं परिज्ञाता त्रिविधा कर्मचोदना ।
करणं कर्म कर्तेति त्रिविधः कर्मसंग्रहः ॥ १८

jñānaṁ jñeyaṁ parijñātā tri-vidhā karma-codanā
karaṇaṁ karma karteti tri-vidhaḥ karma-saṅgrahaḥ

ज्ञानं कर्म च कर्ता च त्रिधैव गुणभेदतः ।
प्रोच्यते गुणसंख्याने यथावच्छृणु तान्यपि ॥ १९

jñānaṁ karma ca kartā ca tridhaiva guṇa-bhedataḥ
procyate guṇa-saṅkhyāne yathāvac chṛṇu tāny api

सर्वभूतेषु येनैकं भावमव्ययमीक्षते ।
अविभक्तं विभक्तेषु तज्ज्ञानं विद्धि सात्त्विकम् ॥ २०

sarva-bhūteṣu yenaikaṁ bhāvam avyayam īkṣate
avibhaktaṁ vibhakteṣu taj jñānaṁ viddhi sāttvikam

15) These five components of action apply to every activity, be it with body, mind or speech, whether proper or improper.

16) The person who regards himself alone as the performer possesses an incomplete understanding, and being ignorant, cannot see things as they are.

17) However, that person who has no sense of "I am the performer," whose intelligence is not tainted, even though engaged in killing, kills no one. Such a person is never bound by the results of actions.

18) Knowledge, the object of knowledge and the knower are the three factors that initiate action. The instrument, the action, and the performer form the threefold basis of action.

19) Knowledge, action and the performer are also divided according to the three *guṇas*. Now hear how these are described in terms of these *guṇas*.

Knowledge and The Three Qualities of Nature

20) That knowledge by which a person sees one indestructible state of being in all creatures, undivided amongst the divided, is of the nature of *sattva*.[8]

---

8. According to Śaṅkara the "one indestructible state of being" (*ekaṁ bhāvam*) means the one and only Self that is seen in all creatures. Rāmānuja says it is the same indestructible entity, the soul as a class that is seen. According to Madhva it is God, Viṣṇu who is seen.

पृथक्त्वेन तु यज्ज्ञानं नानाभावान्पृथग्विधान् ।
वेत्ति सर्वेषु भूतेषु तज्ज्ञानं विद्धि राजसम् ॥ २१

pṛthaktvena tu yaj jñānaṁ nānā-bhāvān pṛthag-vidhān
vetti sarveṣu bhūteṣu taj jñānaṁ viddhi rājasam

यत्तु कृत्स्नवदेकस्मिन्कार्ये सक्तमहैतुकम् ।
अतत्त्वार्थवदल्पं च तत्तामसमुदाहृतम् ॥ २२

yat tu kṛtsnavad ekasmin kārye saktam ahaitukam
atattvārthavad alpaṁ ca tat tāmasam udāhṛtam

नियतं सङ्गरहितमरागद्वेषतः कृतम् ।
अफलप्रेप्सुना कर्म यत्तत्सात्त्विकमुच्यते ॥ २३

niyataṁ saṅga-rahitam arāga-dveṣataḥ kṛtam
aphala-prepsunā karma yat tat sāttvikam ucyate

यत्तु कामेप्सुना कर्म साहंकारेण वा पुनः ।
क्रियते बहुलायासं तद्राजसमुदाहृतम् ॥ २४

yat tu kāmepsunā karma sāhaṅkāreṇa vā punaḥ
kriyate bahulāyāsaṁ tad rājasam udāhṛtam

अनुबन्धं क्षयं हिंसामनपेक्ष्य च पौरुषम् ।
मोहादारभ्यते कर्म यत्तत्तामसमुच्यते ॥ २५

anubandhaṁ kṣayaṁ hiṁsām anapekṣya ca pauruṣam
mohād ārabhyate karma yat tat tāmasam ucyate

मुक्तसङ्गोऽनहंवादी धृत्युत्साहसमन्वितः ।
सिद्ध्यसिद्ध्योर्निर्विकारः कर्ता सात्त्विक उच्यते २६

mukta-saṅgo 'nahaṁ-vādī dhṛty-utsāha-samanvitaḥ
siddhy-asiddhyor nirvikāraḥ kartā sāttvika ucyate

21) Knowledge that recognizes diversity and thereby perceives different natures in all creatures is characterized by *rajas.*[9]

22) But knowledge that is attached to one thing, as if it were the all in all, that is meager, that does not perceive a cause, and cannot see what is real, is declared to be of the nature of *tamas.*

Action and the Three Guṇas

23) Action that is restrained, that is performed without attachment, desire or hatred, and that does not seek a result, is of the nature of *sattva.*

24) Action that is performed to gratify desires, that is performed with tremendous effort and out of egotism, is of the nature of *rajas.*

25) But action that is undertaken out of illusion, without considering the consequences, losses or harm to others, and without regard for one's strength, is said to be of the nature of *tamas.*

The Performer and the Three Guṇas

26) One who performs an action free of attachment, without speaking of one's self-worth, who works with determination and energy, and who is unchanged in success or failure is a person who acts acccording to *sattva.*

9. Śaṅkara says that this verse condemns all forms of dualism.

रागी कर्मफलप्रेप्सुर्लुब्धो हिंसात्मकोऽशुचिः ।
हर्षशोकान्वितः कर्ता राजसः परिकीर्तितः ॥ २७

rāgī karma-phala-prepsur lubdho hiṁsātmako 'śuciḥ
harṣa-śokānvitaḥ kartā rājasaḥ parikīrtitaḥ

अयुक्तः प्राकृतः स्तब्धः शठो नैकृतिकोऽलसः
विषादी दीर्घसूत्री च कर्ता तामस उच्यते ॥ २८

ayuktaḥ prākṛtaḥ stabdhaḥ śaṭho naikṛtiko 'lasaḥ
viṣādī dīrgha-sūtrī ca kartā tāmasa ucyate

बुद्धेर्भेदं धृतेश्चैव गुणतस्त्रिविधं शृणु ।
प्रोच्यमानमशेषेण पृथक्त्वेन धनंजय ॥ २९

buddher bhedaṁ dhṛteś caiva guṇatas tri-vidhaṁ śṛṇu
procyamānam aśeṣeṇa pṛthaktvena dhanañjaya

प्रवृत्तिं च निवृत्तिं च कार्याकार्ये भयाभये ।
बन्धं मोक्षं च या वेत्ति बुद्धिः सा पार्थ सात्त्विकी ॥ ३०

pravṛttiṁ ca nivṛttiṁ ca kāryākārye bhayābhaye
bandhaṁ mokṣaṁ ca yā vetti buddhiḥ sā pārtha sāttvikī

यया धर्ममधर्मं च कार्यं चाकार्यमेव च ।
अयथावत्प्रजानाति बुद्धिः सा पार्थ राजसी ॥ ३१

yayā dharmam adharmaṁ ca kāryaṁ cākāryam eva ca
ayathāvat prajānāti buddhiḥ sā pārtha rājasī

अधर्मं धर्ममिति या मन्यते तमसावृता ।
सर्वार्थान्विपरीतांश्च बुद्धिः सा पार्थ तामसी ॥ ३२

adharmaṁ dharmam iti yā manyate tamasāvṛtā
sarvārthān viparītāṁś ca buddhiḥ sā pārtha tāmasī

27) One who is full of attachment, desiring the fruits of action, who is greedy, injurious, unclean, and filled with joys and sorrows is a person who acts according to *rajas.*

28) One who is inattentive, vulgar, stubborn, deceitful, dishonest, lazy, despondent and procrastinating is a person who acts according to *tamas.*

Understanding and the Three Guṇas

29) O conqueror of wealth, Arjuna, listen as I explain how understanding and determination are also characterized according to the three *guṇas.*

30) The understanding that knows when to act and when not to act, that knows what is to be done and what is not to be done, that knows what is to be feared and what is not to be feared, and that knows what is binding and what is liberating is understanding that is of the nature of *sattva.*

31) O Pārtha, the understanding that cannot distinguish between *dharma* and *adharma,*[10] and between what is to be done and what is not to be done is of the nature of *rajas.*

32) The understanding that considers *adharma* as *dharma* and *dharma* as *adharma,* that sees all things contrary to truth is covered by ignorance and is of the nature of *tamas.*

---

10. For information on *dharma* and *adharma* see: BG 1.1 and BG 4.7.

धृत्या यया धारयते मनःप्राणेन्द्रियक्रियाः ।
योगेनाव्यभिचारिण्या धृतिः सा पार्थ सात्त्विकी ॥३३

dhṛtyā yayā dhārayate manaḥ-prāṇendriya-kriyāḥ
yogenāvyabhicāriṇyā dhṛtiḥ sā pārtha sāttvikī

यया तु धर्मकामार्थान्धृत्या धारयतेऽर्जुन ।
प्रसङ्गेन फलाकाङ्क्षी धृतिः सा पार्थ राजसी ॥ ३४

yayā tu dharma-kāmārthān dhṛtyā dhārayate 'rjuna
prasaṅgena phalākāṅkṣī dhṛtiḥ sā pārtha rājasī

यया स्वप्नं भयं शोकं विषादं मदमेव च ।
न विमुञ्चति दुर्मेधा धृतिः सा पार्थ तामसी ॥ ३५

yayā svapnaṁ bhayaṁ śokaṁ viṣādaṁ madam eva ca
na vimuñcati durmedhā dhṛtiḥ sā pārtha tāmasī

सुखं त्विदानीं त्रिविधं शृणु मे भरतर्षभ ।
अभ्यासाद्रमते यत्र दुःखान्तं च निगच्छति ॥ ३६

sukhaṁ tv idānīṁ tri-vidhaṁ śṛṇu me bharatarṣabha
abhyāsād ramate yatra duḥkhāntaṁ ca nigacchati

यत्तदग्रे विषमिव परिणामेऽमृतोपमम् ।
तत्सुखं सात्त्विकं प्रोक्तमात्मबुद्धिप्रसादजम् ॥ ३७

yat tad agre viṣam iva pariṇāme 'mṛtopamam
tat sukhaṁ sāttvikaṁ proktam ātma-buddhi-prasāda-jam

विषयेन्द्रियसंयोगाद्यत्तदग्रेऽमृतोपमम् ।
परिणामे विषमिव तत्सुखं राजसं स्मृतम् ॥ ३८

viṣayendriya-saṁyogād yat tad agre 'mṛtopamam
pariṇāme vaṣam iva tat sukhaṁ rājasaṁ smṛtam

Determination and the Three Guṇas

33) That determination which upholds the activities of the mind, the vital-breath and the senses by steadfast discipline is characterized by *sattva.*

34) That determination by which one holds to *dharma,* enjoyment and wealth, with the aim to secure the fruits of labor, O son of Pṛthā, is of the nature of *rajas.*

35) But that determination by which the foolish cannot let go of sleep, fear, sorrow, despondency and pride is of the nature of *tamas.*

Happiness and the Three Guṇas

36-37) And now, O best of the Bhāratas, hear from Me about the three kinds of happiness. The happiness that a person enjoys after long practice and that leads to the cessation of suffering—that in the beginning is like poison, but in the end is like nectar—is of the nature of *sattva.* It arises from the serenity that comes from the perception of the soul.

38) The happiness that arises from contact of the senses and their objects—that in the beginning is like nectar, but in the end is like poison—is regarded as happiness characterized by *rajas.*

यदग्रे चानुबन्धे च सुखं मोहनमात्मनः ।
निद्रालस्यप्रमादोत्थं तत्तामसमुदाहृतम् ॥ ३९

yad agre cānubandhe ca sukhaṁ mohanam ātmanaḥ
nidrālasya-pramādotthaṁ tat tāmasam udāhṛtam

न तदस्ति पृथिव्यां वा दिवि देवेषु वा पुनः ।
सत्त्वं प्रकृतिजैर्मुक्तं यदेभिः स्यात्त्रिभिर्गुणैः ॥ ४०

na tad asti pṛthivyāṁ vā divi deveṣu vā punaḥ
sattvaṁ prakṛti-jair muktaṁ yad ebhiḥ syāt tribhir guṇaiḥ

ब्राह्मणक्षत्रियविशां शूद्राणां च परंतप ।
कर्माणि प्रविभक्तानि स्वभावप्रभवैर्गुणैः ॥ ४१

brāhmaṇa-kṣatriya-viśāṁ śūdrāṇāṁ ca parantapa
karmāṇi pravibhaktāni svabhāva-prabhavair guṇaiḥ

शमो दमस्तपः शौचं क्षान्तिरार्जवमेव च ।
ज्ञानं विज्ञानमास्तिक्यं ब्रह्मकर्म स्वभावजम् ॥ ४२

śamo damas tapaḥ śaucaṁ kṣāntir ārjavam eva ca
jñānaṁ vijñānam āstikyaṁ brahma-karma svabhāva-jam

शौर्यं तेजो धृतिर्दाक्ष्यं युद्धे चाप्यपलायनम् ।
दानमीश्वरभावश्च क्षत्रकर्म स्वभावजम् ॥ ४३

śauryaṁ tejo dhṛtir dākṣyaṁ yuddhe cāpy apalāyanam
dānam īśvara-bhāvaś ca kṣatra-karma svabhāva-jam

कृषिगोरक्ष्यवाणिज्यं वैश्यकर्म स्वभावजम् ।
परिचर्यात्मकं कर्म शूद्रस्यापि स्वभावजम् ॥ ४४

kṛṣi-go-rakṣya-vāṇijyaṁ vaiśya-karma svabhāva-jam
paricaryātmakaṁ karma śūdrasyāpi svabhāva-jam

39) The happiness that is self-deluding in the beginning as well as in the end—that arises from sleep, idleness, and intoxication—is declared to be of the nature of *tamas.*

40) There are no beings on earth or even amongst the gods in heaven that are free from these three *guṇas* born of *prakṛti.*

The Four Classes of Society

41) O scorcher of the enemy, the actions of the *brāhmaṇa,* the *kṣatriya,* the *vaiśya* and the *śūdra* are also distinguished according to the *guṇas* that arise from their inner natures.[11]

42) Calmness, self-control, austerity, purity, patience, honesty, as well as learning, wisdom and religious faith are the actions[12] of the *brāhmaṇas,* born of their inner nature.

43) Heroism, power, determination, resourcefulness, steadfastness in battle, generosity and leadership are the actions of the *kṣatriyas,* which arise from their inner nature.

44) Agriculture, cow protection and trade are the actions that arise from the inner nature of the *vaiśya.* The action that consists of service to others is similarly born from the inner nature of the *śūdra.*

---

11. According to Śaṅkara, the *brāhmaṇa* is established in *sattva* alone; the *kṣatriya* is a mixture of *sattva* and *rajas;* the *vaiśya* community is a mixture of *rajas* and *tamas;* and *śūdras* are of darkness with a small amount of *rajas.* Rāmānuja says that one's present position as a *brāhmaṇa, kṣatriya, vaiśya* or *śūdra* is the result of actions performed in previous births. Madhva suggests that priests may have a small amount of *rajas* mixed with *sattva.*
12. According to the *Gītā* a state of mind is considered a form of action.

स्वे स्वे कर्मण्यभिरतः संसिद्धिं लभते नरः ।
स्वकर्मनिरतः सिद्धिं यथा विन्दति तच्छृणु ॥ ४५

sve sve karmaṇy abhirataḥ saṁsiddhiṁ labhate naraḥ
sva-karma-nirataḥ siddhiṁ yathā vindati tac chṛṇu

यतः प्रवृत्तिर्भूतानां येन सर्वमिदं ततम् ।
स्वकर्मणा तमभ्यर्च्य सिद्धिं विन्दति मानवः ॥ ४६

yataḥ pravṛttir bhūtānāṁ yena sarvam idaṁ tatam
sva-karmaṇā tam abhyarcya siddhiṁ vindati mānavaḥ

श्रेयान्स्वधर्मो विगुणः परधर्मात्स्वनुष्ठितात् ।
स्वभावनियतं कर्म कुर्वन्नाप्नोति किल्बिषम् ॥ ४७

śreyān sva-dharmo viguṇaḥ para-dharmāt sv-anuṣṭhitāt
svabhāva-niyataṁ karma kurvan nāpnoti kilbiṣam

सहजं कर्म कौन्तेय सदोषमपि न त्यजेत् ।
सर्वारम्भा हि दोषेण धूमेनाग्निरिवावृताः ॥ ४८

saha-jaṁ karma kaunteya sa-doṣam api na tyajet
sarvārambhā hi doṣeṇa dhūmenāgnir ivāvṛtāḥ

असक्तबुद्धिः सर्वत्र जितात्मा विगतस्पृहः ।
नैष्कर्म्यसिद्धिं परमां संन्यासेनाधिगच्छति ॥ ४९

asakta-buddhiḥ sarvatra jitātmā vigata-spṛhaḥ
naiṣkarmya-siddhiṁ paramāṁ sannyāsenādhigacchati

सिद्धिं प्राप्तो यथा ब्रह्म तथाप्नोति निबोध मे ।
समासेनैव कौन्तेय निष्ठा ज्ञानस्य या परा ॥ ५०

siddhiṁ prāpto yathā brahma tathāpnoti nibodha me
samāsenaiva kaunteya niṣṭhā jñānasya yā parā

45) A person who is content in one's particular duty achieves perfection. Listen as I tell you how that person finds the highest goal.

46) Through the performance of prescribed duties mankind can achieve perfection by worshipping the One, who is the source of all beings and who pervades[13] this entire universe.

47) Better to perform one's own duty imperfectly than to perform another's duty perfectly. For one never incurs sin performing duties prescribed according to one's own nature.[14]

48) O son of Kuntī, actions that are natural to one's being should never be abandoned even though they may be faulty, for all undertakings in this world are covered by some fault, as fire is covered by smoke.

49) One whose mind is unattached in all circumstances, who is self-controlled and without desire achieves the highest perfection of work, namely, freedom from reaction.[15]

Attaining Brahman

50) O son of Kuntī, having obtained perfection, now listen as I tell you in summary how one can attain *brahman*, which is the highest stage of knowledge.

---

13. The word "pervades" (*tatam*) has been used twice before. See BG 2.17 and BG 8.17.
14. Compare this verse to BG 3.35.
15. "Freedom from reaction" (*naiṣkarmya-siddhim*) is literally "the success of actionlessness."

बुद्ध्या विशुद्धया युक्तो धृत्यात्मानं नियम्य च ।
शब्दादीन्विषयांस्त्यक्त्वा रागद्वेषौ व्युदस्य च ॥ ५१

buddhyā viśuddhayā yukto dhṛtyātmānaṁ niyamya ca
śabdādīn viṣayāṁs tyaktvā rāga-dveṣau vyudasya ca

विविक्तसेवी लघ्वाशी यतवाक्कायमानसः ।
ध्यानयोगपरो नित्यं वैराग्यं समुपाश्रितः ॥ ५२

vivikta-sevī laghv-āśī yata-vāk-kāya-mānasaḥ
dhyāna-yoga-paro nityaṁ vairāgyaṁ samupāśritaḥ

अहंकारं बलं दर्पं कामं क्रोधं परिग्रहम् ।
विमुच्य निर्ममः शान्तो ब्रह्मभूयाय कल्पते ॥ ५३

ahaṅkāraṁ balaṁ darpaṁ kāmaṁ krodhaṁ parigraham
vimucya nirmamaḥ śānto brahma-bhūyāya kalpate

ब्रह्मभूतः प्रसन्नात्मा न शोचति न काङ्क्षति ।
समः सर्वेषु भूतेषु मद्भक्तिं लभते पराम् ॥ ५४

brahma-bhūtaḥ prasannātmā na śocati na kāṅkṣati
samaḥ sarveṣu bhūteṣu mad-bhaktiṁ labhate parām

भक्त्या मामभिजानाति यावान्यश्चास्मि तत्त्वतः ।
ततो मां तत्त्वतो ज्ञात्वा विशते तदनन्तरम् ॥ ५५

bhaktyā mām abhijānāti yāvān yaś cāsmi tattvataḥ
tato māṁ tattvato jñātvā viśate tad-anantaram

सर्वकर्माण्यपि सदा कुर्वाणो मद्व्यपाश्रयः ।
मत्प्रसादादवाप्नोति शाश्वतं पदमव्ययम् ॥ ५६

sarva-karmāṇy api sadā kurvāṇo mad-vyapāśrayaḥ
mat-prasādād avāpnoti śāśvataṁ padam avyayam

51-53) The one who is endowed with a pure intellect, who controls the mind with determination, and who has abandoned attachment to the object of the senses, who lives without passion or hatred, who exists in solitude, eating meagerly, who restrains body, mind and speech through meditation, who seeks renunciation and exists without a sense of "I am a doer" is a *yogī*. Such a soul is free from harshness and pride, desire and anger, possession and proprietorship. Such a person is peaceful and is qualified for the state of *brahman.*[16]

54) One who has attained *brahman* and who has become serene neither laments nor desires. Being equally disposed to all, such a *yogī* obtains unalloyed devotion to Me.[17]

55) Through such devotion one who knows the truth of my greatness, at once enters into My nature.[18]

56) Though performing all kinds of activities, ever trusting Me, such a person, by My grace, attains to the eternal and imperishable abode.[19]

---

16. Śaṅkara interprets "qualified for the state of *brahman*" (*brahma-bhūyāya kalpate*) as, "becomes fit for becoming *brahman.*" Rāmānuja says it means, "fit for the state of *brahman.*" Madhva takes it as, "becomes fit for resting the mind in *brahman.*"
17. What is here translated as "unalloyed devotion" is a rendering of *para-bhakti.* Śaṅkara explains *para-bhakti* as devotion having the characteristic of knowledge. Rāmānuja explains it as the first step in a series followed by *para-jñāna* and finally *parama-bhakti.* In other words, Rāmānuja speaks of *para-bhakti, para-jñāna* and *parama-bhakti* as three successive stages in the development of devotion to God.
18. "At once enters into My nature" (*māṁ…viśate tad-anantaram)* is literally, "immediately enters Me."
19. "Eternal and imperishable abode" (*śāśvataṁ padam avyayam*) as in other instances may be read as the "eternal and imperishable *state.*" See fn. BG 15.4 and 18.62.

चेतसा सर्वकर्माणि मयि संन्यस्य मत्परः ।
बुद्धियोगमुपाश्रित्य मच्चित्तः सततं भव ॥ ५७

cetasā sarva-karmāṇi mayi sannyasya mat-paraḥ
buddhi-yogam upāśritya mac-cittaḥ satataṁ bhava

मच्चित्तः सर्वदुर्गाणि मत्प्रसादात्तरिष्यसि ।
अथ चेत्त्वमहंकारान्न श्रोष्यसि विनङ्क्ष्यसि ॥ ५८

mac-cittaḥ sarva-durgāṇi mat-prasādāt tariṣyasi
atha cet tvam ahaṅkārān na śroṣyasi vinaṅkṣyasi

यदहंकारमाश्रित्य न योत्स्य इति मन्यसे ।
मिथ्यैष व्यवसायस्ते प्रकृतिस्त्वां नियोक्ष्यति ॥ ५९

yad ahaṅkāram āśritya na yotsya iti manyase
mithyaiṣa vyavasāyas te prakṛtis tvāṁ niyokṣyati

स्वभावजेन कौन्तेय निबद्धः स्वेन कर्मणा ।
कर्तुं नेच्छसि यन्मोहात्करिष्यस्यवशोऽपि तत् ॥ ६०

svabhāva-jena kaunteya nibaddhaḥ svena karmaṇā
kartuṁ necchasi yan mohāt kariṣyasy avaśo 'pi tat

ईश्वरः सर्वभूतानां हृद्देशेऽर्जुन तिष्ठति ।
भ्रामयन्सर्वभूतानि यन्त्रारूढानि मायया ॥ ६१

īśvaraḥ sarva-bhūtānāṁ hṛd-deśe 'rjuna tiṣṭhati
bhrāmayan sarva-bhūtāni yantrārūḍhāni māyayā

तमेव शरणं गच्छ सर्वभावेन भारत ।
तत्प्रसादात्परां शान्तिं स्थानं प्राप्स्यसि शाश्वतम् ॥ ६२

tam eva śaraṇaṁ gaccha sarva-bhāvena bhārata
tat-prasādāt paraṁ śāntiṁ sthānaṁ prāpsyasi śāśvatam

Surrender

57) Mentally dedicate all your actions to Me, become devoted to Me alone and with a disciplined mind, always think of Me.

58) With mind fixed on Me you will cross all difficulties by My grace. Now, if out of egotism, you fail to listen, you will surely perish.

59) Driven by egotism, if you think, "I will not fight," your intention is mistaken and your very nature will force you to fight.

60) O son of Kuntī, you are bound by the actions that are determined by your very nature. Out of illusion you wish to avoid those things that you will be forced to do all the same.

61) The Lord as controller, O Arjuna, is situated in the heart of all beings, and by divine power[20] directs the movements of all creatures who are seated on this machine.[21]

62) O descendant of Bharata, with your whole being take exclusive shelter of that One[22] by whose grace you will attain the eternal abode[23] of supreme peace.

---

20. Rāmānuja suggests that the expression "by divine power" (*māyayā*) should be taken as "by means of material energy, *prakṛti*."
21. The "machine" (*yantra*) is described by Śaṅkara to be a mechanical contrivance that goes round and round and that all beings are like dolls or puppets placed on this machine. Rāmānuja says the machine is the physical body.
22. "That One" (*tam*) is literally "Him."
23. "Abode" (*sthānam*) may also be taken as a state of being. See BG 15.4 and 18.56.

इति ते ज्ञानमाख्यातं गुह्याद्गुह्यतरं मया ।
विमृश्यैतदशेषेण यथेच्छसि तथा कुरु ।। ६३

iti te jñānam ākhyātaṁ guhyād guhyataraṁ mayā
vimṛśyaitad aśeṣeṇa yathecchasi tathā kuru

सर्वगुह्यतमं भूयः शृणु मे परमं वचः ।
इष्टोऽसि मे दृढमिति ततो वक्ष्यामि ते हितम् ।। ६४

sarva-guhyatamaṁ bhūyaḥ śṛṇu me paramaṁ vacaḥ
iṣṭo 'si me dṛḍham iti tato vakṣyāmi te hitam

मन्मना भव मद्भक्तो मद्याजी मां नमस्कुरु ।
मामेवैष्यसि सत्यं ते प्रतिजाने प्रियोऽसि मे ।। ६५

man-manā bhava mad-bhakto mad-yājī māṁ namaskuru
mām evaiṣyasi satyaṁ te pratijāne priyo 'si me

सर्वधर्मान्परित्यज्य मामेकं शरणं व्रज ।
अहं त्वा सर्वपापेभ्यो मोक्षयिष्यामि मा शुचः ।। ६६

sarva-dharmān parityajya mām ekaṁ śaraṇaṁ vraja
ahaṁ tvā sarva-pāpebhyo mokṣayiṣyāmi mā śucaḥ

इदं ते नातपस्काय नाभक्ताय कदाचन ।
न चाशुश्रूषवे वाच्यं न च मां योऽभ्यसूयति ।। ६७

idaṁ te nātapaskāya nābhaktāya kadācana
na cāśuśrūṣave vācyaṁ na ca māṁ yo 'bhyasūyati

63) Thus I have declared to you this knowledge, which is more mysterious than any mystery. Deliberate on this fully and act as you see fit.

64) Listen once again to My supreme words, the most secret of all secrets. Because you are very dear to Me I am speaking for your benefit.

65) Always think of Me, become My devotee, worship Me, and offer respects to Me. In this way you will truly come to Me. This I promise you because you are very dear to Me.

66) Relinquish all forms of *dharma* and seek refuge in Me alone. I will free you from all wrongdoing. Do not fear. [24]

Who is Qualified to Hear this Message

67) You must never utter this most secret wisdom to one who is devoid of devotion or austerities, or who is envious of Me.

---

24. This verse is probably the most often quoted verse in the *Gītā*. It is called the *carama-śloka* or highest of the *Gītā*'s teachings. The first word of the *Bhagavad Gītā* begins with the word *dharma* and there we defined *dharma* as that by which the world is "held together." It was Arjuna's *dharma* to fight. It is the teacher's *dharma* to teach. It is a child's *dharma* to respect and obey the parents. Thus every aspect of society is governed by *dharma*. Yet here, for a higher purpose, we are asked to give up *dharma*. If by doing so we incur some wrong we are told that God will protect us. Śaṅkara adds that the giving up of " all forms of *dharma*" (*sarva-dharmān*) means giving up *adharma* as well. Rāmānuja says that giving up *dharma* includes *karma-yoga*, *jñāna-yoga* and even *bhakti-yoga*. This means that one should concentrate on God alone as the creator, the object of worship, the goal, and the means by which the goal is attained. Madhva says that the giving up of *dharma* is the renunciation of the fruits of *dharma* and not directly the giving up of one's responsibilities in life. Otherwise, he asks, how can there be any commandment to fight? Madhva quotes BG 18.11.

य इदं परमं गुह्यं मद्भक्तेष्वभिधास्यति ।
भक्तिं मयि परां कृत्वा मामेवैष्यत्यसंशयः ॥ ६८

ya idaṁ paramaṁ guhyaṁ mad-bhatkeṣv abhidhāsyati
bhaktiṁ mayi parāṁ kṛtvā mām evaiṣyaty asaṁśayaḥ

न च तस्मान्मनुष्येषु कश्चिन्मे प्रियकृत्तमः ।
भविता न च मे तस्मादन्यः प्रियतरो भुवि ॥ ६९

na ca tasmān manuṣyeṣu kaścin me priya-kṛttamaḥ
bhavitā na ca me tasmād anyaḥ priyataro bhuvi

अध्येष्यते च य इमं धर्म्यं संवादमावयोः ।
ज्ञानयज्ञेन तेनाहमिष्टः स्यामिति मे मतिः ॥ ७०

adhyeṣyate ca ya imaṁ dharmyaṁ saṁvādam āvayoḥ
jñāna-yajñena tenāham iṣṭaḥ syām iti me matiḥ

श्रद्धावाननसूयश्च शृणुयादपि यो नरः ।
सोऽपि मुक्तः शुभाँल्लोकान्प्राप्नुयात्पुण्यकर्मणाम् ७१

śraddhāvān anasūyaś ca śṛṇuyād api yo naraḥ
so 'pi muktaḥ śubhāl lokān prāpnuyāt puṇya-karmaṇām

कच्चिदेतच्छ्रुतं पार्थ त्वयैकाग्रेण चेतसा ।
कच्चिदज्ञानसंमोहः प्रनष्टस्ते धनंजय ॥ ७२

kaccid etac chrutaṁ pārtha tvayaikāgreṇa cetasā
kaccid ajñāna-sammohaḥ pranaṣṭas te dhanañjaya

अर्जुन उवाच ।
नष्टो मोहः स्मृतिर्लब्धा त्वत्प्रसादान्मयाच्युत ।
स्थितोऽस्मि गतसंदेहः करिष्ये वचनं तव ॥ ७३

arjuna uvāca
naṣṭo mohaḥ smṛtir labdhā tvat-prasādān mayācyuta
sthito 'smi gata-sandehaḥ kariṣye vacanaṁ tava

68) One who declares this supreme mystery to My devotees, who cultivates unalloyed devotion, will come to Me without a doubt.

69) Amongst mankind there is no one more dear than this person; nor in the future shall there be another more dear to Me.

70) One who studies this sacred dialogue worships Me through the sacrifice of knowledge. This is My judgement.

71) A person of faith, who is without envy or who simply hears these teachings, becomes liberated and attains the realm of the pious.

72) O conqueror of wealth, have you heard this with a concentrated mind? Has your illusion due to ignorance been destroyed?

73) Arjuna said:
O Infallible One,[25] by your mercy my illusion is now destroyed and my memory is restored. I am fixed and my doubts are dispelled. I will carry out your words.

---

25. Kṛṣṇa is here referred to as Acyuta, the infallible One.

संजय उवाच ।
इत्यहं वासुदेवस्य पार्थस्य च महात्मनः ।
संवादमिममश्रौषमद्भुतं रोमहर्षणम् ॥ ७४

sañjaya uvāca
ity ahaṁ vāsudevasya pārthasya ca mahātmanaḥ
saṁvādam imam aśrauṣam adbhutaṁ roma-harṣaṇam

व्यासप्रसादाच्छ्रुतवानेतद्गुह्यमहं परम् ।
योगं योगेश्वरात्कृष्णात्साक्षात्कथयतः स्वयम् ॥ ७५

vyāsa-prasādāc chrutavān etad guhyam ahaṁ param
yogaṁ yogeśvarāt kṛṣṇāt sākṣāt kathayataḥ svayam

राजन्संस्मृत्य संस्मृत्य संवादमिममद्भुतम् ।
केशवार्जुनयोः पुण्यं हृष्यामि च मुहुर्मुहुः ॥ ७६

rājan saṁsmṛtya saṁsmṛtya saṁvādam imam adbhutam
keśavārjunayoḥ puṇyaṁ hṛṣyāmi ca muhur muhuḥ

तच्च संस्मृत्य संस्मृत्य रूपमत्यद्भुतं हरेः ।
विस्मयो मे महान्राजन्हृष्यामि च पुनः पुनः ॥ ७७

tac ca saṁsmṛtya saṁsmṛtya rūpam aty-adbhutaṁ hareḥ
vismayo me mahān rājan hṛṣyāmi ca punaḥ punaḥ

यत्र योगेश्वरः कृष्णो यत्र पार्थो धनुर्धरः ।
तत्र श्रीर्विजयो भूतिर्ध्रुवा नीतिर्मतिर्मम ॥ ७८

yatra yogeśvaraḥ kṛṣṇo yatra pārtho dhanur-dharaḥ
tatra śrīr vijayo bhūtir dhruvā nītir matir mama

Epilogue

74) Sañjaya said:
Thus I have heard this wonderful conversation between the son of Vasudeva and the great soul Arjuna. My hair stands on end.

75) By the grace of Vyāsa I have heard this supreme secret of *yoga* spoken directly from Kṛṣṇa, the master of *yoga.*

76) O king, I am thrilled at every moment remembering this sacred and wonderful conversation between Keśava and Arjuna.

77) As I repeatedly remember that extraordinary form of Hari, I am amazed. O king, I am thrilled again and again.

78) Wherever there is Kṛṣṇa, the master of all *yoga,* and wherever there is Arjuna, the holder of the bow, there will surely be fortune, victory, prosperity and morality. That is my opinion.[26]

End

---

26. This verse plainly tells Dhṛtarāṣṭra that his sons' defeat is certain.

The Devanāgarī Letters

Vowels (*Svara*)

अ a आ ā इ i ई ī उ u ऊ ū ऋ ṛ ॠ ṝ
ए e ऐ ai ओ o औ au

Consonants (*Vyañjana*)

Gutturals (*Kaṇṭhya*)
क ka ख kha ग ga घ gha ङ ṅa

Palatals (*Tālavya*)
च ca छ cha ज ja झ jha ञ ña

Cerebrals (*Mūrdhanya*)
ट ṭa ठ ṭha ड ḍa ढ ḍha ण ṇa

Dentals (*Dantya*)
त ta थ tha द da ध dha न na

Labials (*Auṣṭhya*)
प pa फ pha ब ba भ bha म ma

Semivowels (*Antarstha*)
य ya र ra ल la व va

Sibilants (*Ūśman*)
श śa ष ṣa स sa

Aspirate (*Mahāprāṇa*)
ह ha

Sanskrit Glossary

ācārya–traditional teacher or theologian of Hindu doctrine, head of *sampradāya* or school of religious thought.

adharma–the opposite of *dharma.* The term is often used in the sense of unrighteousness, impiety or non-performance of duty

adhibhūta–the manifestation of *brahman* as the perishable nature of matter.

adhidaiva–the manifestation of *brahman* as the Universal Person or *puruṣa* who is the foundation of the gods.

adhiyajña–the principle of divinity that dwells within all things and is the recipient of all sacrifice.

adhyātmā–the manifestation of *brahman* as the individual soul.

advaita–non dualism, the name given to the theological position of the Śaṅkara school of thought.

agni–fire or the fire deity.

ahiṁsā–nonviolence.

akṣara–something that is imperishable, the soul, God.

āryan–one of noble birth, one faithful to the religion of the Vedas.

artha–wealth, not to be understood solely as material assets, but all kinds of wealth including non-tangibles such as knowledge, friendship and love. *Artha* is one of the four *puruśārthas* or "goals of life," the others being *dharma, kāma* and *mokṣa.*

āśrama–one of the four stages of life: *brahmacarya* (studentship), *gārhasthya* (householder), *vānaprastha* (retired), and *sannyāsa* (renounced); a hermitage.

asat–opposite of *sat,* non-being, impermanent, false, evil, unreal, sometimes used to refer to matter or to the body.

asura–an ungodly one, a demon, one who does not follow the path of the Vedas.

ātman–has many meanings in Sanskrit that include: soul, breath, the Self, one's self (as a reflexive pronoun), mind, body, the Supreme Soul, etc.

avatāra–literally, one who decends, an incarnation of God who descends into this physical world, an incarnation of Viṣṇu.

avidyā–non knowledge, ignorance, nescience.

bhagavān–literally, one possessed of *bhaga. Bhaga* means fame, glory, strength, power, etc. The word is used as an epithet applied to God, gods, or any holy or venerable personality.

bhakta–a devotee, one who follows the path of devotion.

bhakti–love, devotion. One of the most common forms of *yoga.*

bhakti-yoga–the spiritual path of connecting one's self to God through devotion.

brahmā–the four headed creator god born of the lotus.

brahmacārī–a religious student in the first stage of life.

brahmacarya–the first stage of life, studentship, celibacy.

brahman–derived from the Sanskrit root *bṛmh* meaning to grow, to expand, to bellow, to roar. The word *brahman* refers to the Supreme Principle regarded as impersonal and divested of all qualities. *Brahman* is the essence from which all created beings are produced and into which they are absorbed. This word is neuter and not to be confused with the masculine word Brahmā, the creator god. *Brahman* is sometimes used to denote the syllable *om* or the *Vedas* in general.

brāhmaṇa–a member of the traditional priestly class. The *brāhmaṇa* was the first of the four *varṇas* in the social system called *varṇāśrama-dharma.* Literally, the word means "in relation to brahman." A *brāhmaṇa* is one who follows the ways of *brahman.* Traditionally a *brāhmaṇa,* often written as brahmin, filled the role of priest, teacher and thinker.

candra–the moon or the moon deity.

deva–derived from the Sanskrit root *div* meaning to shine or become bright. A *deva* is therefore a "shining one." The word is used to refer to God, a god or any exalted personality. The female version is *devī.*

deva-nāgarī–name of the writing script in which Sanskrit and Hindi are usually written.

dharma–derived from the Sanskrit root *dhṛ* meaning to hold up, to carry, to bear, to sustain. The word *dharma* refers to that which upholds or sustains the universe. Human society, for example, is sustained and upheld by the *dharma* performed by its members. Parents protecting and maintaining children, children being obedient to parents, the king protecting the citizens are acts of *dharma* that uphold and sustain society. In this context *dharma* has the meaning of duty. *Dharma* also employs the meaning of law, religion, virtue, and ethics. These things uphold and sustain the proper functioning of human society. In philosophy *dharma* refers to the defining quality of an object. For instance, liquidity is one of the essential *dharmas* of water; coldness is a *dharma* of ice. In this case we can think that the existence of an object is sustained or defined by its essential attributes, *dharmas*.

duḥkha–suffering or unhappiness.

dvaita–dualism, the name given to the theological position of the Mādhva school of thought.

dvāpara-yuga–the third time period (*yuga*) said to last 864,000 years (two times 432,000)

gaṅgā–the river Ganges.

gārhasthya–the third order (*āśrama*) of life, domestic affairs

gāyatrī–a meter used throughout the Vedas comprised of three lines of eight measures totalling twenty-four measures. A sacred chant.

guṇa–quality, positive attributes or virtues. In the context of *Bhagavad* Gītā and *Sāṅkhya* philosophy there are three *guṇas* of matter. Sometimes *guṇa* is translated as phase or mode. Therefore the three *guṇas* or phases of matter are: *sattva-guṇa*, *rajo-guṇa* and *tamo-guṇa*. The word *guṇa* also means a rope or thread and it is sometimes said that beings are "roped" or "tied" into matter by the three *guṇas* of material nature.

gṛhastha–one situated in the second order of life (*āśrama*), a householder.

guru–a teacher. Literally, the word means heavy and so refers to one "heavy" with knowledge, commonly used to refer to a spiritual teacher.

haṭha-yoga–a path of physical discipline meant to control the senses.

Īśā–literally, lord, master, or controller. *Īśā* is one of the words used for God as the supreme controller. The word is also used to refer to any being or personality who is in control.

Īśvara–see Īśā.

japa–chanting.

jīva–the soul, a living being.

jñāna–derived from the Sanskrit root *jñā*, to know, to learn, to experience. In the context of *Bhagavad Gītā* and the *Upaniṣads*, *jñāna* is generally used in the sense of spiritual knowledge or awareness.

jñāna-yoga–the spiritual path of connecting one's self to God through knowledge.

jñānī–literally, "one possessed of knowledge," a scholar.

kāma–wish, desire, love. Often used in the sense of sexual desire or love, but not necessarily. *Kāma* is one of the four *puruṣārthas* or "goals of life," the others being *dharma, artha* and *mokṣa.*

kāla–time.

kali-yuga–one of the four ages, said to last 432,000 years, the age characterized by fighting and diminished spiritual abilities.

kalpa–sacred law, a period of time, a twelve hour period (a day) of Brahmā said to last one thousand *mahā-yuga* cycles.

karma–derived from the Sanskrit root *kṛ* meaning to do, to make. The work *karma* means action, work, and deed. Only secondarily does *karma* refer to the result of past deeds, which are more properly known as the *phalam* or fruit of action.

karma-yoga–the spiritual path of connecting one's self to God through action or work.

kṣatriya–a member of the traditional military or warrior class. A king, a prince. The *kṣatriya* was the second *varṇa* in the system of *varṇāśrama-dharma.*

kṣara–something that is perishable, the body, the world.

kṣetra–a field, the body, the world.

kṣetra-jña–the knower of the field, the soul, God.

līlā–divine pastime, play of God.

mahā-yuga–a period of time comprised of one cycle of the four *yugas: satya, tretā, dvāpara* and *kali,* a total of 4,320,000 years.

mantra–a Vedic hymn or sacred prayer.

māyā–a trick, illusion.

mokṣa–liberation or freedom of rebirth. *Mokṣa* is one of the four *puruśārthas* or "goals of life," the others being *dharma, artha* and *kāma.*

mukti–see *mokṣa.*

muni–a sage, a silent one.

nirguṇa–without attributes, refers to God conceived to be impersonal.

nirvāṇa–blown out or extinguished as in the case of a lamp. *Nirvāṇa* is generally used to refer to a material life that has been extinguished, one who has achieved freedom from re-birth. The term *nirvāṇa* is commonly used in Buddhism as the final stage a practitioner strives for. The word does not mean heaven.

om–a sacred syllable, the sound of *brahman,* a sound vibrated at the beginning and end of Vedic recitation, the Vedas.

pāpa–literally, *pāpa* is what brings one down. Sometimes translated as sin or evil.

paramātman–the supreme soul, the supersoul, the lord of the heart, an aspect of God that pervades all things.

paramparā–one following the other, the chain of teachers and disciples.

pitṛ–a father, a forefather, an ancestor, a class of celestial beings, the manes.

prakṛti–material nature. In *sāṅkhya* philosophy *prakṛti* is comprised of eight elements: earth, water, fire, air, space, mind, intellect and ego. It is characterized by the three *guṇas*: *sattva, rajas* and *tamas. Prakṛti* is female. *Puruṣa* is male.

prasāda–favor, mercy, blessing, God's blessings, any item that has been offered to God during worship, especially food.

puṇya–the opposite to *pāpa. Puṇya* is what elevates; it is virtue or moral merit. *Pāpa* and *puṇya* go together as negative and positive "credits." One reaps the reward of these negative or positive credits in life. The more *puṇya* one cultivates the higher one rises in life, whereas *pāpa* will cause one to find a lower position. *Puṇya* leads to happiness, *pāpa* leads to suffering.

puruṣa–man, male. In *sāṅkhya* philosophy *puruṣa* denotes the Supreme Male Principle in the universe. Its counterpart is *prakṛti.*

puruṣottama–comprised of two words: *puruṣa* + *uttama* literally meaning "highest man." *Puruṣottama* means God.

rajas–the second of the three *guṇas* of matter. Sometimes translated as passion, the phase of *rajas* is characterized by action, passion, creation, etc.

ṛta–what is proper, right, true, divine law.

ṛtu–season, a period of time, menstruation period.

ṛṣi–an inspired poet or sage, a class of beings distinct from men and gods who were the "seers" of the Vedas.

saṅkhya–calculating, enumeration, analysis, categorization. Modern science can be said to be a form of *saṅkhya* because it attempts to analyze and categorize matter into its constituent elements. *Sāṅkhya* (first *a* long) refers to an ancient system of philosophy attributed to the sage Kapila. This philosophy is so called because it enumerates or analyses reality into a set number of basic elements, similar to modern science.

saguṇa–literally, "with attributes," God conceived as possessing humanlike qualities.

śaiva–a follower of Śiva.

śākta–a follower of Durgā (*śakti*).

śakti–power, energy conceived as female in nature.

samādhi–meditative trance, absorption in the divine.

sannyāsī–one situated in the final stage (*āśrama*) of life, a mendicant.

sannyāsa–the fourth or final stage (*āśrama*) of life, characterized by full renunciation.

śāstra–an order, command, rule, scriptural injunction, sacred writings, science, any department of knowledge.

sat–being, good, virtuous, chaste, the third word of the famous three words: *oṁ tat sat,* refers to what is truly real, eternal and permanent, used to mean God or the soul.

sattva–the first of the three *guṇas* of matter. Sometimes translated as goodness, the phase of *sattva* is characterized by lightness, peace, cleanliness, knowledge, etc.

satyam–truth. The word *satyam* is formed from *sat* with the added abstract suffix *ya*. *Sat* refers to what is true and real. The abstract suffix *ya* means "ness." Thus *satyam* literally means trueness or realness.

satya-yuga–the first of the four *yugas*, said to comprise 1,728,000 years, characterized by virtue, wisdom and spirituality.

śloka–a hymn or verse of praise, a stanza or verse in general, a stanza in *anuṣṭubh* metre (the most common metre used in Sanskrit consisting for 4 lines of 8 syllables), fame.

smṛti–literally, "what is heard," the division of the Vedas written by human beings (*pauruṣeya*), comprised of the later tradition that includes the *Mahābhārata*, *Rāmāyana*, *Purāṇas* etc.

śruti–literally, "what is heard," the division of the Vedas not written by human beings (*apauruṣeya*), said to be "heard" by the *ṛṣis*, comprised of the four Vedas including the *Upaniṣads*.

śūdra–a member of the traditional working class. The śūdra was the fourth *varṇa* in the system of *varṇāśrama-dharma*.

sukha–happiness, pleasure.

sura–a godly one, a god, one who follows the path of the Vedas.

svāmī–controller, a *yogī*, one in the renounced stage of life, a *guru*.

tamas–the third of the three *guṇas* of matter. Sometimes translated as darkness, the phase of *tamas* is characterized by darkness, ignorance, slowness, destruction, heaviness, disease, etc.

tapas–heat, voluntary acceptance of trouble for a spiritual goal, austerity, penance.

tapasya–see *tapas*.

tretā-yuga–the second of the four *yugas*, said to last 1,296,000 years.

tyāga–abandonment, renunciation, the performance of actions without attachment to the results of action.

vaikuṇṭha–literally, "without anxiety," the realm or heaven of Viṣṇu.

vairāgya–renounciation, detachment from the world.

vaiṣṇava–a follower of Viṣṇu.

vaiśya–a member of the traditional mercantile or business community. The *vaiśya* was the third *varṇa* in the system of*varṇāśrama-dharma*.

vanaprastha–one situated in the third order of life, literally, "one who remains in the forest."

vānaprastha–the third order (*āśrama*) of life, the retired stage.

varṇāśrama–the traditional social system of four *varṇas* and four *aśramas.* The word *varṇa* literally means, "color" and it refers to four basic natures of mankind: *brāhmaṇa, kṣatriya, vaiśya* and *śūdra.* The *āśramas* are the four stages of an individual's life: *brahmacarya* (student), *gṛhastha* (householder), *vanaprastha* (retired) and *sannyāsa* (renounced).

veda(s)–knowledge, the sacred knowledge of the Āryans, the hindu scriptures, the *Ṛg, Yajur, Sāma, Atharva,* the *Mahābhārata, Rāmāyaṇa, Purāṇas, Vedānta-sūtra,* etc.

vidyā–knowledge, the goddess Sarasvatī.

vijñāna–derived from the prefix *vi* added to the noun *jñāna.* The prefix *vi* added to a noun tends to diminish or invert the meaning of a word. If *jnana* is spiritual knowledge, *vijñāna* is practical or profane knowledge. Sometimes *vijñāna* and *jñāna* are used together in the sense of knowledge and wisdom.

viśiṣṭādvaita–offen translated as "oneness of the organic unity" or "differentiated monism," the theology taught by the Śrī Vaiṣṇavism associated with Rāmānuja.

viśva-rūpa–God's cosmic form, the universal form, the vision seen by Arjuna in *Bhagavad Gītā* Chapter Eleven.

yajña–sacrifice, the worship of God performed with fire.

yoga–derived from the Sanskrit root *yuj,* to join, to unite, to attach. The English word yoke is cognate with the Sanskrit word *yoga.* We can think of *yoga* as the joining of the *ātman* with the *paramātman,* the soul with God. There are numerous means of joining with God: through action, *karma-yoga;* through knowledge, *jñāna-yoga;* through devotion, *bhakti-yoga;* through meditation, *dhyāna-yoga,* etc. *Yoga* has many other meanings. For example, in astronomy and astrology it refers to a conjunction (union) of planets.

yogī–literally, one possessed of *yoga.* A *yogī* is a practitioner of *yoga.*

yuga–a period of time said to comprise 432,000 years, one of the four ages that rotate like calendar seasons.

Sanskrit Verse Index

A

B

M

General Index

B

J

K

L

U

Notes

Notes

Notes

Notes

Notes